ISBN 972-46-1313-5

© Martin Page

Direitos reservados
EDITORIAL NOTÍCIAS
Rua Padre Luís Aparício, 10-1.º 1150-248 Lisboa
editnoticias@mail.telepac.pt
www.editnoticias.pt

Revisão: Gillian Delaforce
Ayala Monteiro
Capa: 3 designers gráficos

Edição n.º: 01 503 038
1.ª edição: Fevereiro de 2002
4.ª edição Março de 2003
Depósito legal n.º 192.543/03

Pré-impressão:
Multitipo – Artes Gráfica, Lda.
Impressão e acabamento:
Tipografia Peres, SA

THE FIRST GLOBAL VILLAGE
HOW PORTUGAL CHANGED THE WORLD

Also by Martin Page

Non-fiction:

Unpersoned: The Fall of Nikita Khrushchev (with David Berg)

The Year of Three Kings (with Helen Hardinge)

The Company Savage

The Lost Pleasures of the Great Trains

Kiss Me Goodnight, Sergeant Major

For Gawdsake Don't Take Me

The Good Doctor Guide

Fiction:

The Pilate Plot

The Man Who Stole the Mona Lisa

MARTIN PAGE

THE FIRST
GLOBAL VILLAGE

How Portugal Changed the World

4.ª edição

To the memory of Pedro da Cunha,
and the lasting friendship of his family.

MY THANKS TO:

Catherine, who enabled me to research and write this book, despite my lack of sight; Professor Pedro da Cunha, of the Catholic University of Lisbon, without whose encouragement I should never have embarked on the project; Professor Fernando d'Orey, of the New University of Lisbon, for his support, expertise and help; Professor Jaime Reis, of the European Institute, Florence, for his guidance over Portugal's economic history, its effect on the rise of Salazar and Anglo-Portuguese relations; Austin Coates, the doyen of writers about European colonists in East Asia, particularly for his information about the Portuguese transfer of medicines, plants, animals and cooking methods between the Americas, Europe, and Asia; Sister Aedris, OP, of the Convento of Santo António, Lisbon, for helping document the origins of Portugal; our many Portuguese friends, who contributed memories of their personal involvement in their country's recent history; Dr. Tristão da Cunha, for generous access to his library, and much other help; Dr. António Saldano, for his many valuable corrections and suggestions; Ambassador Gabriel Mesquita de Brito, for checking the text, for Portuguese usage, and for his insights into the Portuguese presence in Asia; John O'Connor, for his insights into the cultural life of Sintra; Carlos Fernandes, for his help and friendship, throughout this project; Susan Moore and Geraldine Tomlin, for text-editing.

CONTENTS

A Personal Introduction

A Note on Sources

Suggestions for Further Reading

Web sites

Index

Chapter I: **From Jonah to Julius Caesar**

Old Testament and early Greek and Latin descriptions of the land beyond God's reach; the Carthaginians' discovery of vast mineral wealth; Portuguese horsemen march with Hannibal on Rome; Julius Caesar wins the governorship of Portugal in a lottery, and makes his fortune there; buys his way to power in Rome, and the conquest of France, Belgium and England. (Page 31.)

Chapter II: **Rome on the Atlantic**

The Romans make themselves at home; fostering changes to the country, the people, their laws, diet and language; soaring taxes cause Portuguese to sell themselves into slavery; the isolation of the Roman ruling class. (Page 39.)

Chapter III: **The Rise and Fall of Christendom**

St James's revolutionary "Practical Christianity" arrives from North Africa; the uprising against the Romans; arrival of religious dissidents from Germany, who take over the country; law reform leads to the murder of King Witiza; an Arab raiding party unintentionally becomes an army of occupation. (Page 48.)

Chapter IV: **The Arabs Bring Civilisation to Europe**

An almost peaceful conquest; filling of the vacuum left by the flight of the bishops and the priests; Christian martyrdoms or suicides?; Arabic innovations in farming, education, medicine and architecture; the Prince falls in love with the Chief Minister; the capital of the Algarve becomes an international centre of music and literature, and is destroyed by English Crusaders. (Page 55.)

Chapter V: **The Christian Reconquest**

St Bernard of Burgundy's scheme for a modern Christian state; his cousin, Afonso Henriques, locks up his Spanish mother, and declares himself first King of Portugal; the founding of the Knights Templar and their key role; the exploits of Fearless Geraldo; English and Normans versus Germans and Flemings at the siege of Lisbon; the sacking and the savagery. (Page 69.)

Chapter VI: **The Cistercian Peace**

The monks' post-war revolution, turning the battlefields into orchards, vineyards and forests; King Dinis's new Portugal, innovation in social welfare and university education; the fall of the royals from Burgundy; menace from Spain; a prudish English queen battles licentiousness in court. (Page 80.)

Chapter VII: **Prince Henry the Misadventurer**

The British re-invention of Prince Henrique as "The Navigator"; the myth of the School of Sagres; peace with Spain means financial ruin for military-religious orders; Henrique's looting of North Africa, and disgrace in the royal court; the development of the caravel; the European trade in African slaves begins. (Page 92.)

Chapter VIII: **King João and the Great Adventure**

Meritocracy reforms the royal court; why King João was right to dismiss Christopher Columbus; the council of Jewish and Christian scholars; the West African gold boom. (Page 107.)

Chapter IX: **Pêro da Covilhã: Master Spy**

Pêro travels alone to India; his maps complement those of Bartolomeu Dias, of the route around southern Africa; Pêro fails to return from his second quest, to find Prester John; the royal chaplain sets out, to bring him back to Lisbon, but finds him living in luxury, claiming to be under house arrest. (Page 117.)

Chapter X: **Vasco da Gama and the Lord of the Oceans**

An ambassador, not a discoverer; his voyage no more random than a modern space mission; danger of being identified as Christians; verbal duelling with India's Lord of the Oceans; European goods despised; narrow escape. (Page 125.)

Chapter XI: **India and Beyond**

The contest with the Arabs for the mastery of the Indian Ocean; severing Venice's trade links; the foundation of modern pharmacology; the capture of Malacca, the gateway to the Far East; the sinking of Admiral Albuquerque's $2.5 billion booty; the incredible adventure of Mendes Pinto, and São Francisco Xavier; the Portuguese Jesuits' impact on Japan; transfers of plants, foods and cooking methods between America, Europe and Asia. (Page 135.)

Chapter XII: **The Golden Age in Lisbon; Disaster Abroad**

Europe's new centre of wealth and fashion; Manueline architecture, music, theatre and partying; the da Cunha present an elephant to the Pope; Portuguese advances in science; the depredation of Protestant pirates; King Sebastião's disastrous invasion of Morocco; Portugal falls to the Spanish. (Page 150.)

Chapter XIII: **The Coming of the Inquisition; The Departure of the Jews**

Portugal, the only European nation not to persecute Jews, comes under the Spanish inquisition; the Pope and King Manuel defend the Portuguese Jews; the system of the Holy Office of the Inquisition; de-mythologising the *auto-de-fé*; through banishment and escape, the Jews find diamonds in Brazil, bring tulip bulbs, chocolate, tobacco and banking to Holland; the Dutch take over Portugal's Asian empire. (Page 159.)

Chapter XIV: **Freedom Regained**

Sir Francis Drake's invasion becomes a farce; the Earl of Essex steals the Bishop of Faro's books, and gives them to Sir Thomas Bodley, with which to start Oxford University's library; Portuguese nobility expel the Spanish, install the Braganças as the new royal family; an Irish priest becomes Foreign Minister, swaps Tangier, Bombay and Princess Catarina of Bragança as bride for King Charles II of England, in return for military aid against Spain; marriage a political and personal disaster; the royal profits from the European craze for tobacco; the first gold-rush in the Americas. (Page 176.)

Chapter XV: **Pombal and the King: A Duet in Megalomania**

The Lisbon earthquake's tidal wave reaches the Caribbean; a dictator appointed in the city's ruins; Pombal as propagandist; the true creators of "Pombal's" new Lisbon, and of "Pombaline" architecture; the terrorising of the aristocracy, on behalf of the King; the war with the Jesuits; the destruction of the educational system; the profits of despotism. (Page 192.)

Chapter XVI: **Playground of the Great Powers**

The Braganças flee to Brazil, as the Portuguese people welcome Napoleon's troops as liberators; under French military dictatorship, the country is vandalised; the Duke of Wellington allows the French to retreat, on British ships, taking as their loot, the nation's art treasures; the French military dictatorship replaced by a British one; once freed, the Portuguese engage in devastating civil war, encouraged by Bismarck. (Page 205.)

Chapter XVII: **The Fall of the House of Bragança**

Hans Christian Andersen's report on Portugal, as the model of a modern nation in democracy, technology and social advance; an inept new King; British threats in the race for Africa; the King and Crown Prince are assassinated; the new King exiled to a London suburb. (Page 215.)

Chapter XVIII: **The Slide to Dictatorship**

Too many elections, new presidents and governments lead to anarchy, and violence spreading from the streets into parliament; the republicans try to eradicate Catholicism; the bishops counter with the miracle of Fátima; a military coup ends democracy and creates Salazar as civilian dictator; the state as family, with Salazar as father; the founding of the secret police, and the first Portuguese concentration camp. (Page 225.)

Chapter XIX: **World War II: Betrayal and the Fight for Freedom**

Portuguese tungsten threatens to devastate London; Graham Greene as head of British secret activities in Portugal; accusations of betrayal of the pro-democracy underground; the origins of James Bond; Galvão's exposé of conditions in Portuguese colonies and his capture of a cruise-liner; Salazar's growing humiliation and anger, as Goa falls to the Indians, and a new generation of Portuguese officers in Africa ask: how long? (Page 236.)

Chapter XX: **Freedom at Dawn**

Rádio Clube Português's call to uprising; the revolution of flowers turns sour; Soares, the democrat, wins TV confrontation with Cunhal, the Stalinist; free elections at last; Portugal's emergence as a "Latin tiger economy"; recovery as hope for other nations traumatised in the twentieth century. (Page 248.)

A PERSONAL INTRODUCTION

It was the middle of the afternoon. The Congo was in the midst of another civil war. I was a novice foreign correspondent, newly arrived from London, and I was standing beside the road from Ndola to Elizabethville. Four of my ribs were cracked. My left shoulder was fractured. The barrel of a sub-machine gun was being pressed gently into my back, by a Katangese militiaman, while his colleagues helped themselves to the contents of my luggage from the wreck of the hire-car.

There was a flow of traffic, of white, southern-African mercenaries in cars and other stolen vehicles, escaping the battle-zone I had been trying to reach. Several drivers slowed, and seeing the militia, accelerated again. It seemed to me that over fifty of them passed me by. Then came a new, white Peugeot estate. The driver slammed his brakes, reversed back towards me, opened the rear passenger door, and shouted: "Jump in."

"There's a gun in my back."

"That's why I'm telling you: jump in."

I obeyed. He sped off. With my shoulder broken, I could not close the door, but the wind shut it. We approached the border-post. The driver sounded his three-tone horn, flashed his head-lights, and accelerated. The guards, apparently fearing he would smash their new barrier, hurriedly raised it. We were out of the self-proclaimed Republic of Katanga. But why had the guards let us through, not opened fire on us?

"They've got no ammunition. They haven't been paid any wages. We give them cigarettes they can trade for food."

I looked at the reflection of his face, in the driving mirror. His grave, slightly wry expression was unmoving. Like his companion, he was in his thirties, with a southern European complexion, dark hair, a carefully trimmed moustache. They were dressed in freshly laundered white shirts. A small crucifix and a medallion of Our Lady hung from gold chains around each of their necks.

They told me they were cigarette smugglers, into the Congo, from what is now Zambia. They drove me to the clinic at the copper mine at Kitwe, where I was x-rayed, injected and bound. They took me to the mining company's rest-house, and introduced me to the English manager.

She said: "Morning tea is at half past five."

"I won't be wanting any. I need to rest."

"I'm sorry," she said. "If I make an exception for you, all the other gentlemen would ask for one, wouldn't they? Last breakfast in the dining room at 6.30."

She put a phone call through for me, to Terence Lancaster, my foreign editor in London. Terry said: "I'm very sorry to hear of your mishap. But there's a riot in Cape Town, at the cigarette factory. If you don't get there by tomorrow, I'll break your other shoulder."

My rescuers bought me a large South African brandy at the bar, gave me 500 *Rothmans*, checked my wallet to see I had enough cash, then left me, delivered back to my native culture, never to see them again. It was the first time I had met Portuguese knowingly – and my first encounter, not only with their extraordinary reaching-out to a stranger in need, but with their blend of bravado, honour, ingenuity and poise.

* * *

I went to Tokyo, to promote the Japanese translation of *The Company Savage*, my satire about the irrational decision-making of business executives. The chief executive of the publishing house first took me to have tea with a reviewer, who had written about it favourably, in *Asahi Shimbum*, the leading business daily. It was clear that I was being honoured. He was one of the most influential and respected gurus in the rising of Japan's economic sun. We arrived at the tower block, which houses the Sofia University, and took a lift to the top. We entered the ante-room of the suite of the Dean of Business Studies, passed a line of people waiting, and into the corner-office of the great man. I found myself in the presence of a Portuguese Jesuit, in an impeccably cut clerical suit, and as fluent, lively and engaging in English as he clearly was in Japanese.

It is easy to overlook, at least if one is English, that Portuguese, under the co-founder of the Jesuits, São Francisco Xavier, lived in Japan, for generations before our own ancestors knew of its existence. They debated theology with Buddhist monks, before the royal court. They introduced words to the Japanese language, which are still current, including "orrigato", from "obrigado", meaning "thank you". They brought the recipe for tempura, the favourite fast-food of the Japanese. They taught the technique of manufacturing guns, and constructing buildings which could withstand both artillery attack and earthquake. These structures, in the Portuguese-built city of Nagasaki survived for centuries, and withstood the atomic bomb of 1945 so much better than those of Hiroshima. Portuguese were advisers to the Emperor of China before Marco Polo claimed to have reached there. They brought the chilli plant to India, enabling the invention of "curry", for the English to discover there, and take home with them as a taste of the British Raj.

The East Timorese won their independence from Indonesia in 1999, after one of the longest and most bitter of such struggles in the post-colonial era. One of their first acts, in the creation of their new state, was to adopt Portuguese as their official language, and recognise the escudo as legal tender. There were powerful emotions behind this decision. The intensity with which people in Portugal espoused the cause of freedom for East Timor was, and is, little understood by other Europeans. To the East Timorese, it was such that the Portuguese language itself became an important symbol of the cause.

From other viewpoints, however, the choice was not as idiosyncratic as many foreigners, particularly Australians, their nearest neighbours and protectors, thought it to be. Portuguese is by far the most difficult of the Latin tongues to master, and so the least susceptible to unwelcome listening-in. It is also the third most spoken European language, after English and Spanish, and before French and German. Brazil and Angola, of course, make a hefty contribution to this little-known statistic. But Portuguese is also the *lingua franca* of cattle ranching in northern California, where bulls are fought in the ring with spears tipped with Velcro, to conform with state laws against cruelty to animals, and of fishing communities on the New England coast, such as Provincetown and Providence, where Portuguese are rated the most courageous and skilled of seafarers. At the Kennedy family's summer parish church of São Francisco Xavier, in Hyannis, two Masses on Sunday are said in Portuguese.

So it is, behind the swing-doors of London's "Italian" *trattorias*, which are predominantly owned and run by Portuguese impersonating Italians. The low profile of the Portuguese in London was tragically typified, when the party-boat, the *Marchioness*, was rammed and sunk in the Thames by a dredger. Virtually none of the media reported that many of those drowned were young Portuguese investment bankers, working in the City, celebrating a colleague's birthday. Portuguese also own and run over 400 restaurants in Paris, some "Latin American", but mostly "French". The city's newest, most glittering icon – the Louvre pyramid – was built by a Portuguese construction company.

Portuguese is the second language of Johannesburg in South Africa, of Newark, New Jersey, of Luxembourg, and of Caracas, the capital of Venezuela. There are locally-born Portuguese-speaking communities in, among countless places, India, Malaysia, Taiwan and China — as well as in Bermuda, Jersey, Toronto, Los Angeles and Brisbane.

This is not reflected in official figures, largely because most Portuguese abroad are citizens of their country of residence. But as Mário Soares said: "Language is the bond. To speak Portuguese is to be Portuguese." They are all around, speaking so quietly, few of us hear their presence.

* * *

On Easter morning, 1988, Catherine and I, and our two sons, Matt and Sam, woke in our new home on the Cabo da Roca, the great peninsula that juts from the Serra da Sintra, west of Lisbon, into the Atlantic. From the terrace, we saw the sun transformed by the rising mist, into a silver disc. The moon was still shining, above the wooded *serra*, behind the house, where, in the night, wolves howled and foxes prowled. In the sky, a white eagle and two falcons hovered. In the meadow beside us, wild flowers, and bushes of rosemary and blackberry, fluttered in the breeze. A donkey pulled a cart up the track to the Sunday market, piled with vegetables, lemons, jams, honey, fragrant bundles of coriander and boxes of edible snails. From the ocean below the cliff, came the slow chugging of the fishing boats taking their morning catch to the auction, around the coast in Cascais.

Sintra has been a refuge for generations of English writers. In 1757, Henry Fielding, the great comic novelist, feeling ill and ill-humoured, abandoned hope that the sun would ever shine on Bath that summer. He boarded a packet-boat at Tilbury, for Lisbon. There, he hired mules and a carriage to carry him up the hill to Sintra town where he rented a mansion. His health and mood seemed to recover almost immediately. He wrote to his brother, declaring Sintra to be the finest place on earth in which to write a new novel, and asking him to send from London a secretary, to whom to dictate it, a conversationalist, possibly a clergyman, to entertain him in the evenings, and two broad-brimmed hats. Before any of these arrived, however, he died of liver failure.

At the end of that century, Robert Southey, future Poet Laureate, and author of *A Portuguese Journal*, brought his wife and children to live in Sintra and urged the other members of the English romantic movement to join him there. Coleridge came and described the region as "a garden of Eden, set by a silver sea". William and Dorothy Wordsworth followed; but Dorothy became incensed that Fielding had been unceremoniously buried, by the local Anglican community, in an unmarked grave. She hurried back to England and wrote a furious pamphlet, denouncing the "philistine" English residents of Lisbon, for their lack of respect.

Alfred Lord Tennyson lingered in Sintra. Lord Byron started *Childe Harold* here. Down the hill, in the Estoril casino, Ian Fleming conceived the character of James Bond, and the plot of his first novel, *Casino Royale*. Until shortly before his death, Graham Greene used to visit Sintra, and stay in a house belonging to the Marquesa de Cadaval. During World War II he had been the London-based director of British secret operations in Portugal. *Our Man in Havana* was the satire that resulted – the change of locale being made to get it past the censor. In it, he parodied himself, for playing with secret service agents as though they were toys, and only realising they were human beings when they were killed. The surviving agents, still living in and

21

around Sintra, continued to dread him, and his visits, for decades after the end of the war.

Christopher Isherwood had come to live in Sintra, in the late 1930s, with Heinz, his German partner, and Stephen Spender, who was accompanied by a Welsh church-organist. Heinz's presence in Portugal was reported to the German consul in Lisbon. He was ordered to report to the consulate as a preliminary to being conscripted into the German army. Otherwise, he would be listed as a deserter, and he could be extradited from Portugal, to face a court martial, and be sentenced to a military prison.

Isherwood took Heinz to the most expensive lawyer he could find in Lisbon, to ask for help. The lawyer regretted, he could do nothing. They took the train back to Sintra. In the café opposite the railway station, a waiter found the couple, both in tears.

He asked them what was the matter. When they explained, he said: "Don't worry. I can arrange it."

Incredulous, they inquired, "How much will you charge?"

"Of course, nothing", the waiter replied. He proved to be as good as his word, and, although Spender and his companion left after a tiff, Isherwood remained in Sintra, with Heinz acting as his housekeeper. Here, he completed *I am a Camera*, which became the Hollywood musical, *Cabaret*. W. H. Auden joined him, and they co-wrote *The Ascent of F6*, getting themselves into the mood in the mornings, by scrabbling up one or another of the *serra*'s rocky crags.

During our first autumn, a week after the Frankfurt Book Fair, we watched and listened, in awe, to a great storm, roaring, flashing and rushing towards us, from the ocean. A lightening bolt struck our chimney, another the village's electricity sub-station, leaving us without power or heat. Water slid beneath the French windows. I slipped on wet floor-tiles, and fell, fracturing my arm.

After an operation to bolt it together, I was recovering from the anaesthetic in a room in a clinic in Lisbon. Catherine was with me, talking as she looked out of the window: "The next door building has a beautiful garden, with palm-trees and baroque murals. The tables are laid with white cloths and buckets of champagne. There are waiters dressed in livery. Beautiful people are walking down from the terrace, dressed in the latest Italian..."

A nurse came in. Giving me another injection in the upper-quartile of my buttock, he explained: "That's the writers' club."

Clubs for writers I had visited had included a sub-basement in Tokyo, a large, shabby wooden hut outside Moscow, and the scrum-bar at Groucho's in London. I had never before encountered one even approaching elegance. Within a few months, after an introduction to Dr. Salles Lane, the Grémio Literário's secretary, we too were on its terrace overlooking the River Tagus, planning the next chapter over sautéed shrimp and casseroled partridge.

* * *

We had moved from London, when I was not yet fifty. My sight had deteriorated, through untreatable retinal failure, by 95 per cent, to a range of ten degrees. To drive a car, with safety, one must have at least 120 degrees. In the USA, where I had been working on a film-script, one becomes "legally" blind, at 20 degrees. If I out-stretched my right hand, and held it in front of my eyes, I could still see four fingers, but not my thumb at the same time.

I had spent most of my adult life, thus far, as a foreign correspondent and a travel writer and editor. Now, I could no longer travel independently. I had fallen down an open manhole on Pushkin Square in Moscow, and across a loading-bay of Lexington Avenue in Manhattan. On my last solo journey, at Brussels airport, I picked up an attaché-case belonging to a European official, instead of my own, and was apprehended, trying to board a plane with it.

By now, my native London had become a dangerous and even a hostile territory. Tumbling down the steps on Ludgate Hill, on my way from St Paul's Cathedral to Fleet Street, or, on my way home from the office, falling across an abandoned luggage trolley at Waterloo Station, I experienced the current of people dividing, to pass around me, then merging again.

I had a wooden shed built at the back of our suburban garden, in Barnes. I took to leaving for work through the front door, and arriving for it, through the side-passage between our house, and the one next door. In the hut, I wrote a novel, *The Man Who Stole the Mona Lisa*. It was wonderfully well-reviewed in New York, and in London named by *The Times* as one of the two best thrillers of the year. My agent told me, over lunch in the Savoy Grill, we would both become rich, from my future fiction.

According to the actuarial tables, my life expectancy (excluding future accidents) was another 24 years. This was twice the prison sentence most convicted murderers serve. Was I to spend it in a four-by-five metre solitary cell, writing stories I could neither read, nor cast from my mind in the middle of the night? It was time to start another life somewhere else.

Our friends were perplexed by our choice of Sintra, instead of the south of France or Tuscany. Even a Portuguese lawyer, practising in London, implored us to try Provence instead. Portugal was Europe's banana republic: too corrupt, impoverished, decayed, illiterate, disease-ridden for people like us. Strikes were endemic. Inflation was rising at a rate that shattered financial thermometers. The escudo was falling. The economy, if you could call it that, was in decline. Experts predicted that it would take two generations of hard work and severe sacrifice to reduce the national debt to a manageable level.

The roads were pot-holed. The Portuguese were the most dangerous drivers in western Europe. The only supermarket in the Lisbon area offered little but cabbage for soup, salted cod, canned tomatoes and margarine.

A lawyer in Lisbon told us of driving with a client, a paramount chief from Nigeria, to the airport. When would his excellency be returning to Lisbon?

"I won't be," the chief replied. "It's too like Africa."

On a visit to Lisbon, we found amputees lying on the pavement, begging. There was mould on the carpet of our four-star hotel room. Making a phone call was a time-demanding challenge. Abandoned, decaying villas stood alongside shacks, housing refugees from the former African colonies. The national shrine, the Jerónimos, was being eaten away, un-checked, by pigeon-droppings.

Yet there seemed to us to be another side to it. Crossing the Spanish border at Badajoz, into the Portuguese province of Alentejo, we were captivated by the change of mood, from seeming despair, to hope. This is less noticeable today, thanks to the aid Madrid and Brussels have given south-western Spain; but travellers before us had been remarking on it, from Hans Christian Andersen in the mid-nineteenth century, on the alertness and courtesy of the guards who policed the border, the fresh paint on the village houses, the profusion of flowers in their well-kept gardens, the improvement in the quality of the cooking and wine-making, the friendly curiosity of the children if they spotted foreigners

24

in a café, the municipal pride that kept the historic towns so well preserved, and so alive. There were local landscape-painters, marble-sculptors, embroider, wood-carvers, poets. Nuns preserved plums in Elvas and invented new cakes: it was from here that Catarina of Bragança brought the institution of afternoon tea to England, including cake-making nuns from Alentejo in her retinue.

The Portuguese had largely lost out in the 20th century. Their mineral rights in central Africa had been seized by the British, their "oldest allies". Their military involvement on the allied side in World War I, had been brief but disastrous. An ineffectual monarchy had collapsed, to be succeeded by anarchy, then an inept military junta, who gratefully passed on their powers to Oliveira Salazar. He rescued the country from bankruptcy, restored its currency, and found investment funds for a huge development programme.

He also became a dictator, and, like other dictators, he did not know how to retire. After keeping Portugal out of military involvement in World War II, he sent waves of young conscript soldiers to Africa and their deaths, in a futile attempt to turn the tide of nationalism there. The armed forces and then the communists seized power. It was the only instance of such coups d'état in a west European country. By the time democracy prevailed, in the late 1970s, Portugal had been brought back to the plight where it had started the twentieth century: bankrupt and in chaos.

Our feeling was that the Portuguese had not deserved their fate. They had no more brought it on themselves than I had inflicted my blindness on myself. We had both been out of luck, casualties of misfortune. It also seemed us that the Portuguese, and hopefully ourselves, had hit bottom, had nowhere to go but up. Many of them showed the energy, ingenuity and determination to re-create the nation, for the twenty-first century. We had been born and brought up in a Britain of gradual decline, which was not being reversed. It was an inviting prospect to watch a country rising again.

* * *

Pedro da Cunha and I first met after midnight, in a car park, outside a fado-hall, off the beltway north of Lisbon. We were both leaving the birthday party for a teacher at St Dominic's, the Irish

Dominican school our children attended. He was one of many Portuguese who had recently returned from abroad, with high qualifications earned in exile – in anything from medicine and computer technology, to museum curatorship and music — with a determination to help get newly democratic Portugal back on its feet. In the dark, I could not see him, but I can still hear, in my mind, the first impact of his voice: warm, confident, alert, full of curiosity and openness, with a wry tinge.

He had returned to become Secretary of State for Educational Reform. He, and his American wife, Susan, met us at Sunday Mass at St Mary's, in Estoril. Over coffee afterwards, our conversations continued. We began to meet for lunches and dinners, long conversations on weekend afternoons. We joined a dining club, which was supposed to study and discuss modern theology, and did so about half the time.

Pedro was extraordinarily knowledgeable, fast-minded, and fascinated by opening new perspectives. Our friendship, which lasted until his death from cancer seven years later, was among the most valued of my life, and the least expected.

Pedro and I had been born within a year of one another – I in London, he in Lisbon. From there, our paths seem to have diverged still further. I experienced, under protest, a Quaker boarding school in the west of England – cold baths in the winter, at seven in the morning; a single change of underclothes a week; suppers of meat with a green hue, or a grey mash smelling of fish oil, we told each other was canned cat-food; mostly mediocre teaching; and a punishment called "running the triangle". Hours of collective, silent meditation were followed by a school outing to a Billy Graham evangelical rally, where my aversion to religion reached the point where I decided I was an atheist.

Meanwhile, Pedro, undergoing the greater rigours of a Jesuit school and house of formation in the north of Portugal, which left several of his contemporaries there physically and mentally bruised, was embarking on priesthood.

While I was at Cambridge, ignoring my studies to immerse myself in undergraduate journalism, Pedro was taking a degree in philosophy at Braga, then another in theology at Granada. As a novice foreign correspondent, I covered train and plane crashes, wars and summit meetings. Pedro was now at Boston College, gaining a master's degree in psychology. While I became a bureau chief in Moscow, Pedro moved to Boston University, and was writing his doctoral thesis, on education.

By the time the call came to return to Lisbon, he had left the priesthood formally (few of his friends thought he ever did so in spirit), and was a US citizen.

Portugal was joining the European Union. Grants, low-interest loans and investment funds were flowing in from the rich north of Europe. A Social Democrat government had been elected, under Aníbal Cavaco Silva, who had a doctorate in economics from Coimbra, and had become a lecturer at the elite, new English University of York. The new minister of finance had gained his second PhD at the University of Chicago, and taught at Yale, before joining the World Bank, to direct its policy towards the Third World. The new foreign minister had taught foreign affairs at Georgetown University. I counted, at the time, that the members of the new Portuguese government had, between them, more doctorates than the British cabinet had bachelor's degrees.

Roberto Carneiro, the new minister of education, had the added distinction, of being the first ethnic Chinese (or, indeed, Asian) to hold cabinet rank in a European country. His department was designated a "super-ministry". He read Pedro's dissertation on problems of educating migrant Portuguese children in New England. He called him, to solve the crisis in education in Portugal itself. It had the lowest scores for adult literacy and numeracy, in western Europe.

Five years after Pedro's appointment as Secretary of State for Educational Reform, *The Financial Times* of London reported that, in literacy and numeracy among 18 year-olds, Portugal, on its way up, had overtaken England, on its way down.

In the impoverished north east he found children at school in the morning, apparently too tired to be attentive. Their mothers gave them breakfasts of dry bread and wine, to stave off their hunger-pangs. He introduced school breakfasts, of ham and cheese sandwiches, fruit and milk. Malnutrition and child-inebriation declined, attendance increased, and so did scores. Teachers throughout the country were given incentives, not so much for the years of service, but for further training. Maximum class sizes were halved. A new curriculum was formulated, to include practical, social and survival skills: how to measure, take a family photograph, swim. Master craftsmen were paid to take on young people as apprentices. Pedro also asserted that Portugal was now a multicultural society. Catholicism, to which he himself was dedicated, no longer had a religious monopoly; other faiths had to be accommodated, and respected.

The economy was growing at much the fastest rate in Europe. Business publications started referring to it as the "Portuguese tiger". The Ford Motor Company reported that Portuguese school-leavers now took half the time to learn to control an electronic robot, than their peers in the industrial north of England. Volkswagen joined with Ford to create, near Setúbal, south of Lisbon, a plant to produce all the world's Galaxies and Sharans. Such vehicles overtook cellulose for paper-making, to become Portugal's largest single export.

The speed with which Portugal was emerging from its third-world plight was startling. In some areas, it was leap-frogging over "developed" countries. A study by BNP, the French bank, found that Banco Comercial Português had achieved the highest standards of customer-service in all Europe. When we arrived, there had been no credit-cards. Now, it was the first country where you could buy a railway ticket, and reserve a seat on the train, through almost any ATM. Portuguese *autostradas* became the first anywhere with fully-electronic toll-gates. New methods of extracting and refining copper, led to the reopening of mines, unworked since Roman times. Hospitals acquired high-tech equipment, consultants in Britain could only dream of.

Suburban sprawl spread westward from Lisbon, along the new highway, which was soon filled, in early mornings and late evenings, with near-stationary *Alfa Romeos, BMWs* and *Volvos,* their drivers speaking on their mobiles, dictating into their recording machines, smoothing their faces with electric razors, the *Wall Street Journal Europe* pressed against their steering wheels. Land, ear-marked to be a university campus became, instead, a Japanese golf-club. Pastures where sheep and goats had grazed, became the sites of some of the biggest shopping malls in Europe, containing Au Printemps from France, C&A from Holland, Captain Tapioca from Spain, Divani & Divani from Italy, The Bodyshop and Mothercare from England, and from across the Atlantic, along with McDonald's and Pizza Hut, Warner multi-screen cinemas.

It was easy for foreigners living there, comfortably, to regret – and many of us did openly – the loss of quaintness and charm, symbolised by the replacement of the donkey and cart with the *Toyota* pick-up. There were instances of corruption in granting building permits and awarding public works contracts. Drug-abuse, street-crime and stress-related illnesses were increasing, though from among the lowest levels in Europe.

However, there were now specially-designed planes and helicopters, to fight the forest fires which had annually ravaged the countryside in summer. Families could afford to heat their homes in winter, to install electricity and telephones. Sewerage systems had been installed. Inflation was among the lowest in the western world. Unemployment was the lowest in the EU, and workers received their wages regularly. Tuberculosis and other diseases of poverty were in decline. The gap between the richest and the poorest narrowed, to become less extreme than in the UK.

But was Portugal losing her identity? On the contrary, it was here that the process known as globalisation began, and now the country had returned from its long isolation, to take up a role in the world again.

Lisbon is often likened in guide-books to São Francisco, because of its streets that rise so dramatically from the waterfront, and Rome, because it is built on seven hills. In truth, there is, and surely never will be, any mistaking the Portuguese capital for anywhere else. So far from surrendering its compelling character to the twenty-first century's forces of homogeneity, the new prosperity has instead revived Lisbon's justifiable pride in its distinctiveness.

* * *

Two days before Pedro da Cunha died, courageously, refusing those pain-killing drugs which might diminish his mental alertness, he telephoned me in the morning. He said he had spent the night reading the first chapters of this book. He questioned my dating of the building of the aqueduct at Alcântara (since corrected). The rest of my account of Portugal's early years, he fully endorsed, and readily gave me his leave to cite his support. Another friend, Professor Fernando d'Orey of the New University of Lisbon, read through my manuscript three times, after it was completed. He said its most important contribution was its perspective on Portugal's origins.

29

The birth of Portugal as a nation-state, the only one in Iberia to be independent of Spain, is a significant landmark in the shaping of the modern world beyond. My account differs radically from previous versions. Between Portugal's foundation, in the middle ages, and the restoration of democracy near the end of the twentieth century, there had been censorship for all but about 50 years. Many documents which were not suppressed or altered by the censors, were destroyed in the Lisbon earthquake, the Napoleonic invasion, the British occupation, or by neglect.

Thus each succeeding regime was free to re-invent history. Portuguese of Pedro's and my generation, were taught, under Salazar's dictatorship, of a medieval, Christian, Che Guevara figure, who inspired his people to rise up against, and overthrow their Islamic oppressors. The new nation then discovered and exerted power in Africa, Asia, and the half of South America it had not ceded to Spain, with Bible and breech-loading cannon, in the cause of Christ and trade.

This myth of national destiny led Salazar himself into committing Portugal to his disastrous wars in Africa. It also underlay a persistent self-doubt, among an older generation of Portuguese, about their national identity: a feeling that while they were Europeans, they belonged elsewhere.

The reality is strikingly different. It is revealed by reference to sources outside Portugal itself. The most notable of these are the records of the twelfth century Council of Troyes, between kings of France and Germany and the Pope, over which St Bernard of Clairvaux, presided. There and then, the Order of the Knights Templar was established, with the specific task of creating a new European nation, which came to be called Portugal. It did not come into being as a lone entity, but as an organic part of an emerging Europe, with which it is now re-united.

Tourists visiting Portugal are taken to see the great abbey at Batalha, built to commemorate a celebrated victory over the Spanish. This confirmed Portugal's nationhood; but Pedro held that the nation's soul is to be found nearby, at the Cistercian abbey at Alcobaça, built by monks from Burgundy, where a new, humanistic civilisation was created, and from where it spread. The role of the Portuguese has not been as conquerors, let alone the conquered, but as a pivot, a conduit, by means of which ideas, knowledge and technologies have moved through Europe, and the world.

CHAPTER 1

FROM JONAH TO JULIUS CAESAR

The Book of Jonah was written in around 700 BC, and is still read in synagogues on the Day of Atonement. It is one of the shortest books in the Bible, and also the oldest surviving satire.

Jonah, according to the anonymous author, was a prophet. God ordered him to hurry to Nineveh, and warn its residents that He was angry with them, for their sinful ways. Unless they repented quickly, God would destroy their city, with them in it.

Jonah detested the people of Nineveh. Instead, he went to the seaport of Jaffa, and bought a ticket on board a ship bound for a destination beyond God's reach. Soon after the ship sailed, a violent storm blew up. The captain and crew threw Jonah overboard.

Jonah was swallowed by a giant fish, which disgorged him on to the shore, where God repeated His orders. Then God calmed the sea, and the ship continued to its Godless destination, Tarshish.

Tarshish was identified in the tenth chapter of Genesis as a distant nation, founded after the flood by a great-grandson of Noah. The forty-eighth Psalm described how even great Kings could be "filled with alarm and panic, and trembling, and toss in pain... like the ships of Tarshish, when the east wind strikes them".

Herodotus, the Greek geographer and historian, wrote in the fifth century BC, that Rex Argentonius, The Silver King, of Tarshish was 120 years old, and that access to his realm was guarded by giant sea-monsters and serpents, waiting for ships to wreck and sailors to devour. Strabo, another leading Greek scholar, who lived during the time of Jesus, wrote in his treatise *Geographia*, that this was the land of the adventures of Ulysses.

In as famous a series of Greek legends, Hercules came to Tarshish, and first stole King Gades' herd of red bulls, then the golden apples of Hesperides. It has been suggested that the latter were oranges; today, in some east Mediterranean languages, the word for orange is "Portugal".

For at least a thousand years, the Pillars of Hercules, on the narrow strait which separates the Mediterranean Sea from the wild Atlantic Ocean, had been regarded as the western boundary of Europe (which was calculated to occupy half the world's surface), and so where civilisation ended. Tarshish was the land that lay beyond: today, the west of Andalucia, and Portugal south of Lisbon. (Tarshish survives as a name of a small town in Spain, six kilometres from the present Portuguese border, and of a shellfish found uniquely off the west coast of Portugal.)

In 241 BC, Carthage, for five centuries the great North African merchant power of the Mediterranean, master of its sea-routes and its trading cities, was defeated by its upstart northern neighbour, Rome. After a war which had lasted twenty-three years, the Romans, as the new super-power of the civilised world, imposed terms of surrender which their own official historian, Livy, was later to describe as "grasping and tyrannical".

The Romans, in Livy's words, "added insult to injury" in their humiliation of Hamilcar, Carthage's military commander-in-chief, superior in honour and skill, but hopelessly out-numbered. He was in effect banished from the Mediterranean, and exiled to Tarshish. As Livy was to relate, over more than 600 pages of his *History of Rome*, it was to prove the costliest mistake the rising empire could have made.

Before Hamilcar left Carthage, he was begged by his eight-year-old son, Hannibal, to take him with him into exile. Livy recounted that Hamilcar took Hannibal to the Temple of Melqart, the city-state's chief god. "Hamilcar led the boy to the altar, and made him solemnly swear that as soon as he was old enough, he would become the enemy of the Roman people." Then they set off together.

Those who survived a rarely risked journey by sea, of a little more than a hundred kilometres beyond the Pillars of Hercules, came to a long, sheltered bay. Apparently unknown to the Romans then, it is today called the Bay of Cadiz. It was formed by the estuaries of three rivers. On the banks of the first, the Guadalquivir, the great cities of Cadiz and Seville were to be built. The second, the Rio Tinto, the Red

River, was so named from the colour of the vast copper deposits on its bed; one of the modern world's largest mining companies, Rio Tinto Zinc, is named after it.

The Guadiana, the third and westernmost of the rivers, is today the border between Spain and Portugal. Generations of travellers have remarked how, on crossing it, one leaves a rather arid, Mediterranean terrain and climate, and enters an Atlantic one, more fertile and more temperate in its weather. The bay itself was full of fish, the land rich with flowers, fruits, nuts, wild asparagus, honey-bees, rabbits, hares, foxes, wolves, bears, deer, and wild boar, the air with partridge and pheasant, and with their hunters, white eagles and falcons.

Echoes of a local religion, recorded in the second century after Christ, are of a god-King, Gargaris, inventor of cultivation, and of Abis, who forbade the nobility from working, and divided the rest of the people into five tribes.

It was on the banks of the Guadiana that the Romans were later to build the city of Merida, one of the finest in the empire, as the capital of what was to become Portugal, which they called Lusitânia.

Archaeologists have discovered, from the evidence of graves, that Tarshish had already been known for centuries to other people from the Mediterranean: Jews, Phoenicians, Cypriots and Greeks had settlements here, long before Hannibal arrived. Carthaginian settlers had built at least one great temple, about 150 kilometres north of the Guadiana's estuary, whose pillars now form part of the portico of Portugal's University of Évora. The settlers had an alphabet, and a legal code, written in rhyming couplets, so that it could be learnt by heart.

The Romans had yet to realise that in the Sierra Morena, the hills and mountains to which the River Guadalquivir led upstream, were huge quantities of silver — sufficient to pay for the recruiting, equipment, training, maintenance and wages of a large army. Under the Carthaginians, the number of workers employed in these mines grew to over 20,000.

On the west bank of the River Guadiana, which is now the Portuguese province of Alentejo, were vast deposits of copper, tin, zinc and phosphorous, the ingredients for making bronze. Bronze was the alloy from which weapons, shields and armour were manufactured, and with which wooden warships were held together.

At the point at which the Guadiana became navigable, the Carthaginians built a town, Myrtilis, and docks, where rafts could be loaded with the minerals, and sent down the river to the estuary, where they built a harbour, smelters and weapons factories. Myrtilis is known now as Mértola. Until the 1960s, convoys of mineral-carrying ships took the copper etc. into their holds there, and carried it to England for processing. Today, more than 2,000 years after the Carthaginians left, the Portuguese government and RTZ are still mining ores in Alentejo, which still has the largest known copper and the richest tin reserves in Europe.

In south-west Iberia then, there was no nation in the sense we understand it. It was populated by the tribes mythologically created by the god-King Abis. None fought back more fiercely and bravely against Hamilcar's attempts to subdue and colonise them than the Lusitanians, who lived by and to the north of the River Tagus. Hamilcar was killed by them in battle, in 230 BC.

Hannibal was seventeen years old then, and became Carthaginian governor of Iberia when he was twenty-six. He seems to have spent most of the intervening years in Gades (Cadiz), studying under a Greek tutor and Carthaginian military officers. During those years, his brother-in-law Hasdrubal, as the interim governor, had sought and achieved conciliation with the Lusitanians and other tribes, through gifts and trade. The Carthaginians were now wealthier, as masters of southern Iberia, than they had been as masters of the Mediterranean.

"The troops received Hannibal with only enthusiasm," Livy wrote. The older soldiers thought it was as though he was his father reincarnated. In "the features and expression of the son's face, they saw the same vigour, the same fire in his eyes. Very soon, he found he no longer needed to rely upon his father's memory to make himself loved and obeyed. His own qualities were sufficient. Under his leadership, the men always showed outstanding dash and confidence. He was reckless in courting danger; and when he was in it, he showed brilliant tactical ability."

Hannibal married Imulce, daughter of the lord of the Silver Mountains, and the legend is that they had one son. The partnership was short-lived. "From the very first day of his command," wrote Livy, "Hannibal acted as if he had definite instructions to take Italy, to make war on Rome. Speed was the essence of his plan. The violent death of his father reminded him that he was not immune from an early end, and had no time to spare."

Twenty-four elephants were brought by ship from North Africa. Roman sources later identified and named the landing place, in the Algarve, as Portus Hannibalis, now known as Portimão. They were joined by over 1,000 Berber horsemen, also from North Africa, wielding spears.

Hannibal went to the temple of Hercules, and prayed for strength. He called a great gathering of Iberian fighting men, and rousingly offered them the opportunity "to begin a war against Rome which, with God's help, will fill your pockets with gold and carry your fame to the world."

This is not the place to re-tell the story of how Hannibal led his elephants and his army of North Africans and Iberians through the Pyrenees and over the Alps into Italy, and came within ten kilometres of destroying Rome. The importance to us, in the history of Portugal, was Rome's response.

By the spring of 218 BC, Hannibal had crossed the Apennines, won a major battle, and, with reinforcements newly arrived from Iberia, was marching towards Rome. The Roman Senate sent a large force, under General Gaius Cornelius Scipio, to Iberia. They seemed to have had no thought at that time of conquering, let alone colonising, the peninsula. Their task was to help save Rome, by cutting off Hannibal's source of reinforcements and money.

In the eastern part of Iberia, Scipio and his troops found little resistance. The tribespeople had become accustomed over centuries to foreign domination of one kind or another. The Romans spent heavily, buying local supplies, and were relatively humane in their treatment of the native population. When Scipio's soldiers marched inland, however, and reached what is now Portugal, in 197 BC, they came face to face with the Lusitanians.

During the fifteen years of war that followed, the Lusitanians fought without armour, lightly clothed, and often on horseback, wielding swords, poisoned javelins, and slings. They declined the set-piece battle, and hid in the hills and mountains of the Serra da Estrela, from which they launched sudden, devastating attacks. According to Roman accounts, they carried poison pellets, with which to commit suicide if they were captured. If taken prisoner alive, they would withstand any amount of torture, until death, rather than reveal information.

It took 150,000 Roman troops to impose a tense peace on Lusitania, requiring the Romans to introduce permanent, professional military service for the first time. Then, there rose among the Lusitanians a new leader, a shepherd named Viriatus, who called his people again to rise against the Romans. For eight years, he led his followers in lightning raids on the foreign forces. The Roman generals sued for peace, which they accepted on humiliating terms. These, the Senate rejected. Under the pretext of wishing to negotiate with him further, the Romans hired agents, who posed as intermediaries, gained access to Viriatus and poisoned him.

The Romans divided Iberia into two provinces, the peaceful Hispania Citerior, whose borders were approximately those of today's Spain, and rebellious Hispania Ulterior, to the west, of which today's Portugal was the largest part.

Two important differences between the two provinces were that Citerior was, like Rome, a Mediterranean country, climate and culture. Ulterior was an Atlantic one. Such was the intransigence of the Lusitanians living, often in hiding, in the central highlands, that Rome's effective rule did not reach much further north than the River Tagus.

In 61 BC, in Rome, in a lottery conducted among a small group of senior officials, the governorship of Hispania Ulterior was won by Julius Caesar. His win, which few at the time thought to be an enviable one, was not only going to transform his fortunes. It was to change fundamentally the course of the history of western Europe.

His exact birth-date is unknown, but he was probably under forty years old. He had been until recently the chief priest of the city of Rome. He had just caused great scandal by divorcing his second wife, on grounds of alleged, but unproved blasphemy, making his famous but somewhat lame remark: "Caesar's wife must be above suspicion."

Caesar was also deeply in debt. Instead of waiting for the Senate's ratification of his prize, thus giving his creditors time to learn of it and to obtain a court order to stop him leaving the city until he settled with them, he slipped out of Rome without delay, and sailed to Cadiz.

This was not his first visit to the province. He had served, ten years before, as an assistant to a previous governor. Nor did he seem to have any hesitation or doubt as to what he was to do here. Plutarch, the Roman biographer, wrote that on arrival, Caesar read a life of Alexander the Great, put the book down with a sigh, and said: "At my age, Alexander was already a King, and I've yet to achieve anything really remarkable."

Julius Caesar recruited 10,000 soldiers, and added them to the 20,000 which had come under his command on taking up the governorship. He marched them over the River Tagus, and into Lusitania. It was a route many of his predecessors had attempted, with disastrous consequences. Caesar's motive, however, was different. He had come not to conquer, but to loot, plunder and exact tributes in return for mercy. This proved a more practical tactic. Both Lusitânia and the region to its north were rich in gold and silver, which the Lusitanians and their neighbours had refined, and made into jewellery and coin in immense quantities. These the Romans took from them by surprise and superior force, and hurriedly withdrew with their spoils.

Caesar had a fleet sail north, to terrorise the people who lived along the River Douro. "Douro" means "of gold", and at that time its waters glittered with it. On its banks were open-cast mines, great strips cut in the hillsides, as much as 200 metres wide, and a kilometre long, in which worked as many as 1,000 men a mine. Caesar's warships soon left, laden with ingots.

Under Julius Caesar's supervision, the spoils were split three ways: one third to be sent to the treasury in Rome, one third to be shared between the looting soldiers, and one third for Caesar himself. In the already pacified area south of the River Tagus, near the town of Beja in the region now known as Alentejo, he owned and operated gold-mines in his wife's name, Juliana. Legionnaires who guarded the routes down which the gold bullion was transported, were rewarded with the right to mine and smelt the copper ore on the roadsides, and to create prosperous farms, growing olives, grapes and wheat. They married locally and never returned to Rome. Their descendants are there still.

After two years, Caesar left and returned to Rome, without awaiting his successor's arrival. His plunder of Hispania Ulterior had been acclaimed as a "triumph" by the Senate. He had not only repaid his debts, but had amassed sufficient fortunes to engage in, among other things, large-scale electoral bribery. He arrived back in time to stand for election to one of the two vacant consulships, and to pay for more than enough votes to secure it. Thus he obtained the means, the position and the power to invade and occupy Gaul, the Low Countries, and England.

For centuries before the Romans had come to Tarshish, merchant mariners, described as "shy and dark", from its south-west coast, today's Algarve, had been navigating their way up the coast of continental Europe, and then across the Bay of Biscay to Cornwall. There, they bought tin, in exchange for bronze and gold. Many of the legionnaires who marched overland with Caesar across the continent, and invaded England in 55 BC, were their descendants, rather than Italians, and had never set foot in Rome itself. Hadrian, who became the governor of England, was from Cadiz. British archaeologists have found, as far north as Hadrian's Wall, jars made in and shipped from Beja, in Portugal, which had contained olive oil.

CHAPTER II

ROME ON THE ATLANTIC

As you enter the village of Almoçageme, forty minutes west of Lisbon, you pass, on the right, the ruins of a house. Over its whole area, a corrugated metal roof has been erected, and earth temporarily re-covers its mosaic floor, to protect it from the Atlantic's salt winds.

This house was the westernmost point of the Roman empire. It overlooks rough pastures abounding in the wild lilies unique to this region. A path leads down to a cove, with caves and grottoes carved out by the ocean's pounding waves. Early in the first century AD, a group of Roman tourists visited here, and were convinced that they saw sea-nymphs and goddesses dancing in the grottoes. So moved were they by the experience, they wrote a letter (preserved today in the Hamilton Collection in the Public Records Office in Edinburgh) to the Emperor Tiberius, describing their experience, and commissioned a messenger to take it to him in Rome.

It had taken the Romans 200 years of recurrent warfare to pacify the land they now called Lusitânia, whose borders were not much larger than Portugal's today. What they had fought so hard to win, they set about enjoying in peace.

As word spread of its attractions, Italians came and settled, adding to those who had opted to stay on after serving in the military and make new homes here. Their numbers were not recorded, but the archaeological evidence is that there were clearly very many of them. Farmers today use ploughs which dig deeper into the earth than previously; and it is almost commonplace for them to turn up chunks of mosaics and inscriptions and patterns carved in stone, which they leave at the side of the field or incorporate into walls.

Road construction and other public works are uncovering villas, temples and settlements. Several times, new highways have been re-routed. Fourteen major Roman sites have been excavated recently or are still being dug. Roman bridges, including that on the road north from Sintra to Mafra, are still in use, as are the two-storey Roman buildings. The parish church at Egitania, now called Idanha-a-Velha, on the main road the Romans built from Mérida to Viseu, is an adapted Roman temple.

At Torre de Palma, in northern Alentejo, on the Roman road that goes eastwards from Lisbon, archaeologists from Louisville University, in the USA, uncovered in 1947 a marble mosaic, wonderfully preserved, depicting the muses. It is one of the finest to have been discovered so far in Rome's western empire. The Americans remained for a further twenty-eight years, uncovering the everyday life in a small town in Roman Lusitânia — the residential district, with the houses of the Italians, the quarter for their Lusitanian servants and slaves, and the industrial zone, with its workshops and warehouses.

In southern Alentejo, at Santa Cucufate, is a wealthy Italian's country mansion, in a remarkable state of preservation. Large parts of its walls, its arched doorways and its carved pillars are still standing. So soundly did its first owner build it, it was maintained in continuous occupation for the next 1,500 years.

In a square in Alentejo's capital, Évora, is a raised, pillared temple. At Milreu, near the Algarve's capital, Faro, are pillars, walls and mosaics of a much larger temple, thought to have been a major place of pilgrimage.

In Lisbon, the vast Roman theatre is well preserved, as it has been only partly excavated because of cost and practicality. At Conímbriga, a Roman spa south of today's Coimbra, extensive excavations have revealed a large part of the town, and the museum has a major display of utensils and decorative objects.

The jewel in all this archaeological treasure is Mérida. Founded by Emperor Augustus as Lusitânia's capital, it is just across today's Portuguese border with Spain, reached by a bridge of sixty spans, first built across the River Guadiana in AD 25.

Here is the most dramatic display of imperial Rome in western Europe, far excelling Arles or Nîmes in France, or Verulamium, in England. In the 15,000-seat circus, gladiators fought wild animals or one another. It was designed so that it could be flooded, to stage mock naval battles between rival fleets of miniature galleys: Romans versus Carthaginians.

Mérida's 6,000-seat, almost 2,000-year-old theatre is still in use, dominated by large statues of the gods, and with a veranda for promenading. Among other buildings being restored as I write, is a three-storey temple of Diana.

Pavements lead to and between the shops — the baker's, the goldsmith's — and beyond, to the remains of mansions. Mérida's Roman museum is as exceptional for its displays of, for example, the workings of the bakery, as for its outstanding collections of mosaics, sculpture and jewellery.

Remarkable though they are, the archaeological remains are not the major part of the Roman heritage. Nowhere else on the coasts of the Atlantic, except Galicia, the Spanish province immediately to Portugal's north, is still so permeated by Latin influences.

Romans make up a substantial portion of the ancestry of the Portuguese people, perhaps equalled only by their Celtic forbears. The Portuguese language, like Galician, from which it developed, and which it still closely resembles, remains more faithful to Latin than other Romance languages.

Villages like Almoçageme, which to many Portuguese are the heart of the nation, are built on the Roman model: a central forum, where men stand in groups, talking, and where markets are held, bounded by the temple (church), the school, the café and the gymnasium, the latter housed these days in the Volunteer Fire Brigade building.

Portuguese laws are founded on Roman ones. This is for reasons distinct from those of other European countries, which took on the Roman model through adopting the Napoleonic Code, at the beginning of the nineteenth century. For 2,000 years now, the Portuguese have shown a consistent preference for the Roman legal system. The attempt of the Visigoths, from Germany, to impose a Teutonic legal system in exchange for their embrace of Roman Catholicism, led to a rebellion, which opened the way for the Moors to enter and take control of the country. On the expulsion of the Moors, the founding fathers of the new Portugal promulgated a Roman legal system again.

Portugal was one of the first western countries to which Christianity was brought. It remains western Europe's second most Catholic nation, after Ireland: most of the rest of Atlantic Europe has adhered, for centuries, to a rugged Protestantism. Roman architecture influenced the design of many of the country's finest churches. Roman influence in cooking is to be found in duck cooked with orange or olives, and in *cozido à portuguesa*, offal boiled with cabbage, which was the legionnaires' standard fare. In adapted form, it was later fed to the African slaves being transported on board Portuguese ships to the Americas, and evolved into "soul food". Similarly, the Romans introduced to the Portuguese the method of frying fish in egg batter, *tempura*, which the latter later took with them to Japan. The Romans showed the the Portuguese how to preserve fish by salting and drying it; and *bacalhau*, cod preserved in that way, remains a national addiction. As cod was fished out from their coastal waters long ago, Portuguese fishermen went ever further afield in search of it, as far as Newfoundland. Norway's negotiations to join the European Union foundered on the insistence of the Portuguese and the Galicians on a share of its cod-fisheries. They now import it, in huge quantities, from Scandinavia and England.

The Portuguese concept of nationality is distinct from that of its neighbours, and is based on the ancient imperial Roman one. To the Spanish, nationality is essentially based on ancestry, and when a child's birth is registered there, his or her lineage, for three generations before, is recorded. The English concept, at least traditionally, has been based on ethnicity, on being "Anglo-Saxon". For the latter, where you were born has also been an important consideration.

As with being a Roman citizen, so being Portuguese is essentially a state of mind, an acceptance of the national culture, in an all-embracing sense, and way of life. Some of the most eminent Romans were not Italian. Seneca the Elder and Hadrian were southern Iberians; the former never set foot in the imperial capital. Most Portuguese have long taken pride in their society's relative lack of racial discrimination, and on their long tradition of inter-marriage with Indians, Africans and Chinese, as well as with English and Germans. It is often the foreign spouse, of whichever sex, who integrates into Portuguese society, rather than vice-versa.

From the earliest days of the Portuguese in India, and in marked contrast with the English policy there of strict separatism, they were encouraged to form relationships, including intimate ones, with local women. Whether or not these fell short of marriage, which they often did, the imperial government strictly enjoined them, under threat of punishment, to acknowledge and take responsibility for the care and upbringing of the children that resulted.

The state itself did likewise. As in the case of so many of Rome's citizens during the empire, large numbers of Portugal's citizens, holding full Portuguese passports today, whose only European ancestor may have been a century or more ago, have never visited their "home" country. They include Euro-Chinese in Macao and Hongkong, the "Burghers" of Sri Lanka, and Indians, many of them in Bombay, originating in Goa.

Many Italians were drawn to Lusitania by its gold. Pliny the Elder, who was governor here, from AD 70 to 75, described the goldfield that ran through Lusitania and Galicia, to Asturias, as "the largest gold-producing area in the world". (The known world then was twice the size of Europe.) He said that under an old Senate decree to preserve these reserves, gold-mining enterprises in Iberia were restricted to employing a maximum of 5,000 miners per seam. Now the constraint had been removed, Pliny estimated that the western Iberian mines were producing 3,200,000 ounces of gold a year. Yet so huge were the deposits in Portugal, it was only in 1992 that the Jales mine near Vila Real, in the north-east, first worked by the Romans, was closed. It had until then been producing a little over 100,000 ounces of gold a year, in addition to more than twice the amount of silver. Geologists estimate that the lodes contain a further billion dollars' worth; but the cost of extracting it with existing techniques is too high.

Pliny became deeply depressed by his fellow Italians' greed for gold, and the lengths they would go, or have others go, to obtain it. He described one method then in use in northern Portugal, as follows: "By the light of lamps, long tunnels are cut into the mountainside. Men work in long shifts, measured by lamps, and may not see daylight for months on end. The roofs of these tunnels are liable to give way and crush the miners. Diving for pearls or getting purple-fish from the depths of the sea seem comparatively safe. How dangerous we have made the earth!"

Another method was by open-cast mining. One scar left by the Romans in northern Portugal, from using this method during 200 years, is 350 metres long, 110 metres wide and 100 metres deep. Over 2,000 miners were employed here. Pliny recounted: "The method used is to crush the earth with iron wedges and crushers. The mixture of clay and gravel is regarded as the hardest of all things — except the greed for gold, which is even more stubborn."

Eventually, as the miners attacked the mountainside, a fissure would appear. "With a shout or a wave," Pliny wrote, "the look-out gives the order for the miners to be called off, and at the same time, rushes down from his vantage-point. The ruptured mountain falls asunder with an unimaginable crash, and is accompanied by an equally incredible blast of air. Like conquering heroes, the miners gaze at their triumph over nature."

The lumps of clay and granite were smashed into smaller pieces. Then the sluices of reservoirs, which had been built in the mountain above, would be opened. Water would come rushing down steep conduits. To carve these, miners were lowered over cliff edges, on ropes. "Viewed from a distance, the operation seems to involve not so much a species of strange animals, as of birds," Pliny observed. "Most hang suspended as they take the levels and mark out the route. Thus man leads rivers to run where there is no place for him to plant his footsteps."

In the rush of water, very rarely, nuggets weighing up to 3,000 ounces would be exposed. In any case, it swept the clay-gravel fragments down flights of steps carved in the rock by the miners. These were covered in gorse, which collected the particles of gold. The gorse would then be dried and burnt, and the gold recovered from its ashes.

The Romans' mining technology was so advanced that over hundreds of years afterwards, after succeeding invasions had disrupted Portugal, many of their mines had to be abandoned, because nobody could figure out how the water had been pumped out to keep the mines dry enough for continuous working. It was not until the nineteenth century that a successful method was again devised.

South of the Tagus, in the Alentejo, the Romans took over the copper, silver, tin, zinc and iron mines that the Carthaginians had worked under Hannibal, and greatly expanded their operations. There were also large deposits of white lead, valuable as an additive to iron, to prevent it from rusting.

The two most notable copper fields were San Domingos, which continued to be open-cast mined by a British company until the 1960s, and Aljustrel, where Roman shafts, some more than 200 metres deep, are still being worked.

All the gold mines in the north were state-owned and operated. In Alentejo, concessions were sold to individual entrepreneurs and groups of miners. The conditions under which they worked were rigorous. On buying a concession, they had twenty-five days in which to begin mining it, otherwise it was forfeit to the state again. High taxes were imposed on the ore and metals produced, before they could be sold. The roads to the docks on the banks of the River Guadiana were guarded and patrolled, to prevent smuggling. Some, it seems, succeeded in clandestinely moving metals at night; but those that were caught, suffered long terms of forced labour.

Mining, though by far the most profitable activity, was concentrated in a few areas of the north and the south. In the country as a whole, the greatest Roman impact, on the Lusitanian way of life as well as the economy, was through the introduction of new farming techniques. Olives, grapes and cereals were already being cultivated, but on a very small scale. Italian migrants brought with them more sophisticated plant varieties. They bought out small land-holders, and pieced together large farms, some of over 2,000 hectares.

Wheat, fruits (preserved in honey, or dried) and esparto grass (used to make ropes and sails) were exported to Belgium, Holland and England, as well as to Italy. The best grades of Lusitanian olive oils were regarded in Rome as the best in the empire, and were sold for premium prices.

In the eighth decade AD, huge surpluses of unsold wine had accumulated in the Roman empire, much like the European wine lakes at the end of the twentieth century. In Lusitânia, a decree of Emperor Domitian was imposed, that grape-vines growing on land which could be used for other crops, such as cereals, had to be uprooted. By his order, production was halved. This seems to have had the effect of making the wineries concentrate more on improving quality, and exports of premium Lusitanian wines thrived. Almost 2,000 years later, wines produced in vineyards first planted by the Romans, south of the River Tagus, are still being shipped to and sold in Italy — including 3,500,000 bottles a year of Lancer's Rosé, from the José Maria da Fonseca winery in Azeitão.

By AD 212, there was a high degree of homogeneity in the population, through generations of inter-marriage. In that year, Emperor Caracalla decreed that everyone, other than slaves, who lived in a municipality and was not already a Roman citizen, was automatically granted citizenship. This removal of official distinction between immigrant and native was intended to bond the latter to Rome. Ironically, it had the effect of helping them to unite with the migrants, against it.

Rome's state enterprises controlled the mining industry. Large farms and factories were privately owned, but with few exceptions by upper-class Italians who, so far from integrating, were in many cases absentee landlords, living in Rome. The bulk of state and private profits were remitted to Rome; but Rome did not consider them to be sufficient.

Millions of words have been written about how Rome itself became so insatiable in its greed for extravagance and opulence, that it effectively bankrupted itself, and lost the will as well as the means to keep the barbarians from entering its gates. As Rome's power declined, so it demanded ever more remittances from its colonies. There, the price for the increasingly dubious privilege of citizenship was the obligation to pay taxes to a foreign state, and these came to seem increasingly intolerable.

During the long period of *Pax Romana* in Lusitânia, the municipalities had been allowed to evolve into democratic and, to a considerable degree, self-governing communities. The townspeople elected magistrates from among themselves, and these ran the municipality. They collected taxes; and the archaeological evidence is that for generations they spent them in large part on public works: roads, bridges, aqueducts, temples, bath-houses and theatres.

As Rome's tax demands increased, so the amount spent on services and improvements to the community declined. To avoid paying the taxes, people moved out of the municipalities. An edict was issued from Rome, making it illegal to do so, on pain of pursuit and, on capture, severe punishment. Some men, without the means to meet their tax bills, sold themselves into slavery, as the lesser evil than the debtors' prison. When nobody any longer came forward to stand for election to the magistracies, Rome decreed that the positions were hereditary. Lusitanian son succeeded Lusitanian father as Rome's tax-collectors, on pain of death.

As their means of escape, many young Lusitanian men signed up in the Roman foreign legions, and were sent to suppress uprisings in other colonies, including North Africa, Gaul and Britain. Some went with Constantine from there on his march to relieve the siege of Rome, only to find the Goths already occupying the city.

Those Italians in Lusitânia who had eschewed integration with the locals, and formed a wealthy elite, could now only survive as a caste by the consent of the majority. Of the three legions that had been maintained to defend them, two had been disbanded to save money. Then Rome's authority in Italy itself became under challenge. The Italian elite of Lusitânia, at odds with the people around them, learned that their home country was being invaded by "barbarian" north Europeans.

CHAPTER III

THE RISE AND FALL OF CHRISTENDOM

So sparse is the documentation of the period in Portugal that followed the eclipse of Rome's authority, some historians have simply passed over it. One recent chronology jumps straight from AD 104, when the Romans completed a bridge over the River Tâmega at Chaves, in the north, to 409, and the take-over of the country by religious refugees from Germany.

What evidence there is from the years between, however, is of events of such importance that they are not to be ignored; we must piece them together as best we can.

Archaeologists have discovered, over a wide area of Portugal, rubble left by a clearly terrible wave of destruction, which swept across the country around AD 250. Traditionally, the damage has been blamed on invading hordes of Vandals. But Professor Jorge de Alarcão has established that, in reality, there is a total absence of clues through which to implicate them, or any other group of outsiders. The first wave of the devastation occurred long before the Germans arrived, and was clearly inflicted by locals.

The archaeological findings show that the wreckers and pillagers were not undiscriminating. Their targets were those wealthy Italians who owned so much of the property and controlled so many of the profitable parts of the economy, and who treated their slaves and their paid employees harshly. Both their factories and the large and lavish villas in which they lived, were destroyed. A protective wall was hurriedly erected around Conímbriga, the luxuriant spa town where the foreign upper class gathered to relax. It seems to have been demolished by a mob soon afterwards.

Prominent among the many objects buried then, apparently to hide them from the looters, were temple lamps and ornaments of pre-Christian cults. This adds to the supposition that this huge uprising was an early expression, not merely of resentment towards the Italians, but of militant Christianity: a revolt of converts to the early Church, against the economic and social injustices of the pre-Christian Roman order.

Its immediate provocation is likely to have been an edict issued by Emperor Domitian ordering everyone to pay homage and make tributes to Roman gods, in official temples, and to carry a certificate showing that this had been done. Quintilian, the Iberian historian who lived earlier in the second century, wrote that by his time, Christianity had reached as far as the Atlantic coast. Adherence to it was far from universal, however: it was the most recent of several rival religions to have come here from the opposite extreme of the decaying Roman empire, the east Mediterranean. Some of Christianity's concepts, which seem to us today to be among its most characteristic, were no longer novelties to the Lusitanians, when the first missionaries came among them. From the Egyptian cult of Isis, they were already familiar with the theology of the death and resurrection of the Son of God, and from the Persian cult of Mithras, with the sacraments of baptism and the sacred meal (Eucharist). Some priests officiated over both Mithraic and Christian rites, in separate temples. The cult of Mithras was to co-exist with the cult of Christ in Lusitânia, for at least another two centuries.

What was it that nonetheless caused such a strikingly rapid growth of Christianity, in competition against at least half a dozen other faiths, with such disruptive results? As well as Jesus's teachings, there was of course the revelation that he was a divinity, who came to earth in the recent past, was killed by the same imperial Roman ruling class that oppressed them, to be triumphantly resurrected by God.

In addition to this, in Atlantic Iberia, there was the particular impact of James, the disciple whom Jesus called "Son of Thunder". The enduring local legend is that it was James who first brought "the good news" of Christianity here, between the crucifixion of Jesus in AD 32, and his own beheading on his return to Judea, ten years later.

According to the legend, his body is in the tomb beneath the basilica at Santiago de Compostela (which means, in English, St James of the Field of Stars), in Galicia, just north of the Portuguese border.

49

His head was supposedly preserved nearby in Braga, Portugal's oldest cathedral city. Still today, each year, hundreds of thousands of pilgrims, and perhaps almost as many sight-seers, travel to Santiago, in respect or curiosity.

It seems as unlikely that St James ever visited Iberia, as is the fable that his body, wrapped in pontifical robes and surrounded by stars, flew here after his execution in Judea. This would have to have been without his head, which the Bishop of Braga found in Jerusalem, while on a pilgrimage there in the twelfth century, and which he brought back with him to northern Portugal. There, it was stolen by agents of the King of Leon, who sent it to Santiago de Compostela. The tomb at Santiago may also contain the bodily remains of a German missionary charged with heresy, executed in the fourth century on the orders of Emperor Maximus, and brought here by his followers, fleeing from persecution in northern Europe.

The strength and persistence of the cult of St James here reflect more than superstition. At least as much of its impact has arisen from the teaching attributed to him. The sermons of St James, called in the New Testament his *Letters to All Christians*, or *Practical Christianity*, was probably the first Christian text to reach Atlantic Iberia. It is likely that it was written a generation before Mark wrote the earliest of the synoptic gospels, in AD 72. It seems to have been brought here by Lusitanian mercenaries, returning home after service with the Roman VII Legion in North Africa, where they themselves had been converted by missionaries from further east.

The *Letters to All Christians* were known in the early Church as the "universal letters", to distinguish them from St Paul's, which were addressed to specific people and communities, and were concerned in large part with spiritual awakening and communal Christian living. St James, contrastingly, described his message as "the perfect law of freedom". His writings read like a rousing call to a holy rising against the rich.

Nowhere, in the seven very similar manuscript versions of the "universal letter" which have survived, did St James condemn the rich for being rich. He warned only incidentally of the transience, of the inevitable decay of physical property. His protest was against the rich because, in the course of their pursuit for ever greater wealth, they abused the well-being and the rights of their fellow human beings.

"Is it not the rich who lord it over you?" asked St James. "Are they not the ones who drag you into court, who insult your good name?"

He asked the rich: "Can you hear crying out against you the wages you kept back from the labourers mowing your fields?" And he warned them: "The cries of the reapers have reached the ears of the Lord."

To him, belief was not enough. Religious conviction must be expressed through action. "It is by my deeds that I will show you my faith. Faith without deeds is useless ... Anyone who looks steadily at the perfect law of freedom, and keeps to it — not listening and forgetting, but putting it into practice — will be blessed in every undertaking."

He forbade his followers from verbal, let alone physical violence, remarking: "Mercy can afford to laugh at judgement... It's the rich who condemn and kill the upright."

Herod Agrippa II was to condemn and kill St James in AD 42, in Judea. The poor of Lusitânia, 4,000 kilometres to the west, received his evocation with the same immediacy as though he was among them.

The class franchised by Rome to rule here had lost both Rome's purchasing of its minerals and farm produce, and Rome's military protection. As the living and working conditions of the slaves deteriorated, they increasingly refused to work. Their owners, having no longer any means of making them do so, found themselves obliged to negotiate contracts, through which the slaves would be freed, and be guaranteed wages, in return for which they would return to work.

But there was no longer a market for the produce, and the wages went unpaid. The Roman bureaucracy and judiciary in Lusitânia, for so long surviving on the basis of a fictitious power, publicly caved in. The rule of the mob took over, with the result of the mass destruction I have described. The only people who by now commanded sufficient respect and popularity to bring about peace and order, were the Christian bishops. They were also the only group able to claim the recognition of the new order in Rome, from its bishop or pope. By the end of the third century, the Church had become the effective administration and purveyor of justice, a kind of government, in so far as Lusitânia still had one.

The Bishop of Mérida, the capital, was criticised for spending the gifts of the faithful to the Church, on himself, and on over-lavish vestments and altar vessels. However, he also built the town's first hospital, where the sick were treated without charge, and a hospice, to accommodate visitors, which was also free. He founded, too, a bank which lent money at modest rates of interest, for the development of business enterprises, to create more prosperity.

Early in the fourth century, Priscilian, Bishop of Ávila, gathered a huge following in the poorer districts of the Portuguese countryside. He publicly rebuked fellow clergy, for their wealth and greed. He dignified poverty and deprivation as being specially valued by God. He preached a rigorous self-denial, advocating celibacy and vegetarianism.

In these matters, he echoed St James. He proceeded to challenge orthodox Christianity, by denying the doctrine of the Trinity. He denied that Jesus had been born the Son of God, but as mortal as the rest of us. He had been filled by God with the Holy Spirit later. This had not been a unique happening. Some prophets had been endowed likewise, and men who made themselves pleasing enough to God, could be so blessed by Him now and in the future. Women were as likely as men to be imbued by God, and so were equally eligible to serve as priests.

At almost any other time, Priscilian, and the poor who took up his challenge to try to become Christ-like, would have been condemned by the official Church as heretics. There seems to have been then a remarkable tolerance in the Christian world. The wealthy property-owners demanded that the Pope, St Martin of Tours, and other pillars of orthodoxy, outlaw "Priscilianism". But while disagreeing, they refused to condemn. Their estates were by now all but paralysed by this cult of the irrelevance of material possessions. They themselves seized Priscilian and executed him anyway. This had the unsought effect of greatly increasing his popularity.

Particularly in their concept of Christ, the Priscilians had much in common with German tribes, in the north of Europe, which followed the teachings of Arian. Their unorthodoxy had caused these tribes to have lived for over a century in a state of constant oppression by the armed might of official, Roman Christianity. Sometimes in search of a homeland, sometimes of plunder, sometimes of revenge, they moved across Europe from the Balkans to Greece. For a while, they ruled much of France. They invaded and wrecked Rome itself, and then retreated to Iberia, to settle there among their co-religionists.

These Visigoth tribes have often been portrayed as conquerors, who imposed their foreign rule. In Portugal, however, whatever their military prowess, the immigrants probably numbered less than 50,000, against a native population of perhaps twelve times that. St Martin, Catholic Bishop of Braga, enthroned and anointed their leader as king — but at the price of his public conversion to Catholicism. And king of what? The German laws and customs they had brought with them were applied only to the German settlers. The rest, the vast majority, continued, unchanged, to live according to their own custom and law, administered as before by the Church.

St Martinho of Braga was a monk, originally from Hungary, who is credited with introducing monasticism to Portugal. There came into being a series of large communities of highly educated priests and monks, skilled in both religious and secular affairs, who lived in simplicity, and were known for their incorruptibility. With St Martin, they declared that the only valid liturgical language was Latin. By then, the Gothic language from Germany had fallen into disuse, except in a handful of churches. Gothic missals were destroyed, and the language disappeared almost completely.

In council in Braga, St Martinho outlawed any view of Jesus which did not comply with Catholic teaching of the Trinity. At the same time, he ended the ban on local Catholics marrying Goths.

Then, however, the Visigoth King Reggeswinth riposted to St Martin's decrees, by himself decreeing that only German ones were henceforth valid. This was to lead not only to his downfall, and that of his people, but of Portuguese Christendom as a whole.

Under the traditional local law, which again applies in Portugal today, the property of a parent of either sex, on death, is shared between his or her spouse, if surviving, and equally between the children. Women had the same rights to inherit from their parents, as their brothers, and to themselves bequeath their property, in their turn. By the imposition of the German law, women lost their property rights. Also, an inheritance was no longer to be divided between surviving children, but to go in its entirety to the eldest son. This was to contribute to the growing disaffection towards the monarchy.

In 710 the Visigoth King, who was by then Witiza, was assassinated, apparently by the younger sons of noblemen. They refused to acknowledge Witiza's oldest son, Agila, as the new monarch, acclaiming instead one of their own, Roderic.

Agila sent an ambassador to North Africa, to ask the Khalif for support in his claim to the throne. It seems that Agila had in mind the landing of an army of Berbers, who would topple the new regime, engage in plunder as a reward for their efforts, and then withdraw with their loot back to North Africa. According to the Arab chronicles, the Khalif's response was tepid: "Send a small unit to explore, but do not, at least at present, expose a large force to the dangers of an expedition across the seas."

In 711, General Tariq ferried across to Europe 7,000 troops. They landed at the great rock whose name today still derives from that of the North African commander: Jabal Tariq — Gibraltar.

Roderic marched his much larger army to meet Tariq. He personally led into battle the central division of elite Visigoth warriors. The other two divisions, one to each side of him, were commanded by officers who were secretly in a conspiracy against him. Their troops were southern Iberians, press-ganged into military service in defence of a regime which they detested. Obeying orders, willingly enough, the southern Iberians ran towards the Moslems, and welcomed them as liberators. Roderic was presumed killed in battle; no trace of him was ever found, alive or dead.

Tariq led his army on into Iberia, finding little resistance, and often a welcome. Together with the deposed Visigoth royalty and nobility, the bishops fled north, into Galicia. The Metropolitan, the head of the Church in Iberia, did not stop until he reached the safety of Rome.

CHAPTER IV

THE ARABS BRING CIVILISATION TO EUROPE

The Khalif, Musâ ibn Nasser, crossed the straits from North Africa to Iberia on a visit of inspection. By the time he reached his army's front line, it was more than 200 kilometres north of the coast. His commander, Tariq, greeted him, and dismounted respectfully from his horse. According to the Arab chronicles, the Khalif lashed him angrily with his whip, and shouted at him, in front of his men: "Why did you advance so far without my permission? My orders were to make a raid, and return to Africa."

It did not take Musâ long, however, to see the extraordinary potential of the situation. The land was more fertile than any in Mediterranean Africa, with plenty of rain and a mild climate. It faced the Atlantic, "the dark ocean", as the Arabs called it, whose challenge had for so long tantalised them. The country was rich with minerals and gems. Much of its ruling class had fled, after the first battle. Now that most bishops, priests and monks had gone, the most educated group were the Jews, who were also prominent in commerce. They had welcomed the Arabs as liberators from the anti-semitism which had been taught and practised by the Church. A large number of Christians, who had been almost as exploited by the Church, seemed ready to accept the Arabs, as likely to be preferable to the past regime.

In June 712, Musâ landed a force of 18,000 Arab horsemen and foot-soldiers. Jews in Seville opened a little-guarded city gate, and ushered them in. Mérida, the Lusitanian capital, under the rule of its bishop, resisted strongly, but fell after a siege of almost a year. Elsewhere, the conquest was mostly bloodless. The Arabs advanced through the north of Iberia, over the Pyrenees, as far as Tours, 200 kilometres south of Paris, before they were halted, and began to be forced into retreat.

To the Witiza princes, who had invited Musâ's invasion, he granted estates totalling 3,000 farms, and gave them senior positions in his new government. He issued a decree, guaranteeing that commoners who readily accepted Arab rule would be allowed to lead their lives in peace. Those who resisted would suffer confiscation of all their property.

The Arabs stayed in Portugal for the next 400 years (and were to remain in southern Spain for a further 250). Their civilisation here developed and flourished beyond anything they had achieved in the Middle East and Mediterranean Africa. It reached its peak in the tenth century, under the rule of the Abd-al-Rahman family, from Syria.

The founding members of this charismatic, shrewd and cultivated royal dynasty established their capital at Cadiz, and extended their rule over most of Iberia. They named their nation al-Andaluz: Andalucia, land of the Vandals — the generic name by which they called north Europeans. Much of what is now Portugal was governed for much of this era as three emirates: al-Qunu, today's Algarve; al-Qasr, which included what is now Alentejo; and the region north of the Tagus, including Lisbon, Sintra and Santarém, which they called al-Balata.

Historians in the nineteenth century were to dispute what inspired this surprising conquest. Was it, as Américo Castro portrayed it, a *jihad*, a holy war, to deliver west European Christendom to the God of Islam — by the sword, if its infidels resisted conversion? Or was it, as Richard Konetske proposed, no more than the enactment of a desire to possess a land more pleasant and profitable than the one from which they had come?

The debate between these historians was based on a shared fallacy, that people act from singular motives. More usually, they do so from an imprecise mixture of them. The dispute had a valuable outcome, which was to bring to light evidence that had lain in obscurity for 800 years.

The commitment of Iberia's Arab conquerors to Islam was uncompromising. It was reinforced by the death penalty for any of their own people who tried to defect from the faith, or even to dissent from it. In 1862, Reinhart Duzy, the great Belgian Arabist, published a series of his translations of ninth-century Islamic court records of trials of Moslems who converted to Christianity in Iberia. The customary sentence was to be crucified by the roadside, between two pigs. By contrast, a Christian who publicly insulted Mohammed or the Koran was executed straightforwardly.

Halfway through the ninth century, a group of Christians formed, who called themselves "The New Zealots". Like many other Christians throughout Europe, they believed that the world was soon to end, in the year 1000, when Christ would come again, in judgement. Their particular goal was to be granted by him prior and direct entry to heaven, without passing through purgatory. Their chosen means of making themselves sufficiently pleasing to Christ, was to have themselves beheaded by the Moslems, for publicly insulting the Prophet Mohammed.

The Arab officials had no stomach for the role in which they were cast by their would-be victims. A Brother Isaac travelled from his monastery at Tabanos, to Córdoba. There, he went before the unsuspecting governor, and shouted: "Your Prophet has lied and deceived you. He is cursed, who has dragged so many innocent souls down to hell with him."

The governor slapped the monk's face. Brother Isaac responded: "You bruise God's own image. How dare you?"

The governor said: "Maybe you're drunk, or you've lost your reason. Don't you realise that the legal punishment for speaking like that is death?"

"I have never drunk wine in my life, and I know what I am saying," the monk replied. "I yearn to be sentenced to death. Blessed are they who are persecuted for speaking the truth, for theirs is the kingdom of heaven."

The governor reported to his superior, the Khalif, that Isaac was obviously mad, and recommended a pardon. The Khalif disagreed. On 3 June 851, the monk was hanged head down on a gibbet. To prevent the New Zealots from turning his funeral into a display of triumphalism, the corpse was burnt, and the ashes thrown into a river. Isaac was promptly declared a saint by the New Zealots, who attributed many miracles to him during, after and even before his "martyrdom".

A priest named Sisenand claimed to have seen, in a dream, Isaac coming down to him from heaven, and urging him towards a martyr's death. On awakening, he went to the office of an Arab official, blasphemed against the Prophet, and was executed. Before mounting the scaffold, he urged his deacon, Paul, to follow his example. Four days later, Paul did so.

These martyrdoms were recorded at the time, in often sickening detail, by a New Zealot teacher and author, Eulogius, in his book, *Memorial to the Saints*. It is from his name that the word "eulogy" is derived.

A few days after Paul's execution, a pupil of Eulogius, named Sancho, urged on by his teacher, insulted the Prophet, and was beheaded. This gave Eulogius enough material for an entire chapter. His book continues to relate how, the next Sunday, six more monks from Tabanos, including Isaac's uncle, went before the governor and — according to Eulogius — cried: "We echo the words of our holy brothers Isaac and Sancho. Now avenge your accursed Prophet. Inflict on us your cruellest tortures."

They were beheaded.

Then came the turn of Isaac's sister, Maria, to have a dream. She told it to her friend, Flora. Maria was destined to be re-united with her beloved brother, and Flora to become united with Jesus himself. They, too, went before the governor, and both insulted the Prophet. The long-suffering governor pleaded with them not to be so foolish. Although they persisted, he still decided not to sentence them to death, and had them locked up in prison.

The governor sent a judge to them, to try to frighten them into their senses, by threatening them, unless they recanted, with the one fate both men prayed the devout virgins would consider worse than death: a lifetime of forced prostitution.

The governor also asked Christians opposed to the New Zealots, to visit Maria and Flora in prison, and try to dissuade them from sacrificing themselves so pointlessly. Tragically, they also allowed access to the girls, to Eulogius. He was, of course, loathe to lose, for his next chapter, the tale of two beautiful young virgin martyrs. He prostrated himself before them. He told them in tones of awe, that he could see that God was already causing them to radiate like angels; and the heavenly crowns prepared for them were already shimmering above their heads.

There was no such punishment in law as forced prostitution. Eulogius had his way. Maria and Flora went to the scaffold on 24th November 851. They do not seem to have faced the moment rejoicing — unlike Eulogius. Later that day, he wrote: "The Lord has been most gracious to us, and given us great joy. Our virgins, instructed by me, with bitter tears, have won their palm of martyrdom."

Eventually exasperated by Eulogius, the governor sentenced him to 400 lashes. Fearful of the pain, he pleaded for a quick death instead. The Arab chronicler recorded him crying out: "Restore my soul to its creator. I will not allow your whip to tear apart my body."

They beheaded Eulogius in 859, in due course. Later, his bones, along with those of several of the "martyrs" he had written about, were retrieved by Arab traders, who sold them to ambassadors of Christian Kingdoms of northern Europe. There, they were venerated; and many miracles were attributed to them.

Most of the Christians who lived under Arab rule were appalled by these events. An open letter to Eulogius, published several years before his own execution, protested: "The khalif allows us Christians to freely exercise our religion. He does not oppress us. Those you call martyrs are nothing of the kind. They are suicides. Had they read the Gospel, they would have found there: 'Love your enemies; do good to those that hate you.' Instead of slandering Mohammed, they should have listened to St James: 'Slanderers will not enter The kingdom of God.'"

The letter continued: "The Muslims say to us: 'If God had intended to prove that Mohammed was a false prophet, and had inspired these Christian fanatics, he would have worked miracles through them, to convert us to your faith.' But He does not. Christianity gains nothing by these executions, and Islam comes to no harm from them."

To slaves owned by Christian farmers and businessmen, Islam proffered a prospect of real freedom, on earth. The Koran states that to liberate a slave is to please God. Slaves who escaped from a Christian to a Moslem community, and there proclaimed before at least two witnesses, "There is one God, and Mohammed is his prophet", were given sanctuary. So long as they accepted instruction in the Koran, and showed that they were trying to live by its teaching, they enjoyed many rights, including property ownership and marriage.

Christian slave-owners sent out posses on horseback into Moslem territory at night, to try to re-capture their slaves, sometimes successfully. To many of those who evaded being caught, the Moslems gave plots of land, large enough to grow fruits, lettuces, vegetables and medicinal herbs in commercial quantities. These were lands that had been confiscated from the Christian bishops after they had fled.

Irrigation was introduced by the Arabs, in a technological revolution, previously unknown in Europe. It was brought here from Alexandria. Two Egyptian agronomists who came to southern Iberia in the tenth century — Ibn al-Basaal and Ibn al-Awaam — wrote manuals in which they adapted their expertise to local conditions. These books covered the design, construction and operation of water-wheels, pumps and conduits, land management, animal husbandry, plant propagation and cultivation, land conservation and marketing of crops.

Replicas of the innovative water-wheels can be seen today, working in the riverside gardens at Tomar. Driven by the River Nabão's current, they scoop up water, and dump it into irrigation channels. Plant varieties introduced from the Middle East included bananas, coconuts, sugar-cane, oil palms, maize and rice. As important, the Arabs encouraged the growing of such foods as lettuces, onions, carrots, cucumbers, apples, pears, grapes and figs.

The impact of this on the diet of the Portuguese is still marked, and investigated by north European medical researchers for clues as to the low rate of heart disease. Part of Portugal's surviving Arabic heritage are the words for many foods, and for irrigation systems which watered them, and the warehouses in which they were stored.

The pattern initiated by the Arabs, in place of the big Italian, German- and Church-owned estates, of family-owned and cultivated horticultural plots has also survived to this day in Sintra, among other regions, although the income from them now is usually supplemented by wage-earning jobs in local factories and shops, and on building sites. The plots tend to be intensely cultivated, with vines beneath the orange and lemon trees, and flowers as well as salads grown between the rows. Government agronomists complain that this is inefficient, but the peasants have so far resisted all attempt to group them into more rational farming units, just as they have rejected the new "Euro varietals" of plants, from loyalty to the varieties their families have been growing for centuries. They are among the last Europeans to hold out in this way; and the crowds that throng their produce markets at weekends show how popular their conservatism remains. These are a people who have not returned to organic farming. They have never practised any other kind.

Before the Arab conquest, the people of rural villages and small towns were ruled by their landlords, which had come to mean, increasingly, the Church. The parish priest, in an ironic reverse of the life of St Paul, had become the extortionate tax-collector. The priest had acted as squire, mayor, magistrate, and welfare-provider, and, with honourable exceptions, had grown much richer than his parishioners, at their expense.

Under the Arab regime, Moslems, whether by birth or conversion, were exempt from most taxes. The chronicles record successive protests by the state treasurers against Islamic missionary activity, because of the loss of revenues. The taxes were no heavier than those the Church had exacted, and could be paid in kind. The Arabs had no interest in filling the administrative vacuum the priests' departure had created. This led to a remarkable movement, of "os Homens Bons", literally, The Good Men. They formed village and small-town juntas, which met in the square, raised revenue and organised maintenance, repairs and other public works, with voluntary labour. They administered local justice, arbitrated local disputes, and provided social welfare, particularly for widows and orphans. They organised co-operative olive pressing, for oil, and wine production, and also the collective marketing of their produce to Arab merchants. Some celebrated the Catholic liturgy, as best as they remembered it, in the absence of priests, and arranged baptisms, marriages and funerals. The young men were trained and formed into fire-fighting brigades.

The Vatican has since recognised the oral tradition of the Mass that has come from that time in northern Portugal, as "The Braga Rite" (sometimes mistaken to be Visigothic), and it is still sometimes celebrated. The confession was simpler and less humiliating than the Latin Mass. The chalice was prepared at the beginning of the Mass, and not in the middle.

The institution of "The Good Men" continues to flourish in rural Portugal. Its communities remain among the most independent-minded and self-sufficient of any in the western world — markedly more so than those in some regions of the USA, where such virtues are upheld more in talk. The name given them is Associations of Volunteer Firemen. In a country of forest fires, they are unpaid, and highly professional in training, in equipment and in actually fighting fires. Yet this is a small part of their function.

The Volunteer Firemen's Association of Almoçageme, of which I have been a member for some years, owns a site on one side of the town square, and about five times its size. Here, it is "The Good

Men", rather than the municipal council, who provide a secure pre-school playground, a library, a museum, a computer room, a sports hall with gym and indoor hockey-rink, a helipad, a legal advice centre and a medical clinic. The latter offers the services not only of first-aid nurses and family practitioners, but specialists who visit weekly from Lisbon. One recent appeal resulted in a state-of-the-art *Mercedes* ambulance. Another will soon enable the construction of a community swimming pool.

Our volunteer fire brigade does not stop at a brass band. It runs, in addition, a jazz band, a dance band, a chamber orchestra and a Gregorian choir. It also preserves one of Portugal's more gruesome social rituals, the pig-killing party.

To replace the slaves they freed, the Arabs bought others from north European traders, and from local pirates, who engaged in kidnapping at sea. The first wave of these were Slav prisoners of war, captured by Germans in their invasions of eastern Europe. Slav women were bought at premium prices, for harems. Some of the Slav men won favour and prominence in the royal court. They were so numerous by the reign of Abd-al-Rahman III, that "Slav" had become the term for all European foreigners, and the Arab king dyed his fair hair black, for fear of being mistaken for one. Other slaves were brought from southern Italy, Belgium and France. The latter was the major source of eunuchs for the staffing of the harem, and the main processing and forwarding house for the trade in boys destined for such service was Verdun.

In the towns, the innovations the Arabs introduced included schools, often free ones, and universities, the first in Europe by several hundred years. Previously, virtually the only people who could read and write had been priests and the members of religious orders — it was a skill which not even kings nor aristocrats acquired.

The Arab rulers of southern Iberia set out to achieve mass literacy. The reading and writing which was taught in the schools was of course Arabic, which was also the language of instruction for mathematics, history and geography. This aroused indignation in an older generation of Latin speaker. A pamphlet, *Indiculus luminus*, dated 854, protested that "Our Christian young men, with their elegant airs and fluent speech, are intoxicated with Arab eloquence. They eagerly devour and discuss the books of the Mohammedans, and praise them with every flourish of rhetoric, knowing nothing of the beauty of the

Church's literature. The Christians are so ignorant of their own law, they pay so little attention to their own Latin language, there is hardly one man in a hundred who can write a letter to so much as ask about a friend's health intelligibly, other than in Arabic."

These Arab-educated Christians in the towns, who did not change their religion, in many cases not only adopted Arabic as their main language, but also Arab dress, diet, culture — the entire lifestyle, save for embracing Islam itself. They became known as Mozarabs. The Jews, also respected by the Arabs as "the People of the Book", made a similar adaptation; and some, like their Christian contemporaries, became noted Arabic scientists and scholars.

Towards the end of the Abd-al-Rahman era, early in the twelfth century, al-Idrisi, the renowned Arab geographer, toured what is now Portugal. It is from him that we have learnt the above information.

Al-Idrisi found the mines, which had fallen into disuse along with so much else during the Visigoth era. They had been extended and deepened. Workers were divided into gangs, for digging, smelting, and extracting mercury. This last was used, in part, to make decorative pools.

Farmers in the Lisbon region boasted to al-Idrisi that Arabian wheat varieties were ready here for harvesting forty days after being planted. In the south, there were particularly fine orchards of "delicate and delicious" figs.

He noted that a distinct and pleasing architectural style had been developed, in which Arab mathematics and local aesthetics came together in horseshoe arches, decorative plaster-work and painted tiles. Ceramics and glass- and metal-working were highly developed crafts. As the Christian crusaders were soon to discover, Lisbon and the other major towns were not only well provided with mains water, public baths and sewerage, but well fortified.

Setúbal, south of the Tagus estuary, was surrounded by plantations of pine trees, the raw material of the town's thriving shipyards. At Coimbra, al-Idrisi praised the gardens on the banks of the Mondego; as I write, in 1996, these are being restored. To the north, he reported, lived tribes of marauding horsemen.

These latter, with help from France and England, invaded the country soon afterwards. In the name of Christ. they then set about systematically destroying the Arabic creations of four centuries — buildings, works of art, irrigation systems, wind- and water-mills, warehouses and ships. The scale of the destruction was such, that it has often been said since that virtually every trace of Arabic influence had been eradicated. As we shall see, this is fortunately far from true.

The distinction between "Arabic" and "Arab" is important here, because so many of the achievements — for example, in medicine, philosophy and education — were those of Arabic-speaking Jews and Christians, working with, or under the patronage of Moslems. Under the royal and scholarly Abd-al-Rahman dynasty in southern Iberia, followers of all the three religions collaborated together, and achieved the most artistically and scientifically advanced society the western world had yet seen.

Today, when "Islamic" is so often the prefix of "terrorism" or "fundamentalism" and of reactionary movements against the rights of women or of free speech, there is a great need to recall and appreciate the Islamic contribution to western civilisation which took root in and then spread from southern Iberia, to more northern parts of Europe. In Santarém, in central Portugal, the mosque, after more than 700 years of disuse as such, is being restored, alongside the synagogue and the monastery of São Francisco. Here, as in Spain, there is a move by Catholics, Jews and Moslems, not just to promote tolerance, but eventually to experience once again the synergy, the intellectual and cultural dynamism, that was here.

It was in Cordoba that the existence of zero was first discerned, leading to the creation of mathematics and, in turn, of means of architectural calculation, which enabled the construction of tall, vaulted buildings. These and other Arabic architectural techniques survived the expulsion of the Arabs, through Christians they had taught. They can be seen clearly today in the design of the National Palace in Sintra, and the still more exotic abbey of Batalha.

Medicine was developed to new levels of sophistication. The care of a child, from conception to adolescence, became a distinct field of specialisation. By the middle of the tenth century, 'Arib bin Said had completed the writing of a major textbook on gynaecology, embryology and paediatrics. It was a watershed in world medical literature, based as it was on bedside clinical observation and pathological investigation, rather than Hippocratic and other abstract Greek theories.

The empirical study of the effects of environment and diet on human beings developed rapidly. New surgical techniques and instruments were devised, which remained in use in western Europe into the sixteenth century.

Long after the expulsion of the Arabs from Portugal, Pedro Hispano, the son of a Jewish physician in Lisbon, translated into Latin his summaries of Arabic medical texts that survived (some written by Jewish and Christian doctors). He published them under the title *Thesaurus Pauperum*, or *The Treasury of the Poor* — one could consult it, even if you could not afford a physician's fee.

Pedro went on to become the first and only Portuguese Pope, John XXI, in 1276. He was crushed to death within months of his election, when the ceiling of the library he had built, at the papal palace in Viterbo, north of Rome, collapsed on to him. This tragedy followed his sharp exchange of correspondence with the King of Portugal, over whether the Church should defer to the state, or vice-versa; and it was widely suspected that the "accident" had been royally commissioned.

With the advent of printing, *The Treasury of the Poor* was translated into and published in most European languages. It remained the standard medical reference work for two centuries after Pedro's death. He also wrote a treatise on madness, asserting for perhaps for the first time in writing, at least other than in Arabic, that it was not a manifestation of being possessed by a demon, but an illness in need of clinical treatment. This was followed by the pioneering work of Portugal's St John of God, in developing psychiatry as a medical speciality, 500 years ago. He is still widely respected by modern psychiatrists, as the first of them.

The Arabs had brought with them from the Middle East the writings of the ancient Greek philosophers, previously unknown in western Europe, in Arabic translation. Here, these were re-translated, into Latin. In this field too, Pedro of Lisbon, before he became Pope, made a notable contribution, through his ground-breaking explanation of Aristotle's theory of logic. This was to remain an important work well beyond the middle ages. Indeed, the gnomic rhymes he composed, as an aid to memorising the steps of Aristotelian logic, are still taught to children in philosophy lessons, which are compulsory in Portuguese secondary schools.

The next chapter describes how the Arabs came to be driven out of Portugal, 250 years after which they were finally sent from Spain as well. It is pertinent to this stage of their story that, despite repeated attempts to dislodge them, the Arabs remained in the Algarve for a century after their expulsion from the rest of the country.

The Algarve takes its name from the Arabic *al-Gharb*, which means "the west". Its capital, Xelb (today's Silves), north of the coast, on the River Arade, developed into a centre of Arabic culture of international importance. In the eleventh century, scholars, writers, artists and musicians migrated here from as far east as Baghdad and Yemen. The linguistic purity and elegance of the Arabic spoken and written in Xelb was renowned throughout Arabia itself, where the town became known as "the Baghdad of the west".

Mohammed ibn Ámmar, a famous poet, was governor of the Algarve and presided over its golden age. He was born in the Algarve, the son of peasants who had migrated from North Africa. After schooling, he studied at the institute for creative writing. His parents could not support him. The Arab chronicles relate that he composed a poem celebrating the re-capture of Xelb from Berber raiders, in 1040, by Arab forces commanded by Prince al-Mu'tamid of Seville. In fact, the Prince's command was nominal, as he was eleven years old at the time. The Prince felt highly flattered by the verses. He bought them for a large sum, and arranged to meet the author. When he did so, he fell passionately in love with him.

Al-Mu'tamid was by now twelve years old. His father proclaimed him ruler of Seville. One of the Prince's first appointments was of Ibn Ámmar, the poet, to be his chief minister. The Prince and the poet went together to the Algarve, where they rode through the streets of Xelb at the head of a huge triumphal procession. One of Ibn Ámmar's first acts as chief minister was to settle an old score. Years before, he had written and sent a poem to one of the town's richest merchants, begging for food, to appease his hunger. The merchant had him sent a bag of barley, commonly regarded as animal feed. Now, Ibn Ámmar sent the merchant a bag of similar size, containing silver. His accompanying note read: "Had you sent me wheat, when I was hungry, I would now be sending you gold."

Descriptions of the town of Xelb, as it developed under the new rulers, include that of an ornate bazaar, devoted to luxury goods imported from the Middle East and the Orient — silks, glassware, perfumes, spices, gold filigree — of ornamental rose gardens on the banks of the river, and of palaces rising above one another, up the hill behind. At its summit was the fabled Palace of the Verandas. Here, the royal court met for concerts and poetry readings, dances and banquets with wine. The Islamic ban on alcohol had long been relaxed in the Algarve. When the call to evening prayer came, the Prince and the governor walked hand-in-hand to the mosque, extemporising verse. One exchange, recorded at the time, was:

Prince: "Listen as the muezzin calls the people to prayer."

Governor: "And hopes that God will forgive him his many sins."

Prince: "May he be forgiven, for proclaiming the truth."

Governor: "So long as he believes in his heart what he says with his tongue."

The Prince's father, the king of Seville, became scandalised by his son's infatuation and cohabitation with Ibn Ámmar. He ordered the poet into exile in Zaragoza, in northern Spain. He summoned the Prince back to Seville, and ordered him to marry. The Prince bought a slave-girl, and married her.

Two anecdotes about his wife, both posing the question as to which one was the slave, have survived. It rarely snows in Andalucia, and when it did in an exceptionally cold winter, she looked at the hillsides covered in white and burst into tears.

She told her husband: "I am weeping because of your selfishness. Why haven't you arranged this every year?"

The story is that the Prince ordered the hills to be planted with enough almond trees to produce a covering of white blossoms, annually.

Riding in their carriage, according to the second anecdote, they passed a building site where a gang of bare-footed slave-girls was treading clay, to be made into bricks. The Princess burst into tears of jealousy, complaining to her husband that life at the royal palace was too enclosed for her. She yearned for the days when she, too, had trodden clay with her friends. The Prince ordered that the palace courtyard be covered with brown sugar and spices, and sprinkled with rose-water, so the Princess could have her ladies-in-waiting tread this designer-mud to her heart's content.

Prince Mu'tamid's father died, and he assumed the throne and dismissed his wife. He re-called Ibn Ámmar, and appointed him governor of the Algarve. Christian crusaders, on a diversion from their voyage to the Holy Land sailed up the River Arade. They were met by Portuguese troops who had marched overland, commanded by the bishops of Lisbon, Coimbra and Porto. Together, they stormed the city of Silves, and captured it.

The Portuguese bishops settled for the conquest. King Richard and his men, as a reward for having come so far, sacked and looted the city. Then they demolished it with such thoroughness that little but the great mosque was left standing. The bishops consecrated it as a cathedral, and Father Nacalau, a Flemish priest who had come with the crusaders, was installed as its bishop.

The Algarve Arabic poet Ibn al-Labban wrote:

> *We are chessmen in fortune's hands*
> *And the king may fall to a lowly pawn.*
> *Take no care for this world*
> *Or the men who live in it.*
> *For now this world is lost,*
> *Without men worthy of the name.*

CHAPTER V

THE CHRISTIAN RECONQUEST

Hugues de Paynes, of Champagne, returned to Europe in 1126 from a stay in Jerusalem. He did so to seek men, money and the Pope's blessing for a new Order. With Godefrede of St Aumer, another Christian knight, he had had the idea of founding the Knights Templar. Their purposes would be to guard the church built in Jerusalem on what they believed to be the site of the Temple of Solomon, and to protect pilgrims travelling there.

It was not be until a generation later that the Templars began to address themselves at all to these aims. During the first years of their Order's existence, its knights were devoted instead to the creation of a new prototype Christian state, to be called Portugal. And long after the Order was persecuted into extinction in France and elsewhere, it continued to flourish here, in disguise, into the nineteenth century. The histories of the Knights Templar and of Portugal are inter-twined, inter-dependent.

The Order was to become the richest institution in the western world, wealthier than any monarchy, and than the Church to which it ostensibly owed allegiance. At the time of its inception, however, its founders were so poor that its emblem was of two knights — presumably Hugues and Godefrede — mounted on one horse.

Hugues arrived in Burgundy, then the most flourishing western nation. It was the commercial and intellectual crossroads of Europe. According to Cistercian chronicles, Hugues's particular purpose was to petition a monk: Bernard, the Abbot of Clairvaux. Bernard's repute was of a man who determined the election of popes and exercised effective power over them. A cousin of the royal Dukes of Burgundy, he suffered chronically from anaemia, gastric ulcers, hyper-tension and migraine. At the age of twenty-five he had persuaded four of his five brothers and seventeen of his aristocratic cousins to give up their estates and their mansions, and take a particularly austere vow of poverty. Self-denial had been out of fashion in Burgundy's monasteries. The Benedictine monks at the most important of them, the abbey of Cluny, ate the rarest foods and drank the finest vintages. They spent much of the year in their luxurious houses in Paris. Their abbot, while soliciting gifts of land, jewels, artworks and cash, used to explain: "nothing can be too good for God".

In the monastery Bernard built, his brother monks lay at night on straw and without blankets in unheated dormitories. They slept for only six hours a night, and had no free time during the day, dividing it between devotions and physical labour. Bernard, who had lost his sense of taste through one of his illnesses, obliged his whole community to eat, as he did, nothing but boiled vegetables. As head of the newly reformed Cistercian Order, one of his main ambitions was to rid the Church of its gross immorality. He lived in a hermit's hovel in the monastery's grounds, attended by a herbalist. From there, he sent out into the world a stream of letters, homilies, exhortations and pamphlets.

Through these, he publicly denounced the corruption of bishops and priests. Echoing St James, he advocated the rights of peasants against the oppression of his own class. He forbade discrimination against Jews, as the people of Jesus. He promoted respect for womanhood, through the veneration of the Virgin Mary as a divine expression of feminine compassion.

Who first had the idea of creating Portugal, and of diverting the Knights Templar to this task, is unknown. We do know from the monastic chronicles of Burgundy and from Brother Irénée Vallery-Radot's authoritative biography of St Bernard, that the original intention was to create a new, model Christian nation on the western flank of Islam. It was to stretch from the River Minho in the north of Iberia, southwards to what is now Agadir in southern Morocco, just north of the Sahara desert. Three centuries later, when Portugal had become the richest nation in Europe, it was the lasting desire to fulfil St Bernard's plan, by conquering Morocco, that led to the most calamitous downfall in the nation's history and to two generations of servitude to Spanish rule.

St Bernard's family had had an active interest in Iberia since before the end of the eleventh century. His uncle, Count Henry of Burgundy, had gone there with his private army to help Alfonso, King of Leon and Castile (for whom El Cid fought and died), to join the war against the Arabs. His payment was the hand in marriage of Princess Theresa, Alfonso's second daughter. Alfonso gave them, as her dowry, the strip of Atlantic coastal land between the Minho and the Douro rivers, known as Portucale.

By 1126, the year Hugues de Paynes arrived in Burgundy, Count Henry had been dead for 14 years. Princess Teresa was left with an only child, a son, named Afonso after his grandfather and Henriques after his father. Afonso Henriques was now 15 years old. During her regency, his mother had paid homage to her nephew, as the new King of Leon and Castile, in Afonso Henriques's name. On achieving his maturity, Afonso Henriques imprisoned his mother in a castle. He married a cousin of the Duke of Burgundy, Mafalda, daughter of Count Amadeus II of Savoy. He then had himself proclaimed a king in his own right. There are unanswerable questions as to exactly when, where and how this was done. His official chronicle describes his soldiers doing so spontaneously, after a great victory over the Arabs and the Berbers, on the battlefield of Ourique. But there is no written or archaeological evidence that such a battle took place, or of the existence of a place named Ourique.

It is clear, from other sources, that the region south of the River Douro was still under Moslem rule, and that the Berber soldiers from North Africa who guarded it mutinied, over a lack of supplies, and began to fight with their Arab officers. Reports of the uprising reached Burgundy. A plan was prepared to send an elite force, to clear out the warring Moslems, and claim the territory for Christendom.

A council was to be held at Troyes, attended by the Pope and the kings of France and Germany, to discuss the possibility of a great new crusade. Bernard declined to attend. The Pope told him that he, Bernard, was to preside. Bernard pleaded ill health. The Pope sent him a litter and bearers, who carried him to Troyes.

The first business of the council was to authorise the creation of the Knights Templar. There was no longer any pretence that their role would be to protect pilgrims, but rather to defeat the Moslems. Bernard was asked to preach a sermon, soliciting recruits. He refused, saying that every human being is your neighbour. To kill your neighbour, even though he be a Moslem, is against Christ's law. Neither Jesus, nor his apostles had ever preached a holy war, as he was now being asked to do and they would be not on the side of the "Christian" aggressors, but of the victims.

Bernard — perhaps weakened by illness — gave in under pressure. He delivered a sermon, possibly to his own dismay, that while Jesus had ordered St Peter to replace his sword in his scabbard, it was also the case that John the Baptist had offered soldiers baptism without demanding that they first laid down their arms. They had only had to promise not to attack people who did not "bear false witness" (Luke 3: 14). Bernard also pointed out that St Augustine had said that wars were sometimes commanded by God or by lawful authority and so were sometimes just.

The formation of the Order of the Knights Templar was announced by the Pope at Troyes in January 1128. Afonso Henriques sent a pledge of his and his nation's allegiance to Bernard's abbey, Clairvaux. Six weeks later, in the middle of March 1128, Hugues de Paynes and a group of newly sworn knights, reached Portucale. The speed of this has often been remarked upon as astonishing, because of an assumption that they travelled on horseback. But Burgundy was the hub of a complex of waterways, spreading out to all four points of the compass. The Pope came to Clairvaux, to consult St Bernard in his hut in the monastery grounds, by boat up the Mediterranean coast of Italy, and then up the River Rhône from Marseille. Hugues and the other knights took the opposite route, going down the Rhine into the Atlantic. Then they were sped southwards by the current and the prevailing wind. At the estuary of the River Soure, near where the city of Leiria stands today, they captured a castle from the Berbers, and took up residence.

A tendency to glamorise this era of Portuguese history, particularly by writers during the Salazar dictatorship, has recently been corrected by the popular modern historian José Hermano Saraiva. He has pointed out that, for a long period, Afonso Henriques and his knights conducted themselves not so much as an army, but as bandits. They raided enemy territory, to loot and kidnap civilians to make slaves.

The most legendary of the knights was "Fearless Geraldo", who stole from the Moslems and gave to the Christians. His flair was in climbing, unseen, over the walls of Moslem towns at night. Then, just before dawn, "raising such a racket that the townspeople thought at least a regiment was there", he grabbed all he could and disappeared with it.

Fearless Geraldo was finally caught not by Moslems, but by Castilians during his raid on Badajoz, today a Spanish town on the border with Portugal. The rescue party was led by Afonso Henriques. As the King was riding through the city gate, the portcullis was dropped on to him. It shattered his right leg, and he was captured. His family paid a huge ransom for him; but his leg did not recover from its multiple fractures, and he never rode a horse again. Fearless Geraldo escaped. This time, he enlisted with the Moslems, and raided Christian towns with such distinction that they rewarded him, on his retirement, with a fiefdom in North Africa.

To celebrate King Afonso Henriques's fortieth birthday, in 1147, a new initiative was launched. Again, it came from Burgundy; and its aim was to end the Christian-Moslem stalemate. The morale of Christendom in general was at a low ebb. To the east, the Moslems had advanced far forward from the Black Sea. There was a threat from the Slav world. St Bernard and his ex-novice monk, Pope Eugene III, launched an appeal for the launch of the Second Crusade.

A letter has survived from St Bernard to his cousin, Afonso Henriques, addressing him as "the illustrious King of Portugal", and introducing and commending the knights who carried it. When these knights reached Portugal, Afonso Henriques and Hugues de Paynes led them to Santarém, which city occupied a commanding position above the River Tagus. The knights sent a messenger to the Moslem governor, giving him three days to surrender, or to be attacked, but they were few in number, so the governor ignored them.

At dawn on the fourth day, the knights placed a scaling ladder against the city wall. Only three of them reached the top before it collapsed. These three killed the two guards, then fought their way down to and along the street, to the main gate. They succeeded in opening it, and the other knights rushed in. The knights had all vowed, before Bernard, to renounce personal gain, and to fight only for Christ. They attacked the unarmed inhabitants — most of whom were Christians — in what became a blood bath. As they carried off their valuables, the citizens who had survived fled south, to seek refuge in Lisbon.

Afonso Henriques granted the knights ownership of all Santarém's churches. In the great abbey of Alcobaça a painted panel of tiles depicts Afonso Henriques, after the capture of Santarém, writing a letter of thanks to Bernard for the help he had sent.

Encouraged by this success, the Burgundians launched a recruiting campaign for knights, which spread through France, Germany, the Low Countries and England. The latter was under the rule of the Normans, who had occupied England after two unsuccessful attempts to take control of Portugal. In all 3,000 men were signed up. A fleet of 164 ships was gathered to carry them. They floated down the Rhine and the Seine, and down the rivers of England and along its south coast, all to assemble in the harbour at Dartmouth in Devon.

It has often been claimed by British historians, writing on the theme of Portugal's historical indebtedness to Britain, that this was essentially an English expedition, with a few continental followers. It has been accepted, unquestioningly, that the expedition's original purpose was a crusade to the Holy Land, and that it ran into a severe storm in the Bay of Biscay and put into Porto for repairs and fresh supplies of food and water. There, the story goes, the knights were entertained to a lavish meal by the bishop, who read to them, through interpreters, an appeal from Afonso Henriques to delay their onward journey until they had helped him conquer Lisbon.

The evidence of the chronicles of Burgundy is otherwise. These show that from its conception, the expedition's destination was always Portugal. The ships gathered at Dartmouth, and sailed from there, because that had been, since the times of the Old Testament, known as the best shelter from which to proceed across the Bay of Biscay. It was a route which was to continue to be taken by ships of all north European nationalities for hundreds of years afterwards.

This venture was the only success of the otherwise disastrous Second Crusade, which brought disgrace to St Bernard and to his *protégé*, the Pope.

Our knowledge of the siege and capture of Lisbon in 1147 comes from an eye-witness report now in the Library of Corpus Christi College, Cambridge, written in Latin by, it is thought, a Norman priest who accompanied the knights as a chaplain.

Lisbon had been effectively closed to north Europeans for almost 400 years. The knights' chaplain described it as beyond the boundaries of the known world, at the southern extremity of the Atlantic Ocean. The city was reputed to be "the richest in trade of all Africa and most of Europe".

At the time of their arrival, the city's population had been swollen by the flow of refugees from Santarém to over 150,000 men, plus their uncounted wives and children. This compares with Paris's population then of 50,000, and London's of 30,000. The residents of Lisbon included, according to the knights' chaplain, "all the aristocracy of Sintra and Almada and Palmela and many merchants from all parts of Spain and Africa". Lisbon was on top of a hill, "its walls, descending by degrees, extend right down to the bank of the river Tagus, which is only shut out by the wall". Beyond the walls to the west, there were suburbs. The plenty of the surrounding country astonished the northern invaders. "It is second to none," the knights' chaplain wrote, "rich in products of the soil, whether you are looking for the fruit of trees or of vines. It abounds in everything, both costly articles of luxury and necessary articles of consumption. It also contains gold and silver and is never wanting in iron mines. The olive flourishes. There is nothing unproductive or sterile or which refuses to return a harvest. They do not boil their salt but dig it. Figs are so abundant that we can hardly eat a fraction of them. The region is celebrated for many forms of hunting. The air is healthful. In its pastures the mares breed with a wonderful fecundity." The River Tagus was so bounteous it was said to be two parts water and one part fish and shellfish.

Hardly had the crusade arrived, than the English and the Normans went on strike. They declared that they would not try to take the city, unless they could help themselves to its entire contents, and not share them with the Portuguese Christian troops. Afonso Henriques, at his camp to the north of the city, gave way, with nobility: "Having been constantly harassed by the Moslems, it surely has not been our destiny to accumulate wealth. Whatsoever our land possesses we count as yours."

A formal charter was written out, in which Afonso Henriques promised that the knights "who are about to remain with me at the siege of the City of Lisbon may take into their own power and possession, and may keep, all the possessions of the enemy. Myself and all my men shall have absolutely no share in them. If perchance they should take the city, they shall have it and hold it until it has been searched and despoiled. After it has been ransacked to their full satisfaction, they shall hand it over to me." Finally, the city and the land around it were to be apportioned among the invaders, according to rank. They and their heirs would be exempt from Portuguese customs dues and taxes.

Lord Saher of Archelle was the knights' commander. He ordered them to pitch their tents on a hill overlooking the city, "at a distance of about a stick's throw". Lord Saher pitched his own tent, and his fellow nobleman Herbay de Glanvill did likewise beside him. All their men went back to the ships, and stayed on board throughout the night.

At about nine the next morning, knights armed with slings began stoning the city. On the other side of the wall, Moslems and Mozarabs went on to the roofs and hurled the stones back. Other knights, trying to fight their way through the suburbs, met strong resistance. They called for reinforcements. When these arrived, they were met by a rain of arrows, and of rocks shot from ballistae. Casualties were heavy. Just before sunset, the Moslems and Mozarabs retreated, and by nightfall the suburbs were in the control of the knights.

The following days were spent in skirmishes, and exchanges of insults. The Christians shouted that Mohammed was the son of a whore. The Moslems responded by spitting and urinating on crucifixes, and hurling them at the knights. By now, the Normans and the English had taken up positions west of the city wall. The Bretons guarded the river front. The Germans, the French and the Flemings were to the east. The Germans, as an independent initiative, tried five times to dig tunnels beneath the wall, but were successfully repelled. The English and the Normans built a wooden tower, thirty metres high, on wheels. As they pushed it towards the city wall, it stuck fast in the sand. There, "it was bombarded night and day without respite by the enemy until, after four days, when we had expended great labour and suffered heavy losses in its vain defence, it was set alight. Our men were hardly able to regain their courage for a week." A knights' chaplain — not the chronicler — from Bristol urged the knights to mutiny. Relations between the Normans and the English and the rest deteriorated. A story circulated that at morning Mass in the German camp, the Host had turned into blood-soaked flesh. The Normans and the English held that this was a rebuke from God, manifesting His repulsion for their bloodthirsty behaviour.

Once evening, when the siege was in its sixth week, ten Moslems boarded a skiff in the river beneath the wall and rowed towards the opposite bank. The Bretons saw them, and went after them in their rowing boats. The Moslems jumped off the boat and swam back towards the city. They left behind a bag of letters, in Arabic, addressed to the Moslem rulers of Palmela, Évora and other districts south of the Tagus. The letters pleaded for help to "liberate the city from the barbarians". They spoke of the deaths of many of the Moslem nobles, of desperate shortages of bread and other foods. Another messenger was intercepted, with a letter from the governor of Évora to the governor of Lisbon: "having long since entered into a truce with the King of the Portuguese, I cannot break faith and wage war upon him. Buy safety by paying them money."

The Norman knights' chaplain wrote in his account: "The spirits of our men were greatly encouraged to continue against the enemy." A group of knights who had gone to raid Sintra returned, laden with booty, to the others at the siege.

As the Bretons fished from the south bank of the Tagus, a group of Moslems attacked, killing several of them, and taking five prisoners. The English and the Normans set out on a raid of reprisal, on the south-bank town of Almada. They returned the same evening with 200 Moslem and Mozarab prisoners, and more than eighty severed heads, at a cost to themselves, they claimed, of one casualty. They impaled the heads on spears, and waved them above the wall of Lisbon.

"They came out to our men as supplicants. They begged to have the heads which had been cut off," said the knights' chaplain-chronicler. "Having received them, they bore them back within the walls with grief and wailing. All that night the voice of sorrow and the miserable cries of lamentation were heard from almost every part of the city. The daring of this brilliant exploit made us ever afterwards the greatest terror to the enemy."

Some knights, lunching *ao fresco* near to the wall, left some uneaten figs at their picnic spot, and saw people creeping out of the city to fetch them. For several days thereafter, they left food at the same spot. Then they laid booby traps, and laughed uproariously at the torment of the people caught in them. Lisbon was densely built, and there was no burial ground within the walls. The stench of death was everywhere. Poor people were increasingly defecting to the knights. They begged for food, and in return gave valuable intelligence about conditions in the city.

After fifteen weeks, the Germans finally succeeded in tunnelling beneath the eastern wall. Inflammable material was placed in the tunnel and set alight. "At cockcrow about thirty cubits (about sixty-five metres) of the wall crumbled to the ground. Then the Moslems who were guarding the wall were heard to cry out in their anguish that they might now make an end of their long labours and that this very day would be their last; and that they would have to die, which would be their greatest consolation... Moslems gathered from all sides for the defence of the breach in the wall. When the men of Cologne and the Flemings went out to attempt an entrance they were repulsed... When they failed to overcome the defenders in a hand-to-hand encounter they attacked them furiously from a distance with arrows so that they looked like hedgehogs as, bristling with bolts, they stood immovably at the defence and endured as if unharmed."

The Germans retired to their camp, exhausted. The Normans and the English came to take their place but were intercepted by the Germans, who told them to make their own breach. The Normans and the English finished building a new tower, and covered it with ox hides to protect it from burning missiles and stones; the Archbishop of Braga then blessed it and sprinkled it with holy water. The tower was pushed up a slope towards the city tower, and the Moslems brought up their full garrison. The knights pushed the tower ten metres to the west. Norman and English cross-bowmen and archers launched a huge bombardment. Night came and the battle gradually quietened down and ceased. Next morning the knights had been cut off from their tower by high tide. The Moslems took their chance to attack it. "But the sea receded quickly, and the enemy gave up the contest in exhaustion," said the knights' chaplain. The knights massed on the sand and moved the tower to little more than a metre from the wall. They put down the bridge on to the wall. "When the Moslems beheld the bridge extending, they cried out with a loud voice and put down their arms as we looked on, and they extended their hands as supplicants and demanded a truce."

Five men came out of the city to negotiate a surrender, with King Afonso Henriques. A group of knights tried to kill them, but were prevented by the Portuguese. The Normans and the English on the one hand, and the Germans and the Flemings on the other, entered into a violent quarrel as to how the spoils should be shared out. The Moslems and the Portuguese watched, in mutual disgust.

Finally, the terms were agreed: 150 Normans and English, and 150 Germans and Flemings, were to enter the city, and take possession of the tower. There, the citizens of Lisbon were to deliver to them all their possessions. There was then to be a search of all the houses, warehouses and shops. Any Moslems who were found to have tried to conceal their goods, were to be beheaded. The remainder were to be allowed to go free. To the disgust of some of the knights, the Moslem governor of Lisbon and his immediate family were to be allowed to keep their property, with the exception of his Arab mare which was coveted by Lord Saher of Archelle.

The Moslems opened the gates. The knights streamed in, and immediately embarked on a rampage of murder, rape and looting. The attack was not confined to Moslems. The Bishop of Lisbon's throat was cut. Many Christians held out crucifixes and images of Our Lady, in the hope that they might be spared. They were slaughtered, as Moslems blaspheming to spare themselves.

"Oh, what rejoicing there was on the part of all!" recorded the knights' chaplain. "Oh, what special pride on the part of all! Oh, what a flow of tears, of joy and piety, when, to the praise and honour of God and of the Most Holy Virgin Mary, the ensign of the salvation-bearing Cross was placed upon the highest tower in token of the subjection of the city, while our Archbishop and our Bishop, together with the clergy and all the people, not without tears, intoned with a wonderful jubilation the *Te Deum Laudamus.*"

CHAPTER VI

THE CISTERCIAN PEACE

While occupying Lisbon in the name of Christ, unopposed by its citizens, the foreign knights had killed the bishop. They installed on his throne one of their chaplains, Father Gilbert of Hastings.

Portugal's Christians, in 370 years of Moslem rule, and consequent isolation from the rest of Christendom, had developed their own, distinct liturgy. It is now known as the Braga Rite; and thanks to a Vatican decree, it can again be heard in Portugal, on special occasions. At the time, Bishop Gilbert suppressed it as best he could, in favour of the English Sarum Rite. In anglicising the Church in this and other ways, he was assisted by thirty-two of the English and Norman priests who had accompanied the crusaders, whom he appointed his canons.

King Afonso Henriques had a palace and a cathedral built for Bishop Gilbert, and gave a mansion to each of the foreign priests. Many of the lay crusaders neither wished to return home, nor to live within the city they had so effectively despoiled. Afonso Henriques gave them farmsteads east of Lisbon, notably in and around Vila Franca da Xira, on the north banks of the Tagus. There is a Portuguese anecdote, that the king's counsellors protested to him, against giving such barbarians homes in the new nation. Afonso Henriques is said to have replied: "It is because you are such gentlemen, that we need these barbarians to defend us."

To Bernard of Clairvaux, back in Burgundy, the real contest for the religious persuasion of south-western Europe was yet to be fought, on a different field from that of military battle, and by means other than coercion. The Cistercian monks whose Order he headed, had each renounced violence, on pain of excommunication. Neither did they go out as missionaries. The conversions they sought were of their own souls, through a gradual process of becoming personally more attuned to Christ. In the world beyond the monastery walls, the gospels were not to be preached but enacted. Thus, and by no other means, were they to demonstrate the greater attractions of the Christian way of life, to that of Islam.

To the north of Lisbon, Afonso Henriques gave Bernard virtual sovereignty over a large tract of land, known today as the Costa da Prata, the Silver Coast. It extends from the limestone hills of central Portugal, to Nazaré (Nazareth) on the Atlantic, and from Obidos, north to Leiria. The Cistercian monks who came from Burgundy to take possession were free to make their own laws, administer their own justice, collect taxes, and to create and manage whatever enterprises they chose. In religious matters, they were exempt from the supervision of Gilbert and the other bishops, and subject to the Pope through Bernard. But the land they had been given was all but derelict. For the past century, it had been the site of the constantly shifting frontier between Christendom and Islam. Most of its people who had not been captured and enslaved, or killed, by one side or the other, had either run away, or died of plague.

The monks were finally expelled in 1834, with the banishment of religious orders from Portugal. Descendants of settlers they brought with them from Burgundy, in the twelfth and thirteenth centuries, are still farming here; and driving through the region today, off the main roads, it is still much as the Cistercians re-created it 800 years ago. Orchards of apples, peaches, pears and quinces are interspersed with groves of oranges and lemons, fields of melons and strawberries, and beehives in the herb gardens. There are edible snails, quails, several kinds of poultry, and domesticated pheasants. On the stony slopes, there are vineyards, and on the sandy coastal plain, pine forests.

The Cistercians, or Bernardinos, as they became known, brought with them Europe's most advanced plant varieties and agronomy. They also organised the mining, smelting and working of iron, and on the coast, boat-building, fisheries, salt extraction and the drying and salting of *bacalhau*. The making of jams and preserves to Bernadine recipes is still a substantial business, and the major trade fair for these foods, as well as for farmhouse-smoked hams and sausages, is still on the Feast of St Bernard, in Leiria. The Bernardinos introduced the skill of glass-blowing and cutting, and Atlantis crystal is today the region's most internationally known product.

The Bernardinos also brought a new social outlook. In their domain, slavery was outlawed. In their vineyards, as in their other enterprises, the labourers were paid fair wages, and the monks behaved not as their overlords, but worked alongside them at the same tasks. Literacy, and a command of the European *lingua franca*, Latin, had been a preserve of the Church. The Bernardinos instituted free Latin schools. Their abbot sat in the king's council as Chief Almoner, though he was much else. He saw to it that the hungry were fed, the needy clothed and housed, the sick treated and cared for, the young educated and the elderly provided for.

This account would have been challenged as sentimental by Protestant English travellers, who visited the region during its heyday, between the sixteenth and the eighteenth centuries. In 1774, Major Dalrymple was wined and dined by the Bernardinos, and wrote in his diary: "These celestial pastors possess so much worldly wealth, that they wallow in sloth and idleness, a nuisance to society."

Ten years later, however, William Stephens, a Scottish businessman, was blaming the failure of his cambric-weaving shop here on the generosity of the Bernardos to the local people: "The monks encourage idleness, by distributing their superfluous provisions. This makes all efforts of the management ineffectual, and weakens their command over the workmen."

The Bernardinos chose, to become their capital, the valley made by the confluence of the Alcoa and Baça rivers. They named their new town Alcobaça. The castle on the hill above, provided by Afonso Henriques for their protection, has since been destroyed by earthquakes and treasure hunters. The abbey of St Mary of Alcobaça still stands. It is the southernmost of the 340 Cistercian abbeys built across Europe at Bernard's behest during his lifetime, one of two dozen in Portugal. Its church is perhaps the finest surviving example of medieval Cistercian architecture anywhere. It certainly surpasses any in Burgundy itself, even Fontenay. (The Cistercians' mother-abbey at Clairvaux has been converted into a prison for the criminally insane.)

As in their other endeavours, the Cistercians' quest in architecture was to find beauty in simplicity. This has led many commentators to describe their style as "severe"; but that is not a word that comes to mind, on entering the church of Alcobaça. Bernard forbade the use of stained glass, of gilt and of statuary. One finds a long nave — I believe the longest in the country — of slender white pillars soaring to the high, vaulted ceiling, interspersed by broad shafts of light from the clear, leaded window panes. The pattern and the symmetry are repeated in each of the side aisles. More than halfway down, are two chapels facing one another, one containing the tomb of King Pedro I, and the other, that of his wife, Inês de Castro. A noblewoman who had joined the Portuguese royal court as a lady-in-waiting, and whom Pedro had married without his father's consent, she was murdered on the latter's orders. Pedro had her embalmed; and, when he ascended the throne, he had her body propped up next to him, and made the courtiers kiss her hand. At the foot of Pedro's tomb, is a bas relief of his last day, being spoon-fed soup on his death bed, and receiving the last rites. At the foot of Inês, is depicted the last judgement, some walking up a marble staircase to heaven, hands uplifted in joy, others clambering woefully down the rocky slope to hell.

King Dinis, who came to the throne when he was eighteen, in 1279, commissioned the building of the main cloister beside the church. He had included in the design the chapter house, where he often sat in council with the abbot and the superiors, a royal chamber, where at periods he resided with his wife Isabel, and held court, and a royal tomb room. One of the greatest of Portuguese monarchs, he so closely associated himself with the "Brother Agronomists" of Alcobaça as to be called by his chroniclers the "Farmer King". Those who brought land into cultivation were to be exempt from taxes on their crops. Tenant farmers who improved their land usage with the advice of the monks, were to be granted their freeholds within ten years.

It was a personal project of Queen Isabel, to greatly increase the pine forests the Cistercians had begun, on the coastal plain. The Cistercians' yards to make ships from the wood were also developed and expanded. For the first time since the Roman era, Portugal began to trade with the rest of Europe, notably with Flanders and England, and as far away as Thessalonika. In a transfer of skills and technology from the Mediterranean to the Atlantic which was to transform the world, shipbuilders and thirty sea captains were recruited from Genoa. Manuel Pessagna from Genoa changed his family name to the Portuguese form Pessanha and became the nation's first admiral, in charge of warding off pirates, and of the trade itself. At the latter, he and his relatives so prospered, that they became bankers to King Edward II of England. When Edward failed to repay his overdraft, their agents took over the collection of English customs dues, until the account was cleared.

Under King Dinis, Portugal became one of the first countries to innovate insurance. Ship owners paid dues into the newly created Bolsa de Lisboa, from which they were compensated if one of their vessels was raided by pirates or sunk in a storm. King Dinis is also remarkable for founding higher education in Portugal, recruiting professors from Paris. It is said that the first students were so over-indulgent in the big-city pleasures of Lisbon, King Dinis decided to transfer his new university to the more Spartan ambience of Coimbra. He is celebrated too as the father of Portuguese literature. Until his time, few outside the Church were literate; and almost all that was written was in Latin, or Burgundian (often mistakenly termed Provençale). King Dinis espoused the language of the people, Galaico, and began the process of adapting it into a distinctly Portuguese language. In this he wrote a large number of poems and troubadour songs.

Perhaps his least acknowledged achievement internationally was to guarantee the survival of the Knights Templar. All the books which I have seen published about this military and mysterious Order have taken it for granted that it was extinguished by the persecutions of King Philip IV of France and by Pope Clement V. By the beginning of the fourteenth century, the Knights Templar in France had acquired wealth of astonishing proportions, owning a third of Paris itself. The French royal family were among many who were heavily indebted to them. King Philip IV had sought a large new loan to finance further his attempt to militarily occupy Belgium. The Grand Master, Jacques de Molay, refused. Just before dawn on Friday, 13th October 1307 all the Templars in France were arrested by officials of the king, who also confiscated all the wealth that they could find, for the royal treasury. The monks were charged with offences that included spitting on the crucifix, idol worship, and "indecent kissing". A number of them were burnt alive in a field to the west of Paris; most were sentenced to imprisonment for life. Pope Clement V addressed a Bull to All the Monarchs of Christendom, *Pastoralis Praeeminentiae*, ordering them to arrest the Templars in their countries, and confiscate all their property;

and that, according to the conventional accounts, was the end of the Templars.

Some of them, however, escaped arrest. A considerable amount of treasure that they had stored in Cyprus, seems to have remained unconfiscated. In Portugal, King Dinis's reaction to the Pope's letter was derisory. His Kingdom owed its very existence to the Order. He had need of them now to guard the frontiers with Spain, along which he had built a succession of castles. He had the Archbishop of Lisbon head a commission of enquiry into the charges against the Templars. The Archbishop completely exonerated them. King Dinis formally complied with the Pope's demand by decreeing the abolition of the Order in Portugal, and confiscating all of its properties. At the same time he announced the creation of a new order, the Order of Christ. Its master and all its other members were the Templars. To them, in their new guise, he gave all the properties and other wealth he had just confiscated from them. Templars who had escaped the persecutions in other countries came here. It is believed also they brought the Cyprus treasure, which some are still seeking to find buried in the ground.

The Knights of Christ established their headquarters in Tomar, on the River Nabão, near to its confluence with the Tagus. Their magnificent fortified monastery still dominates the town. Its chapel is octagonal, a shape the Templars took to represent harmony between God and Man. They held that the Temple of Solomon in Jerusalem had been built thus. The monks, emphasising their constant military preparedness, used to attend Mass in the chapel on horseback.

To the town, the knights attracted artisans, to make weapons, saddlery, clothes, pottery, furniture and farm implements. A large part of the lands returned to them by the king, they divided into farms, which they gave to a new class of squires. Local records show some of these to have also come from France, perhaps as sympathisers of the Templars. These men did not belong to the Order, and led secular lives. The condition of their freeholds was that they themselves kept in training as cavalry officers, and also trained their farm workers in the skills of riding to battle and sword drill.

King Dinis died in 1325, and his widow, Isabel of Aragon, retired to a convent in Coimbra. They had married when she was twelve and she had become a mother when she was very young. Less than monogamous himself, Dinis was so suspicious of Isabel, that he had her locked up for a while. After her release, she established in Lisbon a refuge for abused wives, as well as a home for abandoned children. Today she remains one of Portugal's most popular saints. There is a legend that, taking food in her outstretched pinafore from the royal kitchen one day, to give to the poor, she was accosted by her husband, who angrily accused her of stealing. At his demand, she let the pinafore drop. Out fell a pile of flower petals.

Queen Isabel devoted much of her life trying to resolve family quarrels. When her son Afonso began an armed uprising against his father, she dissuaded him. On another occasion she rode on horseback between the father's and the son's armies, daring them to attack her first. After succeeding his father, the new King, Afonso IV, marched on Castile. On hearing of this, his mother left the cloister, and rode after the Portuguese army. She succeeded in ending the war before it had scarcely begun, but on her way home, died presumably of the plague. With her died the great days of the rule of the House of Burgundy over Portugal.

This was the era of the terrible plague that swept devastatingly across Europe. According to the Portuguese chroniclers, it killed one person in three. Some survivors thus received inheritances from several relatives in the course of a few months, and became a class of new rich. Merchants from England, Flanders and Genoa opened shops in Lisbon to cater to their extravagant tastes. In the countryside, peasants sought to benefit from the new shortage of labour by demanding better pay and conditions. Many who did not obtain satisfaction moved to the ports, to earn relatively large sums unloading the crates of luxury goods from abroad. The bishops and the king, Fernando I, claimed a lucrative share in this trade. King Fernando was accused of trying to fix the price at which the royal family could purchase wheat, at a level at which they could re-sell it for up to 2,000 times more.

King Fernando was engaged to marry a princess of Castile, in another diplomatic move to promote peace between the two neighbours. But he formed a passion for Leonor Teles, a Portuguese noblewoman, and married her instead. A Lisbon tailor, Fernão Vasques, led a protest march to the palace, and was beheaded.

King Fernando died when he was thirty-eight. His widow Leonor became Regent on behalf of her daughter, whose father was widely believed to be Count João Fernandes Andeiro, John of Gaunt's ambassador to the Portuguese court. The court chronicler named him as the queen's lover. The consensus was that he was the actual ruler of Portugal.

King Juan I of Castile added the Portuguese arms to his standard, and with his army captured the mountain stronghold of Guarda. The military Order of Avis, which had been formed in Portugal under the auspices of St Bernard, was charged with defending the frontiers further south. The commander of these warrior monks was João, the late King Fernando's illegitimate half-brother. News of the Castilian capture of Guarda reached him when he was on his way to the front. He abruptly turned around, and rode to Lisbon. In the palace, he told Queen Leonor and Count João that his army was hopelessly under strength. In the course of the discussion, João and Count João left the queen's chamber for another room. João's entourage saw the two men at the window, talking intently. Then they saw João draw his dagger and strike Count João on the head. They burst through the door and into the room. There, they ran Count João through with their swords.

The queen fled up river to the royal country estate at Alenquer and then to Santarém. There, she was kidnapped by King Juan and transported to Castile, where she spent the rest of her life imprisoned in a convent. People went through the streets of Lisbon, calling out that João, Master of Avis, was being held in the palace and in danger of his life. A great crowd took to the streets, and when João appeared from the palace unscathed, acclaimed him as king. The mood was hostile to foreigners. It was with difficulty that João dissuaded them from sacking the Jewish quarter. The Bishop of Lisbon was a Castilian, so the citizens of Lisbon threw him from the top of the belfry.

This was an era of great social upheaval in Europe generally. But while in England Wat Tyler and his lot were cruelly crushed, as were similar movements in France and Italy, in Portugal the common people prevailed. The old nobility, who had either supported Queen Leonor or the Castilians, fell from grace, along with the pro-Avignon Church. The new aristocracy was of merchants and the craftsmen of the Lisbon guilds. A meeting of parliament, in which the commoners now outranked the aristocrats and the bishops, was called in Coimbra. A letter was read out from the Pope in Rome, refusing to legitimise or support any other claimants to the throne but João of Avis. Whether it was genuine may be doubted, but João was proclaimed king. Fernão Lopes, the royal chronicler, wrote: "A new world came into being.

A new generation, the sons of men of such low class that it is hardly to be spoken of, by their good services and hard work, were made knights. Others got hold of ancient noble titles, which had been forgotten, and their descendants today call themselves noblemen, and are treated as such. Many of whom the Master of Avis made great did so well for themselves, that some went riding with twenty or thirty mounted escorts. In the wars that followed, they were accompanied by subordinates of the ancient aristocracy."

Meanwhile, the Castilians advanced. King Juan I took up residence in Santarém. The Castilian infantry marched on Lisbon, and built a fortified camp. They were joined by others of King Juan's troops, disembarking from ships which had sailed from Viscaya, and began a siege, by land and sea. Their camps were stricken by plague; the death toll reached 200 soldiers a day. After ten days, the survivors retreated, dressed in black, their dead comrades transported in rough coffins tied to the backs of mules.

Intelligence reached Lisbon that King Juan was regrouping his forces for another, much larger attack. The Portuguese, who had probably never exceeded two million in number, had also been smitten by plague, and they lacked the sheer quantity of able-bodied men to repulse the enemy.

João of Avis sent Thomas Daniel, an English cloth merchant of Lisbon, and Lourenço Martins, a Portuguese Jew, to the court of King Richard II in England in 1385. The Plantagenets had grave military problems of their own: England was all but cut off from the rest of the world, by the navies of France and Aragon. English seamanship was as archaic as the Plantagenets' clumsy, tub-like ships. A squadron of fast, manoeuvrable Portuguese galleys, each with 160 oarsmen and a platoon apiece of bowmen and stone-slingers, was sent to rescue the English. (Martins remained in England, where he founded a bank which continued until the 1960s, when it was taken over by Barclays.)

In return, the Portuguese were permitted by the king to recruit mercenary soldiers in England. As the first English troops reached Portugal, King Juan had brought his troops to Ciudad Rodrigo, to prepare for an attack on the strategic Portuguese city of Viseu. They met the Portuguese forces at Trancoso, where they used for the first time a new English style of battle. Instead of riding on horseback towards the Castilians, they dismounted, and dug trenches and other defences. When the Castilians had exhausted themselves in trying to breach these, bowmen suddenly rose to their feet and fired volley after volley of arrows, until the Castilians ran away.

Juan, however, re-gathered his forces, and marched towards Lisbon. At Soure, the Knights Templars' original headquarters, the renowned young Portuguese commander-in-chief, Nun' Alvares, rode out to meet Juan, and formally challenged him to battle. The battle took place at Aljubarrota, near to where the great abbey of Batalha now stands, commemorating it. Nun' Alvares's opening move was to gather his soldiers on a steep, stony ridge barring the Lisbon road. The Castilians marched around it in a sweeping detour, and approached the Portuguese and English from behind. Nun' Alvares had earthworks hurriedly dug, and deployed his troops in a wedge shape. On the evening of 14th August 1385, the Castilians came within range. They were exhausted by the day's long march, and commanded by young noblemen, of no military experience, who were confident that their superior numbers could dislodge the Portuguese and the English without any delay. They galloped their cavalry straight into the Portuguese trap. Portuguese and English soldiers rose above the scrub on either side of them and assailed them with stones and arrows. From the apex of the wedge other troops rushed forward, hacking at the Castilians with swords and axes. The Castilian standard-bearer fell. His comrades began to turn and run for it. In fleeing with his men, King Juan abandoned his royal pavilion. João of Avis had this dismantled, and used it himself on major state occasions. The altar triptych from the king's field chapel is now in the Church of the Vine in Braga. The Castilian army's huge cooking pot is in the cloister at Alcobaça. In Aljubarrota itself is a memorial to the baker's widow credited with killing nine fleeing Castilians with her iron bread-paddle. Thus, in under three hours, a battle was won which procured for Portugal almost two centuries of peace from its neighbour.

In London, in the Star Chamber of Westminster, a treaty between King João of Avis and King Richard II was negotiated and signed. It is held to be, by the English at least, the longest-surviving treaty in the world. Essentially, England pledged to come to Portugal's defence in return for trading privileges in the port of Lisbon. In a parallel agreement, Portugal pledged its support for the claim to the throne of Castile of the English King's uncle, John of Gaunt, the Duke of Lancaster. The marriage was agreed between Philippa, John of Gaunt's eldest daughter, and João of Avis — though the latter was still, technically at least, a monk, whom the Pope had not released from the vow of celibacy.

The Duchy of Lancaster's estates were the largest in the land. In London, John of Gaunt held court on a royal scale in the Savoy Palace. In matters of state, the Duchy of Lancaster was so important as to have a permanent place on the king's council. Today, although the estates have long gone, the Duchy of Lancaster continues as a permanent post in the Cabinet, for a minister without portfolio. In addition to his personal wealth, parliament voted John of Gaunt 3,000 pounds, to help finance his expedition.

King Richard II saw the Duke and Duchess off, as they sailed from Plymouth. First, he presented each of them with a royal crown to wear, once Castile was theirs. This was not to be.

The Duke's army conquered Santiago de Compostela with ease, and the Lancastrian court was set up there. João of Avis went to the banks of the River Minho, and set up the portable Castilian royal pavilion, in which he greeted his future father-in-law. Portuguese troops were placed under the Duke's command to conquer Castile, with the English. The Duke encountered little resistance. His army was overcome by the ferocious summer heat of the Spanish plain, by a failure to obtain supplies or to find any local support, and finally by the plague. John of Gaunt retreated to the coast, and with the remnants of his army and his court moved to Bayonne.

Philippa married João of Avis in Porto. After the nuptial Mass, the couple rode on two white horses to the bishop's palace. There, in a main bedroom, Philippa was undressed by ladies-in-waiting and put in to bed. Her husband was brought in by a group of knights, wine was drunk from the nuptial cup, the King himself was undressed and put to bed, the bishop and his retinue of clergy said prayers over them, and everyone withdrew. Philippa was then twenty-six. Portuguese chroniclers complained of her, that she brought to the Portuguese court an alien English prudishness. One wrote that he was not surprised that the English language was the only one to have a word for "cant". It was without precedent before João of Avis that a Portuguese King should have no acknowledged bastard children. The Queen's insistence on monogamy extended throughout the court. Men and women who belonged to it, and were discovered in compromising situations, received written orders to marry immediately.

Queen Philippa issued more than a hundred of these. It is said that when she found her husband fondling a lady-in-waiting in their summer palace in Sintra, she warned him once. When she caught him a second time, she had one of his page boys burnt at the stake in the palace forecourt. In the course of sixteen years, she conceived nine times, and six children survived. Her oldest son, Duarte, succeeded his father to the throne in 1433. Her second, Pedro, toured the courts and universities of Europe, bringing back to Portugal a great deal of knowledge as well as treasure, including the first Venetian text book on anatomy, and a copy of Marco Polo's *Travels*. Her third son, Henrique, was made Grand Master of the Order of Christ. His English mother instilled in him as best she could the ambition to fulfil a Portuguese destiny, to conquer Morocco, expel the Moslems, and make it part of Portugal.

As he and his fellow knights were preparing for the invasion of Ceuta, the Queen lay dying of the plague. She called Henrique to her bedside, according to the chronicler, kissed his ceremonial sword, and had him swear "that he would wash his hands in the blood of the infidel" and died. As her last act, Prince Henrique the Navigator had been launched on his career.

CHAPTER VII

PRINCE HENRIQUE THE MISADVENTURER

A surprise best-seller of the London publishing scene of 1868 was a biography of a previously obscure Portuguese prince, who had died just over 400 years earlier. *The Life of Prince Henry the Navigator* by Richard Major was the first work to be published about him outside Porto, the city of his birth.

Mr Major, who also called the Prince "the Sage of Sagres", evoked the figure of a Renaissance nobleman, tall, handsome, self-disciplined, filled with purpose, an outstanding scholar and a bold man of action. Through Mr Major, the reader could see Prince Henrique poring over charts and ship designs at the great School of Navigation he had founded at Sagres, the rocky, windswept south-western extremity of Europe, interrogating and debating with the scholars he had gathered around him there — some of the most brilliant minds in all Europe — dreaming of adventure as he stood on the battlements, gazing out over the Atlantic through his telescope.

The reader accompanied the Prince, as he fearlessly set out to sea, to sail to the edge of the world, and the astonishing discovery that there was no edge to fall over, that the world was round.

As Prince Henrique's fame has spread around the world since, it has been left to the new generation of Portuguese historians to apply reality to the portrayal. This has not been a conventional exercise in the de-bunking of past heroes. It is to define the true greatness of the achievement, and to attribute it to those truly outstanding figures who carried it out. That the world was round had been known to southern European scholars at least since the Arab era. By the tenth century its diameter had been calculated within an accuracy of under 20 kilometres. From the cliffs of the Portuguese coast, looking out to sea, one can easily see the earth's curvature for oneself.

Prince Henrique was the third of King João I and Queen Filipa five sons. Accounts left by courtiers of the time rate him as the least intellectual of them. While Duarte mastered the affairs of state, and Pedro toured the courts and universities of Europe, bringing back with him an invaluable library of modern knowledge, Henrique showed a preference for hunting and for that sport of the hooray-Henrys of the middle ages — jousting.

It is questionable that the only portrait said to be of him, is of him. After the account left of him by his official chronicler, the bibliography of the *Grande Encyclopaedia Portuguesa e Brasileira* records no book written about him in Portuguese until two years before Mr Major's, in Porto, the home of the British port wine trade.

Though he lived, in good health, to the then relatively advanced age of sixty-six, he left Portugal only twice in his life, and then for no greater a distance than the north coast of Morocco. On the second occasion, he left behind his younger brother, Prince Fernando, as a hostage in the hands of the Khalif of Tangier, as a token of his good faith. Prince Henrique then broke his promise to the Khalif. Young Prince Fernando died in captivity in Fez, and his body was hung by its ankles from the city wall.

Of the voyages of exploration which sailed from Portugal under royal sponsorship during his lifetime, Prince Henrique was responsible for fewer than a third. None got any further than Sierra Leone, barely half way down the coast of West Africa. King Duarte, his oldest brother, gave him a charter to develop Sagres; but this never went beyond a few modest buildings which Sir Francis Drake blew up, when he called in on his way home from "singeing the king of Spain's beard" at Cadiz. Though Henrique had in his pay a small group of Catalan cartographers, astrologers and Jewish scholars to keep him company, there never was a school of navigation, or anything like it, at Sagres or anywhere else, at that time. Prince Henrique lived in the sheltered Algarve village of Raposeira, near Lagos.

However, Prince Henrique's role in modern history is indeed a prominent one. He was the midwife who brought to life the European trade in black African people as slaves.

But the mid-nineteenth century was a time of major historical re-evaluation. A new era called for new heroes from the past. In the

USA, historians were talking up Cristóvão Colombo, who in reality had died in disgrace as a scoundrel and a liar, as the discoverer of North America. This had little to do with the truth as it was then known, and everything to do with playing down the role of the disliked English.

By the time Mr Major wrote his book, slaving was no longer a socially acceptable activity. He devoted an entire chapter to a meretricious attempt to distance Prince Henrique from the trade. Why portray him as a hero at all? The answer was that Britain was in the process of subjecting the peoples of Africa and Asia, previously under Portuguese rule, in their own homelands. They were being put to work by the millions to cultivate and process food and other products at even lower cost than could be achieved by the slave-owning farmers of the south-eastern USA. Questions were being raised, particularly in continental Europe, as to the morality of such subjugation.

The propaganda significance of Mr Major's work, in the cause of British imperialism, was to identify Prince Henrique as the principal Portuguese discoverer of these lands and peoples, in place of the actual ones. For Prince Henrique had an English mother and an English (strictly speaking an Irish) tutor, was completely fluent in the English language, and had been made a Knight of the Garter by his cousin King Henry IV. In short, if Prince Henrique wasn't entirely English, he was the nearest thing to it there could be. It followed, so the British argument went, that his genius and daring came from the English side of his parentage, as these were English, rather than continental European qualities.

Henrique's truly significant status had been that of Master General of the Order of Christ, as the Knights Templars had been renamed. A major role of the knights had been to protect Portugal from Spain. They had been self-financing, raising their revenues by plundering the Spanish across the border and by demanding protection money from the Portuguese in their localities. The signing of the treaty between the two Kingdoms brought not only peace but the prospect of financial ruin for the Knights of Christ. One Portuguese historian wrote: "Peace was the banquet which nobody wanted to attend." In 1413 a prior of the Knights Hospitaller returned from a voyage to Sicily, where he had negotiated a minor royal marriage. On his way back he had stayed for a while in Ceuta, a major Moslem trading town, on the south of the Straits of Gibraltar. While waiting for a ship to take him onwards he had had ample time to get to know the town and the surrounding countryside. Ceuta was ill defended, because its palace was engaged in civil war with its neighbours. More than 20,000 merchants functioned there, trading in spices, rare oriental fabrics and carpets, precious stones from India and gold from south of the Sahara.

Not only Portugal, but Europe as a whole, was in the grip of gold hunger. Knowledge of the techniques of mining it, which the Romans had developed, and which had so enriched them during their colonisation of Iberia, had been lost during the chaos that followed the fall of the empire. These engineering skills, particularly the pumping out of water from and the pumping in of air to deep shafts, were reinvented only in the late nineteenth century. Gold was the commodity demanded of Europeans by Arab merchants, including those of Ceuta, in exchange for oriental spices. The custom of eating meat had by now spread through Europe, and with it the demand for Asian condiments to make it edible. As the gold went east, national treasuries faced a critical decline in their reserves. They began to debase their coinage, but achieved little for doing so but to create a crisis of confidence in their currencies, damaging commerce at home and abroad

Azurara, Henrique's official chronicler, recounted how on a table in a room of the royal palace in Sintra, with the aids of two sacks of sand, half a bushel of beans, a gruel bowl and a reel of ribbon, the prior of the Knights Hospitaller fashioned a model of Ceuta and its surroundings.

It took nearly two years to organise the raiding and looting party. This is hardly surprising, for when it set out it consisted of 19,000 soldiers and 1,700 sailors. The construction of the ships had in itself been a huge task. There were 240 of them. As well as troop carriers, they included 59 war galleys with two or three tiers of oarsmen and over 60 empty cargo boats. The Portuguese were joined by knights from Normandy and Germany. The Earl of Arundel in England, who was married to Henrique's illegitimate half sister, sent cross-bowmen.

The raid was a private venture. Although Henrique's father, King João I, and his older brother Duarte sailed with Henrique, the Portuguese state played no official part. Parliament had neither been consulted, nor asked for funds. This was a venture financed by and for the enrichment of the Order of Christ. It was not the Portuguese flag, but the Order's symbol, the Templar cross, which emblazoned the sails and the pennants. The Pope sent a message of commendation and encouragement. The basic policy of the Church then was that almost anything which harmed Moslems was pleasing to the God of the Christians.

Just as the fleet was due to sail from Lisbon, Queen Filipa died. Henrique, though portrayed by his chronicler as the most devoted of her sons, declared that there was no time for mourning. Indeed, he claimed that she had expressly told him, with her last breaths, that it was her dearest wish that her death should not delay matters.

After passing through two storms on the way, the fleet anchored off Ceuta at night. Shortly before dawn, Henrique led a massive assault on the city. They quickly broke down the main gate, and found themselves unopposed. The Khalif and his counsellors, having seen the scale of the invasion before it arrived, had concluded that to attempt a defence would be futile, and lead only to the senseless loss of civilian lives, and had withdrawn. Henrique and some knights went to the citadel. They found sheltering there a group of Genoese traders, who gave them the Khalif's document of surrender.

A military chaplain consecrated the great mosque as a church. In a ceremony before the makeshift high altar, the King conferred on his son the dukedom of Viseu. The remaining troops poured on to the shore and into the town, and the looting began. In their hunt for gold ingots and coins, the soldiers ripped open sacks of spices and peppers, smashed rare ceramics, and were well rewarded by the treasure they found. The officers were less narrow-minded in their booty hunting. One had the ornately carved marble pillars of a Carthaginian temple dismantled and shipped home. They now support the main portico of the University of Évora.

After the knights and their men had returned to Portugal with their laden ships, ransacked Ceuta was handed over by them to the Portuguese crown. Cut off from the land around it, it was of virtually no further use but as a transit port at the meeting point of the Mediterranean and the Atlantic. In 1425, D. Pedro the Regent was already complaining to parliament that Ceuta did little but eat up people, arms, and money. The Portuguese royal family's English cousins advised that it be abandoned. Perhaps for fear of losing face otherwise, Portugal held on to Ceuta for more than another 200 years.

Henrique decided to launch another raid in the style of Ceuta, this time on Tangier, in 1437. The knights and royal families of the rest of

Europe this time declined to join him. He received formal refusals from England, Flanders and Germany. There was little more popular enthusiasm for the venture in Portugal itself. Henrique calculated that he would need 14,000 men. Foot soldiers were recruited from the prisons, an amnesty granted to those who submitted. Only 3,000 of these, with 1,000 mercenary cross-bowmen and 2,000 knights with their mounts, squires and grooms, could be assembled. Henrique decided the expedition should set sail without further delay. The Count of Viana, then governor of Ceuta, advised Henrique, because of the risks involved to himself, to remain behind. Henrique set out anyway and did so in the oppressive heat of 23rd August 1437.

He landed his troops near Tetouan, and marched them to Tangier. When they came within sight of the city's walls, they realised that their scaling ladders they had brought with them were far too short. Henrique ordered the setting up of a fortified camp, while he considered the next move. The site he chose had neither wells nor streams, nor any defensible line of supply and retreat to the coast. Ranged against them were 40,000 cavalry and 60,000 infantry. Within days, the siegers found that they had themselves become besieged by a large force of Berber warriors, who had been called down from the mountains by the Khalif. In one skirmish, Henrique's horse was killed under him, and he only just escaped capture.

Their food supplies exhausted, they began to kill and eat their horses, cooking them on fires of wood and hay from pack-saddles. Their water supplies ran out. The official chronicler wrote: "Many died with mud between their lips, trying to suck a little moisture out of it."

By mid-October, Henrique was negotiating a truce. This did not take long. The terms were that in return for being able to return to their ships on the coast, the Portuguese would leave everything behind, including their horses and their weapons, excluding only one set of clothes per man. The Portuguese were also to hand back Ceuta to the Moors. The Moors would hold Henrique's younger brother, Fernando, hostage until Ceuta was returned. As his earnest of good faith, the Khalif gave one of his sons to Henrique, as a reciprocal hostage.

On their way to the coast, the bedraggled and defenceless army was set upon by brigands. Although Henrique and his men escaped, he declared that this was a violation of the terms of the truce, and so Portugal would refuse to hand over Ceuta. His demands that Fernando be returned were rejected. Instead, as each succeeding diplomatic mission went to Tangier to try to negotiate Fernando's release, his conditions of confinement were systematically worsened. The first delegation found him accommodated by the Khalif almost as a house-guest. The second found him reduced to the status of a servant, working in the Khalif's garden, and cleaning his saddles.

The royal court met in Évora, in June, 1438. Rather than receive him there, King Duarte rode south to remonstrate with Henrique in the village of Portela. According to the King's chronicler, Henrique proposed the raising of a force of 24,000 men, to rescue Fernando. King Duarte returned to Évora in apparent despair, and died within the year, aged forty-nine.

In Morocco, Fernando was manacled in a dungeon next to the eunuch's latrines. By the time he was hanged by his ankles on the city wall, to be eaten by vultures, it was not known whether he was still alive or had already died.

Prince Henrique never returned to the royal court. As Master General of the Order of Christ, he was *ex officio* governor of the Algarve; and that was where he spent the rest of his life.

The Algarve, though long captured from the Moors, was not part of Portugal. Indeed, it was to remain a separate and much neglected Kingdom until the twentieth century; and until the twentieth century it was so effectively separated from Portugal by a mountain range that communications between the two countries were by means of ocean-going ships. At the time of Prince Henrique, its small population consisted of little more than market traders, fishermen and artisans. There were virtually no peasants. They had mostly fled to North Africa, in search of a new livelihood, when their lands had been confiscated by the Knights Templar. The Algarve was one of the most fertile regions of southern Europe, with several rivers running through it. It was to be the one place in Europe, for example, where the south China orange tree took root and flourished. Prince Henrique's problem was a lack of labour to cultivate his terrain. It was futile to try to recruit manpower from Portugal itself, which was then also under-populated. Agricultural work was unpopular, and so much of the land there remained uncultivated.

It was well known to Prince Henrique and his council that in the Arab world just across the water, there was a flourishing trade in black slaves, kidnapped or bought south of the Sahara. How was he to procure sufficient to till the Algarve?

Though several had tried, no European had yet reached black Africa, and returned. The most recent attempt had been over a century before, when some Genoans set out on this quest, and disappeared. The obstacle was the infamous Cape Bojador, which juts from the coast of West Africa, 1,500 kilometres south of Tangier. Here, ships were smashed to pieces by the current hurling them at the rocks. Prince Henrique is said to have remarked: "There is no peril so great, that the hope of profit will not be greater."

Prince Henrique's adult life saw some of the most rapid and remarkable advances in the design of ships that there had ever been. His invasion of Ceuta had been by galleys, with sails being hoisted when the wind was right. Within twenty years, the caravel had been developed under the patronage of the Order of Christ. Within another eighty years it was to become obsolete, replaced by the much larger and more sophisticated galleon. But the caravel was the means by which Europe's isolation from the rest of the world was first breached. Its immense commercial potential was realised from the start, and the Order of Christ was determined to protect its monopoly of the new technology from foreign spies. A great deal of secrecy surrounded its development. Thus the legend was created that the centre of this activity was Sagres. It is more likely that the actual centre was Castro Marim, on the River Guadiana. The major record of the design and construction method was among the things stolen from Portugal by the French during the Napoleonic invasion and not yet returned. Early maps of the Atlantic coast of Africa, stolen or otherwise deceitfully obtained by French agents in the Algarve, were discovered not many years ago in the departmental archives of the Gironde.

These new ships were both more slender and lighter than the galleys, weighing about fifty tonnes. Instead of twelve oarsmen, who had been needed to manoeuvre ships, there was a single stern rudder. Triangular sails at the bow and stern were able to propel the ship forward across the wind, and to tack into it. It could achieve a speed of ten knots an hour.

The replacement of oars by sail power reduced the number of crew needed by at least three quarters, from perhaps eighty to twenty. This dramatically reduced the amount of water, food (dried meat and fish, lentils, olives, garlic, cheese, almonds, raisins, ships biscuits and honey) and other supplies that had to be carried, and increased the amount of time a ship could be out at sea without restock.

These innovations were accompanied by equally striking advances in navigational aids and techniques: the compass, the Portalan chart and the astrolabe. The latter had long existed and had probably been brought to Iberia by the Arabs. It had until then, however, been a scientific toy much liked by monks, rabbis and astrologers. Now it was adapted to practical use. The astrolabe enabled a mariner to discern his latitude from the height of the north star and the time from the height of the sun.

Thus freed from having to closely follow the coastline, Gil Eanes became the first European to round Cape Bojador, in 1435. To the south of it, he landed on a deserted shore. There he dug up a previously unknown plant, which he put into a barrel and took back to Portugal, where it was named the Rose of St Mary.

The following year Eanes and another captain, Afonso Gonçalves Baldaia, rounded the Bojador again, and went much further south. They landed in a bay, and saw on the beach the footprints of people and camels.

The first known encounter between Europeans and Africans in Africa took place in the following year, 1437. It was not propitious. Baldaia had set off from Lagos in the Algarve with the commission to kidnap at least one African and bring him back alive. Arriving again at the mouth of the Senegal River, he put on the shore two young men, both aristocrats and both seventeen years old, on horseback. They had been selected for their prowess in hunting. They rode inland for several hours and came across a group of about twenty people. The latter, sensing their hostile intentions, retreated behind some rocks and hurled spears and stones at the two young Portuguese, until they withdrew.

After they returned to the ship with their report, Baldaia and a larger hunting party rowed up river to the spot where the encounter had taken place. This had been abandoned, and they saw no sign of humanity. A little further down the coast, he found some abandoned fishing nets made of palm fibre, and some utensils. These were hardly sufficient to justify the cost of his expedition to the Order of Christ. Encountering a herd of seals, he had his crew kill and skin a large number of them until the value of the hides more than recompensed for his voyage.

In 1441 Nuno Tristão sailed from Lagos with an Arabic interpreter on board his ship. He arrived at the mouth of the Senegal River to find another Portuguese captain, Antão Gonçalves, already there. Gonçalves's purpose was the collecting of seal skins; but seeing a Tuareg man and a black woman watching them from the shore, he had had them captured and held on board his ship. Tristão's interpreter failed to establish communication with them, and they were released.

Under the cover, and in the relative cool, of the night, Tristão led his hunting party inland. At dawn, they came to a Tuareg camp, and immediately attacked it. They killed four Tuaregs and captured ten, including their leader, who proved to be fluent in Arabic. His name was Adahu. Ironically, he was a slave trader. Tristão released six of Adahu's captives, and while he himself sailed on south, Gonçalves took Adahu and three companions back to the Algarve.

In Lagos, Prince Henry received Adahu and his companions with the formal courtesy extended to a captured knight and his squires. They were given European clothes, and were comfortably accommodated. They were naturally a great curiosity and Prince Henrique and his fellow knights spent long hours questioning Adahu through interpreters. What most interested them was his account of a green, lush country that lay beyond the south of the Sahara, the land of the black people.

Adahu eventually succeeded in striking a bargain for the release of himself and his companions, with Prince Henrique. The price agreed was four black slaves for the freedom of each one of the Tuaregs. Afonso Baldaia sailed them back to the Senegal, where the Tuaregs promptly disappeared. After eight days, a Moor on a white camel rode down to the shore. He had with him only ten black slaves to hand over to Baldaia, but made up for the short measure with a leather shield, some ostrich eggs and gold dust. The practice of capture and ransom soon spread along the coast. Why go to the trouble and expense of taking a captive to Europe to sell, when you could sell him back on the spot for as much? Soon afterwards, a party of Portuguese raided the Arab slave-trading post at Cape Não, and captured eighteen Moorish merchants. These they managed to ransom for fifty-one black Guinean slaves, and a lion. This was the first African lion to reach the shores of Europe. Prince Henrique sent it on by ship from the Algarve to Galway in Ireland, as a gift to his boyhood tutor in English, who had retired there.

Tristão, sailing ever further south, reached the island of Arguim, in 1443. Standing on the bridge he and his officers saw what appeared to be two huge dark birds speeding across the water towards them, their great wings flapping and splashing the surface. As they came closer, they proved to be two dug-out canoes, propelled by black men using their arms and legs as oars. Under his orders, Tristão's crew took to the boats, and captured fourteen of them. The remainder sought refuge from the whites on the island, where a further fifteen were captured.

That year, Prince Henrique, as Head of the Order of Christ, asked for and received from the Pope the grant of a monopoly of trade from Cape Bojador as far as the Indies. Reserving a 20 per cent share of all proceeds for himself, Prince Henrique franchised this monopoly to Lançarote de Freitas, the chief of customs in Lagos, and a group of local merchants.

A few months later Captain Bartolomeu Dias reached Cabo Verde and "the country of the blacks". A fleet of six caravels returned to Lagos with a cargo of 235 slaves.

Prince Henrique was there to receive them, on horseback, and to claim his fifth share in person. His chronicler, Azurara, has left us this account: "On 8th August 1444, before dawn because of the heat the sailors landed their captives, and they were herded into a field outside the town. Some of them were comparatively light skinned, lighter skinned than mulattos. Some were slightly darker, and others as black as moles. Some were handsome and well-proportioned, and some so hideous in face and form as to appear that they had come from hell. But who among us was so hard at heart as not to be moved by compassion? They had heads downcast, and faces covered in tears. Some looked up towards heaven apparently praying to whatever God was theirs. I saw some slapping their faces with their hands, and then throwing themselves flat on the ground.

There was a wailing chant, and although we could not understand their words, they spoke their grief to us clearly.

Their anguish reached new heights when the moment of distribution came. For it to be fair, it proved necessary for children to be separated from their parents, wives from their husbands, and brothers from brothers. It was impossible to affect this separation without causing them extreme pain. Fathers and sons, ranged on opposite sides, would break ranks and rush towards each other with all their might. Mothers clasped their infants in their arms, and threw themselves on the ground to cover them with their bodies, to try to prevent their children from being separated from them."

A large crowd had gathered to watch, making the distribution even more difficult. Prince Henrique was the first to receive his share of 46 slaves. He gave them away on the spot to members of his entourage. To him, his reward lay in the accomplishment of one of his dearest wishes: the unspeakable satisfaction of anticipating the Christian salvation of these savages' souls, which, but for him, would have been forever lost to God ...

"They proved to be much less obstinate than the Moors about religion, and readily adopted Christianity."

Each trade engaged in a second dividing up of the slaves, according to Azurara, "doubling their despair. A father remained at Lagos, while the mother was taken to Lisbon and the child sent somewhere else."

On the Atlantic coast of West Africa, the fear of the early European trade in slaves was enhanced by the belief that Europeans were cannibals, and that they were shipping black Africans to the Algarve in order for them to be killed and eaten. The reputation of the Portuguese preceded them. In 1446, a mere two years after the first distribution of slaves in Lagos, Nuno Tristão reached for the first time the mouth of the River Gambia. He set out up river with a hunting party in two boats. Eighty warriors in twelve canoes swept down on them, and rained poisoned arrows at them. Tristão and most of his men died within the hour, and those few who managed to get back to the ship were all dead within a couple of days. The only survivors on board were a wounded sailor, two deck boys, and an African boy, who had recently been captured. Together they set sail for the north, in a nightmare voyage which lasted for over sixty days. Then, they were met by chance by Galicean pirates off the Portuguese coast at Sines, north of the Algarve, and brought to land.

Tristão and his men were not, of course, the only casualties of the pioneering days of the West Africa trade. Among others was a Danish nobleman, known to the Portuguese as Eberhardt, who procured a passage on a ship from Lagos to Cabo Verde. He took with him a tent of his own invention, which, he said, could give shelter to thirty men, and yet was light enough to be carried by only one. It was his plan to barter this for an elephant. The Portuguese left him and his tent on the shore. When they returned, both had disappeared, without trace. From this and other incidents, legends grew about white slaves in the African interior.

The coastal chiefs found the capture of blacks in the interior, and their sale to Europeans, a new and extremely lucrative trade. Already, by 1447, the supply had become so plentiful, and the price thus reduced, that one captain, at least, took on to his ship more that he had supplies for to last the voyage back to Lagos, and so threw the surplus ones overboard. At the same time, the papal monopoly was fiercely protected. A Spaniard, caught trading Andalucian horses for slaves (the going rate was one horse to seventeen men), had all his bones broken by royal Portuguese order, and his still apparently sentient body thrown into a furnace.

Before Prince Henrique's death in 1460, around 1,000 slaves a year were being landed in Lagos. They came to make up a majority of the population of the Algarve, and ten per cent of the population of Lisbon. They were by now being obtained peacefully through a supply contract with the African King Badomel of the Senegal coast. The profit per voyage averaged between 600 and 700 per cent, and did not diminish with decreasing demand in Portugal itself, because of a rapid growth in exports of slaves to the northern Kingdoms of Spain and further north in Europe.

Slavery was not without its Portuguese critics, and these included some of Prince Henrique's relatives. Azurara, Henry's chronicler, wrote: "They are treated with great kindness, and no distinction is made between them and the free-born Portuguese servants. The young ones are taught trades. Those who show themselves able to run farms are set free, and their marriages arranged to Portuguese women. They are given good dowries by their masters to help them towards independence. Widows, who take in girl slaves as servants, bring them up as though they are their own daughters. The widows leave them legacies in their wills, so they can marry well, and they are looked on absolutely as free women. I have never known one of these captives put in irons, nor have I ever known one who was not treated with great kindness. I have often been invited by slave owners to the baptism or marriage of one of them. There is as much ceremony and celebration, as if the slave is a member of the family."

There was a partial truth to Azurara's claim, evidenced by the absorption of these involuntary African immigrants into the free population through inter-marriage and land grants. Today, in the Alentejo (the province immediately to the north of the Algarve), two villages — São Romão and Rio de Moinhos — near Alcácer do Sal remain predominantly populated by black rice farmers. Their slave ancestors brought with them a genetic immunity to malaria. This disease was endemic in the rice paddies of Alcácer, as recently as the 1950s. While the white Portuguese died or moved from the region, so the blacks acquired their properties, and prospered increasingly.

These instances were, of course, the exception rather than the rule. In 1555, soon after the centenary of the beginnings of the Portuguese slave trade, Father Fernando Oliveira published a pamphlet denouncing slavery as tyranny. It was false to blame the kings of the African coast for capturing and selling slaves. Without European buyers, there would be no trade, and therefore no mass kidnappings. He condemned with particular vehemence the defence that Azurara had entered on behalf of Prince Henrique, that their enslavement led to their conversion to, and the salvation of their souls by, Christianity. Father Fernando wrote: "We have invented a vile and cruel trade."

Slavery was not outlawed in Portugal nor the remaining slaves there freed, until 1773. This was a year after England, and thirty-five years before the United States. All slave trading by Portuguese was not outlawed until 1836. As in other parts of the world, so in some Portuguese territories overseas, slavery, known often by other names, such as "indentured labour", remained a reality for much longer.

Slaves were not the only commodity brought back from West Africa. At a fortified trading post in what is now Mauritania, run by a syndicate of Portuguese merchants, there was a busy trade in gum arabic, cotton, ivory, parrots, and a range of plants used in medicine, cosmetics and tenderising and flavouring meat. The spices were not as refined, or as esteemed, as those from the Orient and supplied to the rest of Europe through Venice; but the peppers, particularly, were cheaper by several times, and became a major re-export from the Algarve to northern Europe. By early in the sixteenth century, there were Portuguese spice traders permanently resident in Bruges and in Southampton.

How were all these goods paid for? Europe, as I have already mentioned, was suffering from a gold famine, which would only be eased by the Portuguese, as they ventured further south and east. The kings of the African coast, for their part, sought clothing, blankets, red coral beads and objects made of silver; but the commodity they sought above all was wheat. This, by the 1500s, the Algarve and Portugal were importing in huge quantities, to re-export to West Africa. The island of Madeira, about 1,200 kilometres south-west of Lagos, was discovered in the 1420s. It was unpopulated, and because of the favourable winds was an ideal transit port for ships going to and from West Africa. *Madeira* is the Portuguese for wood, and the island was so named because it was densely covered by forest: the island of wood. Whether by accident or design, the forest was set alight, and burned for two years. Thus richly fertilised, the land was divided between supporters of the Order of Christ. With the use of black African slave labour, they grew wheat in abundance. This was shipped to Africa, and bartered for more slaves.

Having enabled so many others to become rich, Prince Henrique died as he had lived, obedient to his vows of chastity and poverty. He had no money of his own to leave and no direct heir. In his will, he bequeathed his office and the powers which went with it to his nephew Fernando. Fernando leased his monopoly of the West Africa trade to Fernão Gomes, for 200,000 reis a year. This was equivalent to no more than the profit of a single voyage. In addition, Gomes was given the right to extend the area of his concession by 100 leagues a year.

CHAPTER VIII

KING JOÃO AND THE GREAT ADVENTURE

The reign of King João II lasted only fourteen years, until his death at the age of forty — some modern Portuguese historians believe, from poisoning — in 1495. It was one of the most remarkable reigns in the history of Europe. The Count of Ficalho's epitaph to him was: "He may not have been a good man, but he was certainly a great King." In our own time, Oliveira Marques has stated: "It is to him, not to Prince Henrique, that the creation of a comprehensive plan of discovery, and its means and goals, should be credited."

This plan was as astonishing in its ambition, as it was inspired in its execution. It was to reduce the Mediterranean, the centre of power in the civilised world since the time of ancient Egypt, to a backwater, and to make Lisbon the western world's new capital of wealth. Portugal, the south-western tip of Europe, had a population of under 1.5 million — an eighth that of Italy, less than a quarter that of Spain, and less than half that of England. In their great adventure, the Portuguese had the financial support of the Medicis and other Florentine bankers, but no other logistic help from outside the country. Within a generation, in 1531, the King of England was to write to the Doge of Venice, to apologise that his galleons would no longer call at Venice to buy spices, but instead go to Lisbon. By then, in any case, the Venetians had no spices in their warehouses to sell. Its merchants had returned from their annual buying expedition to Alexandria, empty handed. Venice's senators turned on one another in recrimination, as the city began to sink literally as well as financially. In Florence, as the Medicis counted their share of the profits from this shift of power and wealth to a small Atlantic

107

nation, they proclaimed it as "the triumph of the modern over the ancient".

A group of Portuguese noblemen, visiting Italy, had their horses shod in gold, and the shoes attached to the hoofs by a single nail, so as to enjoy, when they fell off, the sight of Italians scrambling for them. Lisbon had become the most fabulously rich city in Europe. Visitors came here from England and other similarly backward countries to gaze upon its opulence, and its pre-eminence in the arts and the sciences, in grand opera and medicine, in architecture and jewellery.

It was King João II who founded the Council of Scholars — eminent churchmen, rabbis, mathematicians, and cosmographers — that later came to be misnamed and mislocated as the School of Sagres. Its deliberations took place mostly in Santarém, and on occasion in the Knights Templar castle at Tomar. It was King João who negotiated the procurement of immense quantities of gold from West Africa, which were used to finance the voyages of Bartolomeu Dias, Vasco da Gama and others. Thus it was he, and not Cristóvão Colombo any more than Prince Henrique, who achieved one of the most momentous events in the history of mankind: the ending, for good and ill, of Europe's isolation from other civilisations.

King João II's inheritance, when he came to the throne, could hardly have seemed less attractive. His father, Afonso V, had engaged in a disastrous conflict with Castile, and had gone to France to appeal for military help from King Louis XI. When King Louis refused, Afonso disguised himself as a common pilgrim, and sought refuge in a monastery in Brittany. There, he was found, and sent back to Portugal. He petitioned parliament to allow him to abdicate, but died before the hearing could take place. He left his son João a state which was worse than ruined financially. Its currency was worthless. The state owed huge sums which it had borrowed from the Church. It had sold the rights to collect tax to a consortium of Jews.

The aristocracy was in the mood for a coup d'état. João's cousin, the Duke of Bragança, had amassed a private army of 3,000 cavalry and 10,000 foot soldiers. King João lured the Duke with a plea to negotiate a truce. Then he arrested him and had him beheaded. He summoned his brother-in-law, the Duke of Viseu, to come and have a chat with him. The door closed, and João stabbed him to death, as the chronicler recorded, "without many words". Those of the old

Burgundian nobility, created at the foundation of the Portuguese nation, who survived, did so in starkly reduced circumstances. Their rights were severely curtailed. In particular, the administration of justice became a royal monopoly. Their estates, ceded to them by past kings, were reclaimed by João. Some, in return for making public vows of loyalty on their knees, were given back life tenancies. Within the royal court, and the institutions of state generally, the positions and the influence these aristocratic families had enjoyed over centuries was decisively destroyed.

João had his advisers conduct a search for men of quality from the rest of the population. They were interviewed, their backgrounds and their credentials were examined. The names of those who passed these tests were placed on "The King's List". It was from this list that positions in the administration, the judiciary and so on were filled. A completely new, centralised and unprecedentedly agile regime came into being, of which the Council of Scholars formed a vital part. Thus began a tradition of academics and intellectuals playing key roles in the governance of Portugal, which has continued to this day. More than a third of Prime Minister António Gutteres's cabinet is composed of university professors.

To many foreign historians, King João II's historical role is confined to being a minor player in the epic story of Cristóvão Colombo. It was he who first turned down Colombo's proposal to find a western route from Europe to the Indies, a decision which is almost universally regarded as a blunder, as passing up one of the greatest opportunities ever offered a ruler. The truth is the opposite. Achievements still often attributed to Colombo include the realisation that the world is round, and the existence of the American continent. That the world is round had been known for centuries. Portuguese and Galician fishermen had been catching cod off the coast of Canada for generations, and had augmented their diet by planting and growing crops on the mainland. This latter Colombo never set eyes on. Instead, he landed on some islands, which he called the West Indies, two years after the Portuguese had discovered the route to the real Indies, which, as they had long conjectured, lay to the east. Worse still for his Spanish sponsors, Colombo's boasting about his minor findings alerted King João and his Council of Scholars, and they used it to negotiate a treaty giving them a monopoly over half of South America — today's Brazil — and all of Africa and Asia. Colombo died in disgrace and was buried in a pauper's grave. The Portuguese became the richest people in Europe.

In the folk memory of northern Europe, the early discoverers of the world beyond Europe were men of such blind courage that they believed they risked falling over the edge of a flat earth, and the existence of great monsters which would rise from the depth, smash their caravels to pieces, and gobble up the crews. This is, however, a reflection of the state of ignorance in northern Europe at the time of King João about the rest of the world, from which the Portuguese had made huge strides. They did so in conditions of immense secrecy. At one stage, the Portuguese parliament proposed that all foreigners should be expelled from Lisbon, for fear that they would find out, and report back home. This the King rejected. Instead, he commissioned a campaign of disinformation, to mislead the rest of Europe.

The northern European vision was rooted in the science fiction fantasies of medieval scholastics. Other lands were peopled by literally faceless and throatless men, with their eyes set in their shoulders, and their mouths in their abdomens. There were one-eyed women, and men with only one foot, but who could jump with greater agility than two-legged humans could walk; there were people with two heads, and some without mouths at all, who sustained themselves by smelling the scents of plants; there were people who ate live fish and drank sea water. Near the Ganges, people ate live cobras, and lived for 400 years. The Portuguese exploited their reputation for seafaring by adding to these myths in northern Europe. There were giant serpents that dissolved on contact with water. In particular, it seemed that Flemish ships which had ventured down the west coast of Africa had been wrecked, and their crew boiled alive in pots, and eaten by the locals for dinner. This was a reversal of the real situation. It was the Africans who had been terrified of Europeans, believing *them* to be cannibals. It is an image which survived 500 years later in the comic books and popular imagination of the north.

According to the biography by his son Fernando, Cristóvão Colombo was a Genoese seafarer, a member of the crew of a ship which sank off Cape St Vincent when he was twenty-two years old. He and the rest of the crew were rescued and cared for by people in Lagos. From there, he went to Lisbon, because his younger brother, Bartolomeu, was working there as a cartographer. He helped his

110

brother for a while, and then signed on ships travelling to Bristol, Galway, Iceland, and "the land of the codfish, a hundred leagues beyond".

Back in Lisbon, he acted as agent for a merchant in Genoa, but the business failed, and he fell into debt. Those were his circumstances when he went to King João II with his request that he finance a voyage across the Atlantic. He showed the King calculations demonstrating that this would be by far the shortest route to Japan and the rest of the Indies. The King did not believe him. His chronicler recorded: "His Majesty saw Cristóvão Colombo to have a big mouth and to be boastful, exaggerated his accomplishments, and more inflated with fancy and imagination than certain on his case."

But nonetheless the King passed him on to the Council of Scholars for a second opinion. They were already familiar with the calculations Colombo put forward. Their source was a Florentine scholar, Paolo Toscanelli, and had been contained in a letter by him, some years earlier, to Canon Martins of Lisbon Cathedral. The Portuguese scholars had already dismissed his sums. In the letter Toscanelli had said, and Colombo repeated to the King and the Scholars: "Antillia was 1,500 miles west of Lisbon, Japan 3,500 miles west, and China 5,000 miles". He had miscalculated the width of one degree of latitude to be 84 kilometres, when Portuguese mathematicians had already calculated the correct answer, of 111 kilometres. This had led Toscanelli to misplace the west coast of the Indies (today known as Asia) at 180 degrees, when the Portuguese calculation was 229 degrees. Furthermore, Portuguese mariners had already sailed far further across the Atlantic than 1,500 miles. They knew at first hand that Japan was not located there. The consensus of modern historians is that Portuguese mariners had already discovered, and were trading with, what became known as Brazil, though they kept this a well-guarded secret, trans-shipping the goods at remote island trading stations off the west coast of Africa, and attributing the origin of the cargoes to Africa.

More than two years before Colombo set sail, Bartolomeu Dias had found the route to the Orient around the Cape of Good Hope. The much lesser-known Portuguese spy, Pêro da Covilhã, had been to India itself, via the Middle East, and returned from there with Arab and Indian maps showing the route from southern Africa to India.

Colombo left Lisbon and his debts, and went to England. There again his plan was dismissed as fanciful. When he eventually set sail, with Spanish royal finance, he reached the Caribbean, which, according to Toscanelli's and his calculations was the China Sea. He named an island on which he landed, Anguilla. He then sailed back to Europe to boast of his achievements. Unfortunately for Spain, he did not return directly there, but instead called in at Lisbon. He went to the royal palace and took what he imagined to be the sweet revenge of telling His Majesty of the prize which could have been his, but was now the property of the Queen of Castile and the King of Aragon. He chided King João for slighting him and disbelieving him.

João replied by pointing out that under his treaty with Spain over their division of the rest of the world, Colombo's discovery lay within Portugal's sphere and was therefore his.

By the time Colombo reached Spain, King Fernando and Queen Isabel had received a letter from King João, threatening to send ships to Anguilla to claim it from them. Unless they had any other proposals. The Spanish hastened to the negotiating table. The talks were held in the remote Spanish town of Tordesillas, set in the mountains close to the Portuguese border. The mediator was the Borgia Pope, Alexander VI, who heard the submissions of each side in Rome, and then appointed a papal legate to represent him at Tordesillas. The agreed boundary was set at 370 leagues west of the Cabo Verde Islands. Any land already claimed by one side in the other's area of dominance, had to be handed over. Each side must inform the other of its seafarers' discoveries. In fact the exact position of the line was to continue to be under dispute for another two centuries. What is most striking is that the line more or less divided South America into two, and that that part which fell to Portugal was by far the nearest to Europe. For officially South America had yet to be discovered. It seems clear that the Spanish had no knowledge of it yet. It is hard to conclude other than that the Portuguese did, and by concealing their discovery, pulled off one of the greatest coups in diplomatic history. Once the treaty had been signed, the west coast of South America was officially "discovered" by Pedro Álvares Cabral.

By the time of the treaty, King João II already had a major, indeed near-miraculous, achievement to his credit. Portugal's currency, worthless when he had come to the throne, was now the soundest in Europe. The Church and the Medici bank in Florence had been repaid in full. The right for the state to collect taxes had been repurchased. For the first time since the beginning of the Portuguese explorations two generations ago, the state itself was now rich enough to finance expeditions instead of selling exploration rights to private adventurers.

João had achieved this by shipping huge quantities of gold from what is now Ghana in West Africa. To obtain it, he had created a radically new style of dealing with African tribal chiefs. Gone was the buccaneering, almost piratical style of behaviour, the kidnapping and ransoming back of royal children, the conduct of trade by means of threats. Instead, members of his new nobility were appointed ambassadors, dressed up in court uniforms, and dispatched with letters from João declaring respect and friendly greetings. Contrary to popular myth, these men, including Vasco da Gama, were not navigators. The ships themselves were in the charge of sea captains and pilots.

João II sent Diogo de Azambuja to negotiate with the Ghanaian chiefs. That the ambassador was a man of peace, was underlined by the fact that he was a cripple. Previous travellers had found at last the original source of the gold that found its way into the hands of the Arabs of North Africa. Vast quantities of it were contained in the alluvial sands around what is now Accra. It was a simple and inexpensive task to sieve out the gold dust. In addition more gold was brought down to the coast from the interior by the great Ashanti tribe, further north.

Diogo presented his credentials. The chiefs, dressed in togas, embellished golden staffs in their right hands, accompanied by their sons and their sub-chiefs, sat on their gilded stools in council together to hear and consider João's proposal to establish a permanent trading post, and to become the monopoly buyers of the gold. The chiefs were impressed by the courtesy and decorum of the Portuguese, contrasting sharply with their limited previous experience of Europeans. They found the terms of trade acceptable, and a treaty was made.

King João sent out a fleet of nine caravels and two round ships, containing a pre-fabricated stone fort, warehouse and chapel. These had been previously assembled in Portugal and then dismantled, with each block numbered and entered into the plan. With this innovative cargo sailed 100 stonemasons and carpenters. They recruited local labour to help them reconstruct the buildings. Over time, Accra

113

developed into a Portuguese municipality — the first European town outside Europe. Its centrepiece, named St George's castle, is still a major landmark.

Accra was known to the Portuguese as S. Jorge da Mina. Gold was shipped from there at least once a month to Lisbon. There, in the Praça do Comercio on the waterfront, João had built, next to his palace, the Casa da Mina in which to store it. He personally received every cargo, and signed and stamped the shipping papers. There were outbreaks of piracy by French and Flemish ships, attacking the gold-bearing caravels on their way to Lisbon. At least one had on board a disaffected Portuguese pilot, to guide them to the main route. They netted 2,000 dobrões of gold in a single raid. At one stage the governor of S. Jorge da Mina reported back to Lisbon, that there were some fifty Flemish, French and English pirate vessels hovering outside the harbour. Despite this, by 1500, the quantity of gold being received every year totalled more than 400 kilograms. If a Portuguese working in S. Jorge da Mina was caught attempting to smuggle gold, the penalties were the most severe. However, each was entitled to spend a part of his wages — the amount being regulated according to his military or civilian rank — buying gold from Africans, in the market. This they could have certified as legitimate, for a fee, by the king's fiscal office in S. Jorge da Mina. They could then send it back to the Casa da Mina, where it would be bought by the treasury. Some amassed considerable wealth.

The gold in the royal treasury was now to be applied to carrying out the great plan. Both the secrecy which surrounded it, and the destruction of so many official records in the great fire which was to follow the Lisbon earthquake, means that we do not know precisely when it was conceived. Its nature was and is bold and clear. The principal source of wealth in the rest of Europe was the trade in oriental spices. Although Genoa played a role in this trade, it was dominated by the Venetians. They had built from the profit their magnificent capital, created an empire that had stretched to Dalmatia and beyond, to the shores of the Black Sea. Less patronising of the visual arts than Florence, they had generously sponsored scholarship in the natural sciences. They were particularly pre-eminent in human anatomy and medicine. A young Portuguese physician was sent by the king from Lisbon to Venice, to attend the anatomy classes and returned with a copy of the first European text book on the subject. It seems likely that the first anatomical text in England was a copy of this copy, acquired in Lisbon by visiting English physicians.

What was to prove the fatal gap in Venetian scholarship was its aversion to Arab science. This is understandable emotionally. While Arabs in Alexandria were the middle men in the spice trade, providing the essential link between the Orient and Europe, Arabia as a whole was Venice's arch enemy.

It was Arab science on which the great Jewish scholars of the day founded much of their secular knowledge. Although the Arabs had become hostile to them, it was not for them a case of learning from the enemy. In happier days, Jews had been as essential a group of contributors to it as had been Moslems. Although Arabic was the language in which it was expressed, the body of knowledge belonged as much to the Jews as it did to Islam. Sporadic anti-Jewish riots in Spain gave King João of Portugal the chance to recruit from there to his Council of Scholars, prominent Jewish intellectuals. He did not waste it. By royal decree, a fine site on a hillside in Lisbon was given to the Jews, on which to build a synagogue. Another site, for the same purpose, was given them by the Knights of the Order of Christ, beneath their castle-monastery and headquarters in Tomar. King João was the Order's Master General, and it was under the Order's ensign, the Templar Cross, that the Portuguese ships of discovery still sailed.

In the order of precedence for formal ceremonies of the royal court, the Chief Rabbi was given the same rank as the Cardinal. The Royal Treasurer was Jewish, as was the Royal Physician, Master Rodrigo — a formidable scholar in fields beyond medicine. These were joined by José Visinio, the eminent mathematician of the great university of Salamanca. It was the latter too who had led the examination of Cristóvão Colombo, and rejected him as a charlatan.

The Arabs had in their turn based their secular knowledge on the wisdom of the ancient Greeks. The works of all the great Greek philosophers, as we have already noted, were translated into Arabic long before western Europeans became acquainted with them through the medium of Latin. Such was the ignorance of Greek in the West that many of them first became available through re-translation from the Arabic. To this treasury of knowledge the Jews had added centuries of their own observations; and on these the Portuguese built still further.

The most important conviction that they developed was of the existence of an Indian ocean, between the east coast of Africa and the western coasts of Asia. Until then, even after Marco Polo's travels, it had been surmised that the River Nile had a second estuary, on the Atlantic coast of West Africa and that to its east, Africa was part of an uninterrupted land mass, ending in the China Sea.

The King and his scholars decided to send a spy overland to Aden, the point at which Marco Polo and his companions had turned away from fear, at the prospect of having to board a dhow to proceed any further. The mission of the spy was not to turn back, but to go on. If the scholars' conjectures were right, he would reach India. The man they selected for the mission was Pêro da Covilhã.

CHAPTER IX

PÊRO DA COVILHÃ: MASTER SPY

We know about Pêro da Covilhã, the fifteenth-century Portuguese master spy, through the account of him written by Father Francisco Reis, the royal chaplain. Father Francisco came to write it because, though Pêro had sent back to Portugal detailed information which was to prove vital to the Portuguese capture of the oriental spice trade, he did not return to Portugal himself. King João II sent Father Francisco to find him. He eventually did so, as we shall see.

That Pêro had no surname — Covilhã is a town in the central highlands, where he was born — means that he was a commoner. His was a striking example as to how the royal court now chose its recruits by the criterion of ability, before nobility. This had not been the situation, during his early adult years. Then, finding all opportunities closed to him in his own country, he had gone to Seville, and joined the household of Alfonso, Duke of Medina-Sidonia, the ruler of Andalucia. As well as Andalucian, he learnt Castilian and, more pertinent to his future career, Arabic: although the Arabs no longer ruled the region, many of them had stayed on, and remained faithful to their language as well as to their religion.

It is not known how he came to the attention of the Portuguese royal court, but he became a member of it after he had spent seven years in Seville. Partly on account of his fluent Arabic, he was sent twice as an ambassador to North Africa. He went first to Tlencin, then the centre for the manufacture of particularly fine carpets. These were bought by merchants of Fez, to send by camel caravans across the desert to West Africa. There, they were traded for slaves. Under King João II, the Portuguese had virtually lost interest in

117

slaving. Years of opposition by sections of the Church had made their impression on the consciences of some merchants. Others found gold trading to be more profitable. The West African traders continued to prize carpets from Tlencin as their most preferred barter, whether the commodity was slaves or gold. Pêro's mission was to persuade the Emir, Abu-Thabet-Mohamet, to grant Portugal a monopoly of the purchase of the carpets. This was the more difficult as Tlencin was formally in a state of war with Portugal. Pêro brought him a letter of peace from the King, and within weeks, the deal was agreed.

His second mission was to King Mulachik of Fez. As already recounted, Prince Henrique the Navigator, on his second and last journey abroad, to Tangier, had left there his younger brother, Fernando, as hostage. In the view of the North Africans, Henrique had then broken the terms of the truce. Fernando's body had last been seen hanging upside down on the walls of Fez. To retrieve his remains had become a cause important to Portuguese national pride. Pêro's approach to this perhaps archaically chivalric challenge was also old fashioned. He kidnapped seven of Mulachik's wives and sons, and then exchanged them for Prince Fernando's bones. On his way back to Portugal, he also carried out a commission from the Duke of Beja, to buy Arab horses for him.

By now, Pêro had perfected his spoken Arabic, more precisely the north-west African dialect of it, to a level at which he was easily mistaken to be one of them. He had also, during his travels in North Africa, familiarised himself with Arab and Berber mannerisms and conduct.

He was forty years old, and had reached the rank of Knight of the Royal Guard. He was called to Santarém by King João II, to find, in the words of Father Francisco, "the sources of cinnamon and other spices in the Orient, and the route by which they reached Venice". In a private mansion in Santarém, in great secrecy, he was given an intensive course in cosmography, geography and other related matters, by members of the Council of Scholars. All this took place in provincial Santarém, not Lisbon, because of the absence of foreigners.

On 17th May 1487 — five years before Colombo was to sail westward from Cadiz – Pêro set off on foot from Santarém eastwards, in search of India. At a final audience, the King had given him 400 cruzados and he took with him a letter of credit, "to all the territories and provinces of the World", guaranteed by Bartolomeus Maschioni, Lisbon branch manager of the Medici Bank of Florence.

Pero reached Valencia, from where he took a passage on a boat to Barcelona, and there, on another to Naples. There he was received by the local branch of the Medicis, who arranged for him to sail to the island of Rhodes, the easternmost point of Christendom. The Portuguese had built a fortified monastery on the island, seven years before. The warrior-monks were expecting him. They had ready for him clothes appropriate for a Majhreb merchant, and a boat with a cargo of honey.

Pope Julian had previously warned Portugal in strong terms against sending a trade delegation to Egypt, claiming it to be within the Venetian sphere of influence. Pêro, now in disguise, sailed from Rhodes across the water to Alexandria, the main port of shipment of spices and other oriental goods to Venice. The city was in the grip of an epidemic and many people were ill with fever. Before he could trade his honey, Pêro succumbed to it, and was given up for dead. By local law, the Emir of Alexandria had the right to all the possessions a visitor to the city had with him, if he died. By the time he recovered, the Emir had already sold the honey. However, he compensated Pêro in cash, which the latter used to buy new trading merchandise, and a place on a camel caravan to Cairo.

Cairo's thriving bazaar had long been closed to Europeans, but Pêro found there merchants of many other nationalities and races. Accepted without curiosity, as a trader from the Majhreb, he found it easy to make enquiries without arousing suspicion. It was here, already, his journey hardly begun, that he first met Indians, spice traders who told him that they had travelled up the Indian coast, and to Yemen and from there, up the Red Sea to Egypt. He met up with a group of merchants from Fez, bound for Yemen, and joined them. They set off in the spring of 1488, four years before Colombo was to set sail.

After five days, their camel caravan reached the town of Suez. From there, they travelled by ship, and reached the town of Tôr a week later. Pêro found it to be a miserable settlement, around a Maronite monastery of Armenians and Greeks, cut off for generations from their fellow Christians, by the religious wars of the Middle East.

It was also the main port of transit for goods from the Orient and for European goods bound the other way. The goods were shipped on dhows, of between twenty and thirty tons, whose timbers were

119

held together by ropes, without nails. They had no decks, and the cargoes were protected from the sun with palm leaves. Each had sparse rigging, and a single mast, with a single, huge lateen sail. They sailed heavily laden, the water coming to within a few centimetres of the top of the sides. It was the sight of these vessels which had made Marco Polo and his companions turn back from the shores of the Arabian Sea, terrified by the prospect of boarding one. Pêro bought himself a passage.

The dhow sailed east to Cananor on the west coast of India. Pêro found a large harbour, bustling with other boats from Aden, Persia and several parts of far eastern Asia. The city market was copiously stocked with ginger and spices. Local people told him that Cananor was but a small trading city compared with the great metropolis of Calicut, further down the coast.

Pêro reached Calicut by the Christmas of 1488. The town had no natural harbour, and the ships that called there, whether dhows of the kind on which Pêro had sailed, or the great junks from China, were pulled up on the beach. This was the capital of the kingdom of Samorim. In the midst of the primitiveness and squalor, Pêro found a dazzling opulence. The king's fingers and toes were smothered in rubies, his ears encrusted with jewels, he was carried in procession through the streets on a golden-plated bier, surrounded by his heavily scented Brahmin courtiers, riding elephants resplendent in semi-precious stones. Within the town, there were foreign resident communities of merchants. The king permitted the Moslems, in their enclave, to be virtually self-governing under Islamic law, presided over by their own judges. There were also merchants from a dozen other countries, including Ceylon, Coromandel, Burma, Malacca, Sumatra, Bengal, and Borneo.

In the market was an astonishing array of goods, most of them very expensive ones. The pepper, so craved by European palates, was grown locally. But most of what was on sale came here on the foreign merchants' ships. Pêro saw camphor, shellac, nutmeg, tamarind and cinnamon. He also saw on sale vast quantities of Chinese porcelain, diamonds, sapphires, rubies and pearls.

To fetch these, and start them on their journey to Europe, the Middle Eastern merchants who acted as middle men between East and West, brought down their dhows in August and September, to take advantage of the monsoon winds, and sailed back in February.

They were laden with the goods the orientals desired. Pêro noted copra, mercury, burnt sienna and other pigments, red coral, saffron, rose water, painted wooden panels, knives, silver and gold.

Goa, to which Pêro now sailed, lacked the glamour of Calicut, but it was of greater attraction to the Portuguese, if they were to establish a trading post in India. The rest of the coast was peopled by Hindus, and governed by Brahmin kings. Goa was an island, and already a foreign colony, in the hands of Moslems. For a Christian European nation to take on the Hindus would not have been impossible militarily, but it would have aroused their enmity and prevented trade. On the other hand, to overthrow the foreign Moslem usurpers, could be a welcome prelude to establishing good relations with the Hindus.

Pero now sailed across the Indian Ocean to the east coast of Africa. This was the beginning of perhaps his most important task of all. Deliberating back in Santarém, King João and his Council of Scholars had conjectured — contrary to the consensus of the time — that Africa was surrounded by sea. So there had to be a southernmost point which could be sailed around. They had sent the great sea captain, Bartholomeu Dias, to find it. Pêro's no less heroic task was meanwhile to find the route from southern Africa to the source of the oriental spices. Sped by the summer monsoon, he sailed via Melindi and Mombasa down to the Mozambique channel, and then back again. He reached Cairo before the end of 1489. He had with him charts, land maps and astrolabe readings. These he gave to King João II's messenger Rabbi Abraham, from Beja in southern Portugal. The rabbi had been chosen for the task because he, too, was able to pass himself off as an Arab, as well as being an accomplished cartographer and cosmographer. He debriefed Pêro at length, and returned to Portugal with the data, arriving there in 1490, two years before Columbus set sail from Cadiz, also in search of India.

Bartolomeu Dias, like Pêro a commoner, had sailed from Lisbon in command of three caravels in 1487. He reached Elisabeth Bay, in southern Africa, on 26th December. Ten days later, a huge storm blew up, sweeping the Portuguese ships southwards for several days. The storm abated. Dias sailed eastwards, expecting to reach the African coast again. No coastline appeared. He changed to a northerly course. After a few days, the African coast appeared to the west of them. Dias and his men had sailed around what he called the Cape of Storms, without ever having seen it. They landed in a bay they called the Bay of Cowherds. Dias had with him African interpreters from the Congo, but they could find no common language. The cowherds withdrew and returned with spears, to attack them. The Portuguese sailed on to what was later known as the Groot-Vis River. Here, the crew announced that they had taken as much as they could endure. Dias held a vote among his officers. They unanimously agreed with the crew. They sailed back to Portugal, arriving there shortly before Rabbi Abraham returned from Cairo. Dias's charts of the route from the Atlantic to the Indian Ocean married almost perfectly with Pêro's of the route from south-east Africa to the Indies.

Pêro da Covilhã did not return to Portugal. In Cairo, Rabbi Abraham had given him his new commission from the king. This was now to go out and find the legendary Kingdom of Prester John. In the popular European imagination for perhaps two centuries, Prester John was akin to one of the great emperors of the outer universe in today's science fiction. As the Moslem forces had swept across eastern Europe and, as we have seen, at one stage, reached within eighty kilometres of Paris, a hope grew in the West, that the Christian Prester John would launch an attack on the Moslems from their rear. With no other source of hope that could be seen, it became embellished into a myth, almost a cult. A map and description of his supposed Kingdom had been published in Vienna in 1185. In it, he was portrayed as the Overlord of All the Indias. He was king over dozens of kings. His palace was made of crystal, its floors mosaics of precious stones, its roof supported by pillars of gold. In the courtyard was the fountain of eternal youth. Prester John sat on his golden throne, attended by lions, tigers, wolves, griffins and unicorns. He had serpents whose colour turned from white to black as they breathed out fire, and elephants which transformed into dolphins on contact with water.

What most interested the Europeans was his reported military strength: 10,000 cavalry, and 100,000 infantry, each carrying the cross in one hand and a sword in the other. At least one historian has argued that this cult served a highly effective purpose, and that without it, Christendom might well have been swallowed up by Islam. It was the one thing that saved the Europeans from despair and capitulation, giving them time to regroup their own forces, and eventually win back their nations.

In 1439, Friar António of Lisbon went to Florence, to attend an ecumenical conference called by Pope Eugene IV. On his return to

Lisbon, he reported to the king that he had met a group of black Abyssinian priests who said that their ruler was a priest king, Presbyter John. Then, a month after Pêro da Covilhã's departure from Lisbon, the king had received a report from his ambassador in Rome, that a second group of Abyssinian priests had set up a monastery there. They confirmed to a Portuguese diplomat that they were ruled over by a Christian priest king, but said his name was Lucas Marco. His Kingdom was now thought to be at the source of the Nile. Before Bartolomeu Dias left Lisbon for his historic journey around the Cape of Good Hope, King João had him take with him a black Congolese couple, a man and a woman who had been adopted by the Portuguese royal court. Following his instructions, Dias had put them on shore, probably in what is now Zaire, to travel into the interior, and make inquiries, to locate the source of the river. They returned to the coast several years later, and were picked up by a passing Portuguese ship. They had found nobody who had even heard of the River Nile.

By 1515, Pêro da Covilhã had still not returned from his quest for Prester John. By now, Portuguese explorers had travelled up the coast of East Africa. They had been told locally the rough location of the Christian Kingdom. Father Francisco disembarked at a port at the southern end of the Red Sea. He had brought with him a letter of greetings from King Manuel to the Abyssinian King, and also gifts. These included crucifixes, tapestries depicting biblical scenes, a jewelled dagger and a portable church organ.

Over the next four months, Father Francisco hiked into the mountains. The ambassador the king had sent with him from Portugal had already died of fever. Now, his Ethiopian guide also expired. There were no paths to follow, only dried up river beds. The countryside was full of predatory wild life: lions, leopards and wolves. He encountered a group of itinerant monks, who agreed to show him the way. After about two weeks' walk, they reached their monastery and refused to take him on to the capital. He must wait for their bishop, they told him. How often did the bishop come? Not for years, they answered. Father Francisco set off alone, buying what food was available in villages. By his account the meals were of uncooked barley flour mixed with water, washed down with ox horns of mead. He claimed that they used cow dung to flavour the soup, and munched cow's udders as though they were apples. Thieves stole his luggage piece by piece, including his swords. There were violent hail storms. In some villages, he was stoned.

When, finally, he reached the capital, the King had him accommodated in a tent, and fed, but refused to see him. After two months, he was awakened one night to be summonsed into the royal presence. But even before he reached the royal gateway, other messengers came out saying that His Majesty had changed his mind. Father Francisco's patience was eventually rewarded. After another lengthy wait, it was admitted to him that Pêro da Covilhã was living near by, and that he could visit him.

He found Pêro da Covilhã living in a large country mansion, owning estates extending over thousands of hectares. He had an uncounted number of wives, Abyssinian knights and squires in attendance, and fine horses and a pack of dogs with which to hunt. Into this scene of pastoral opulence, Pêro da Covilhã received the priest, the first Portuguese he had met in perhaps fifteen years. He availed himself of the chance of confession with absolution, remarking that any confession he made to a local priest was immediately retold by the latter to his neighbours. Father Francisco, a priest strikingly free of bigotry, nonetheless suggested that it was time for Pêro to return to Lisbon and take up again with his lawful wife there. Pêro replied that he would dearly like to do so, but unfortunately he was living under house arrest, and was forbidden from leaving.

Father Francisco complimented him on at least teaching his new family the Portuguese language, and returned to Lisbon, empty handed.

It has often been assumed that the Portuguese adventure in East Africa thus ended. This is not the case. Disappointment over the reality of the priest king was compensated for by discoveries of huge quantities of gold in East Africa. The Portuguese kept secret their discovery of King Solomon's Mines' from the rest of Europe, profiting hugely from them, the meanwhile.

CHAPTER X

VASCO DA GAMA AND THE LORD
OF THE OCEANS

Countless millions of people, including some who have never heard of Portugal itself, or think it to be part of Spain, know of the fabulous deeds of Vasco da Gama: how this great navigator sailed from Lisbon in his caravel, into the unknown, and came upon India. This orthodox view of his exploit, however, is no more truthful than it would be to say that the United States launched a manned rocket into space, and its crew chanced to find themselves landing on the moon.

Vasco da Gama was not a mariner, and had scant knowledge of seamanship. As we have seen, India and its whereabouts had already been discovered by Pêro da Covilhã. Vasco da Gama was taken there by Captain Pêro de Alenquer who had previously steered Bartolomeu Dias round the Cape of Good Hope. So far from it being a haphazard adventure, there have been few journeys, before or since, so meticulously planned and prepared for. Vasco travelled to the Orient as Portugal's first ambassador to the court of the Samorim, the Lord of the Oceans, of Calicut. Few Europeans had ventured into Asia before, and none of them charged with the challenge of negotiating the first-ever treaty between a western and an oriental monarch.

Vasco da Gama was to experience many setbacks and misadventures. He also rarely forgot that he was not an explorer, but a diplomat. His true achievement was more courageous, and more remarkable, than that conventionally attributed to him. He laid the first foundation of what the English historian of the Portuguese overseas, Professor Charles Boxer, has termed "the Seaborne Empire". In the century that followed his epic and mostly single-minded mission, the Portuguese — never more than a million and a half in all — came to be the dominant power over a vast region stretching from Brazil to Japan. Portuguese came to replace Arabic as Asia's *lingua franca*. Portuguese ships not only had a virtual monopoly of trade between Asia and Europe, but made up by far the biggest commercial and naval fleet in the Indian Ocean and the China Sea. Portuguese acted as advisers to the Emperor of China. Portuguese built forts in Bahrain, Persia, the north-west frontier of Pakistan, Japan, and more than a score of other oriental places. Monks and priests from Lisbon added monasteries, churches and – in some of these places – even bishop's palaces. For a long period, the Portuguese even monopolised trade between China and Japan. On land, they were without colonial ambition, but built a string of Portuguese cities from Recife in South America to Mombasa in East Africa, and from Goa in India and Malacca in Malaya, to Macao in the estuary of China's Pearl River, and the Japanese port of Nagasaki.

Britain was to become a colonial power in India through Portugal's gift of Bombay to King Charles II. In 1949, the year after India's independence, the Indian historian Professor K.M. Pannikkar published his masterly obituary of European imperialism in Asia between 1498 and 1945. He described this period of four and a half centuries not, as many might have thought appropriate, as the era of the British Raj, but the era of Vasco da Gama, in which the British presence had been but one episode, and which had culminated in the USA's victory over Japan in their battle for naval supremacy in the Pacific.

The great King João II had died in 1495. His only legitimate son had been killed four years before in a riding accident. By the laws of heredity the throne passed to his alienated cousin, Manuel, then 26 years old. One of Manuel's first acts as King was to restore to favour in the royal court the Braganças and other noble families who had opposed his predecessor. Supported by a majority in parliament, they urged him to abandon overseas adventures: "His Majesty should content himself with what he has."

It has often been supposed that between the return of Bartolomeu Dias in 1490, and the departure of Vasco da Gama in 1497, there were virtually no Portuguese voyages of exploration. There is no official record of any. But the circumstantial evidence to the contrary is striking. The Portuguese historian Armando Cortesão has uncovered the order book of a bakery, near to Lisbon's Restello shipyard. During the seven years of pretended inactivity, it supplied ship's biscuits for over one hundred long voyages.

These were in part to further explore and better define the route from Europe to India. That they explored at least as far as Sofala is implied by the journal of Ahmed ibn Madjid, an Arab pilot of the East African coast. He wrote: "At Sofala, European ships stumbled into the Monsoon winds. The waves threw them on to the sharp rocks. The seamen dived into the water and the ships sank. In 1495, European ships came here, after a voyage lasting two years, and were evidently bound for India." They were also to experiment with and test radically new ship designs, to produce a generation of vessels capable of carrying much heavier loads than before and at much higher speeds. This project was directed by Bartolomeu Dias. The advances he master-minded were such that he made the caravel, of the kind in which he had rounded the Cape, virtually obsolete. There was now the immediate predecessor to the galleon, the "round ship". These were much larger, with a capacity of between 500 and 600 tonnes. They had three masts: two with rounded sails, for speed, and one with a lateen sail, to aid navigation. The bridge had been brought forward to behind the bow. On the upper deck at the stern, were mounted Portugal's newly invented secret weapon: breech-loading cannons, which could rapid-fire mortars on a near-horizontal trajectory. It was to prove a startling and effective deterrent. Few were to stay on, to take on the Portuguese navy in battle, after they had been shown a couple of precisely aimed volleys, screaming over the sea.

King Manuel had inherited, along with the throne, King João's master plan, and as great a determination to carry it through. He was able to face down the old aristocracy and parliament, because the voyage was not financed from taxation, but from royal revenues received directly from the gold mines of Ghana.

The extraordinary mission to the Lord of the Oceans had first been entrusted by the King to Estêvão da Gama, but he had died before the preparations were complete. The king asked Estevão's oldest son, Paulo, to take on the task. Paulo pleaded ill health, and said that while he was willing to sail with the expedition, the ambassadorship and the command should be given to his younger brother Vasco. He also claimed that Vasco was the abler of the two.

Paulo would later die of fever towards the end of the voyage, despite his brother's desperate attempts to save him.

The da Gamas belonged to what José Hermano Saraiva has called "the minor bureaucratic nobility", created by João II. Vasco was born in 1468, the son of a provincial governor. He had showed decisiveness as an official in the Algarve, where he impounded all the French ships in Lagos harbour, in reprisal for the French government's failure to stop its seamen's piracy against Portuguese ships. He was to die in Goa in 1524, as one of the most powerful Europeans on earth, the Viceroy of India.

In Lisbon, Vasco was provided with two "round" ships, the *São Gabriel*, in which he sailed, and the *São Rafael*, with his brother on board. There was also a caravel, to be used for scouting and the taking of soundings, and a large cargo boat, loaded with goods — textiles, silk hats, iron and bronze work, nails, beads of coral and little bells and other nick-nacks — which they hoped to trade for spices and precious stones. The ships carried emergency food and water rations, calculated to be sufficient, if they proved necessary, for the crew for three and a half years.

The crew totalled 170 men. Of these fifty-six were to return alive. As well as ship's officers and sailors, it included carpenters, to maintain and repair the ships during the voyage, chaplains, musicians, an Arabic interpreter and a number of paroled convicts. These latter were young aristocrats, sentenced to jail terms for such crimes as unruly behaviour. As was the established practice with Portuguese expeditions by now, they accepted as condition of their early release from prison, that they would risk themselves by being the first ashore in any unknown country. Also on board was the expedition's reporter, Alvaro Velho, whose task it was to keep a daily diary. In this, he recorded all the navigational and astronomical data of the voyage, for the use of future pilots, and, most valuably for the rest of us, a vivid account of the events which took place on board ship and on land.

Vasco sailed from Belém, the docks in western Lisbon, on the morning of 8th July 1497. The evening before, he had dined with King Manuel, in the monastery on the site on which Jeronimos now stands, and where he is buried. He had spent much of the night with his fellow officers, in the chapel. It is clear from Álvaro's Velho diary from the beginning, that this was no haphazard adventure, and that they were following a prescribed route and timetable. After a week, they reached the Canaries on schedule. They turned south at Lanzarote, reaching the islands of Cabo Verde on 27th July where they took on fresh food. At the latitude of Sierra Leone, they caught, as they had hoped, the mid-summer wind, that swept them westwards in an arc to Cape St Augustine, on the coast of what was later to be named Brazil. On 22nd August, they were already riding the south-easterly winds, followed for some of the way by birds from the South American mainland. Contemporary Portuguese historians reckon Vasco to have been particularly lucky and his pilots particularly well briefed. Portuguese mariners had in the past had to follow the South American coast as far as what is now Argentina, to pick up the winds to carry them to and around the south of Africa.

They reached the island of Mozambique on 29th March 1498. This was to be their first experience of Arab commerce and culture, which dominated the coasts of the Indian Ocean, and the first major test of Vasco's diplomatic skills. In the harbour, Álvaro wrote, there were four ships of the "white Moors" (Turks or Persians) carrying gold, silver, nails, pepper, ginger, pearls, sapphires and rubies in great quantity.

The inhabitants of the town, he noted, were reddish-brown in complexion, with well-proportioned bodies. They dressed well, in striped cotton gowns and turbans with brocaded edges. Most had been converted to Islam, and Arabic was widely and fluently spoken. Two of the paroled convicts were sent ashore to ask, if they were not attacked or otherwise repelled, if there were any Christians living on the island. They were received amicably, and with great curiosity, and were told that the nearest community of Christians was to be found much further up the coast of East Africa, in Mombasa.

Through his Arabic interpreter Vasco requested and was granted an audience with the Sultan. The latter received him warmly in his palace. Vasco presented the ruler with two embroidered and hooded capes, and thirty miticais of gold. In return, the Sultan provided him with two experienced pilots, to guide the Portuguese to Mombasa.

On Sunday, the Portuguese left their ships, and went in their long boats to a small and uninhabited island near to the harbour. Their chaplain celebrated Mass in the open air. On their way back to the ships, they were suddenly attacked by well-armed men in a dozen boats. Back on board the *São Gabriel*, the Mozambique pilot explained that the welcome the Portuguese had received had been based on a complete misunderstanding. It had not occurred to anyone in Mozambique that the Portuguese were Europeans, for the simple reason that Europeans had never been sighted there before. From the colour of their skins, they had been taken to be north Asians. Their enquiries about the whereabouts of fellow Christians had led to the impression that they were of the Hindu religion, and seeking fellow worshippers of the Indian god Krishna. It was with horror that the Sultan and his councillors had watched them erect the crucifix and hold a service very different from that of any Hindu rite. The realisation was as threatening in its way as an invasion of aliens from outer space would be today. So the Sultan had ordered that they be killed.

Under threat of being tortured and thrown overboard, the two pilots steered the Portuguese safely to Mombasa. They arrived on Palm Sunday, and dropped anchor outside the harbour. The ruler sent out a boat containing his gifts of three sheep, and oranges and lemons. The Portuguese had been much lacking in fresh meat. The new larger ships now obviated the need for seamen to subsist on salted beef and pickled pork. They carried on board live goats, chickens and other animals, slaughtering them as the need arose and replenishing their stocks at the same time as they took on fresh water at ports of call. The fresh fruit was received ravenously. Many of the crew were by now sick with scurvy. It seems that the people of the Indian Ocean had already discovered its remedy, the eating of citrus fruit. While the Portuguese recovered within a few days, Álvaro, at least, attributed this rather to the curative qualities of the air.

Two paroled convicts were sent ashore, carrying strings of coral and a message of greetings and peace, in Arabic, from Vasco da Gama. The two men were greeted by a large crowd, who led them to the palace. The Sheikh entertained them generously, and gave them guides, to take them to the house of the "Christian" merchants. There the two convicts were shown an image of Krishna. It clearly did not represent either Christ or Our Lady, and, after puzzlement, they concluded that it was a representation of the Holy Spirit.

The two returned to the Portuguese fleet. Just outside the harbour sound, the two Mozambique pilots deliberately steered the *São Gabriel* and the *São Rafael* into a sideways collision, and took advantage of the ensuing confusion to jump overboard and swim to safety. Vasco da Gama decided it was time to leave.

Out in the open sea, pilot-less, the Portuguese spotted two good-size dhows, laden with cargo and people, and gave chase. One got away but they succeeded in taking the other. They captured a good quantity of fresh food, an elderly and seemingly aristocratic Arab couple, who were travelling as passengers, fourteen crew, and a pilot. By a mixture of threats and blandishments, the Portuguese elicited from the old nobleman, that the ruler of Melindi, further up the coast, was a great enemy of the Sultan of Mombasa. Your enemy's enemy is your friend. The captive pilot guided them to Melindi, which they reached after two days. Vasco da Gama had his ships anchored outside the harbour, and the elderly Arab aristocrat placed on the sand bank. He was picked up by people from the town in a canoe.

Within hours, it was evident that he had passed on Vasco's message of peace and greeting, and spoken favourably of his Portuguese captors, for the ruler sent out to them gifts including six sheep and baskets of fruit and spices. Vasco freed his remaining prisoners. The ruler came down to the beach with an orchestra, to entertain the visitors. Vasco, as ever unsentimental, now took as hostage one of the king's ministers who visited him on board, and demanded, as a condition of his release, that a pilot be put on board, who knew the route to India.

The pilot provided was a Gujerati from Bombay. The Portuguese addressed him in his own language as 'Malemo Kanaka', which means navigator-astronomer. He steered them with the storms across the Indian Ocean, and they reached Calicut safely on 20th May 1498.

Vasco sent two of the paroled convicts ashore, João Nunes and Gaspar Correia. The first recorded conversation between Europeans and Indians took place between them and two Genoese-speaking locals.

"What the hell are you doing here?"

"We have come to look for Christians and for spices."

"Have you been sent by the king of Castile or France, or the Doge of Venice?"

"We are sent by the King of Portugal. He does not allow other kings to send people here."

"God will bless you for coming here."

The Samorim, the Lord of the Oceans, was in his country palace. Nunes and Correia were led there. They told officials that the ambassador of the King of Portugal had arrived. He sought an audience with the Samorim, to present his credentials. The Samorim was so driven by curiosity as to return to his palace in Calicut. He sent a group of courtiers, and a palanquin to the shore. Vasco greeted them with a ceremonial salvo of his cannons, and a fanfare of trumpets. "He was greeted with more honour," wrote Álvaro, "than a King is received in Spain." Then, mounted on the palanquin, escorted by the governor of Calicut's brother and a large band of Hindu musicians, and accompanied by a retinue of thirteen Portuguese, he was carried through the streets, which were filled with welcoming crowds of Hindus. They were taken first to a huge building which they initially took to be a church. Then they saw the soaring lingam, and the images of gods and goddesses, some of them, Álvaro noted, "with four or five arms". Nonetheless, to show respect, they knelt in prayer — though as one officer muttered, "not to these devils, but to the true God".

For half a day more, they progressed through crowds lining their route. The locals invited them to their homes for meals, and pressed the Portuguese to stay with them as their guests. They finally reached the palace. They were ushered through great doors into a succession of four courtyards. At the entrance to the fourth, the Samorim's guru approached Vasco and warmly embraced him.

The Lord of the Oceans sat beneath a purple canopy. His only clothing was a white cotton dhoti, and an embroidered cap. But around his waist he wore two gold belts encrusted with rubies. His arms, from the elbows down, were covered by jewelled gold bracelets. On his fingers were rings of emeralds and diamonds. His earrings were of rubies and giant pearls. By his right hand was a golden bowl of betel nut, and in his left he held a small golden spittoon. Vasco da Gama greeted him in Hindu manner, his hands raised and his palms pressed together, "like a Christian", Alvaro remarked, "saying his prayers". The Lord of the Oceans bade the Portuguese to sit on a long bench facing him. His servants brought them fruit.

In accordance with Indian regal etiquette, Vasco da Gama was invited to explain his business to the attendant courtiers, as it would be a presumption to address the ruler directly. Boldly and firmly, Vasco refused to do this, stating that he was the ambassador of the King of Portugal who was overlord of vast lands, wealthy beyond other kings and he had a personal message for the ears of the Lord of the Oceans alone. The ruler led Vasco into a private room. Vasco told him that he had come both in search of fellow Christians, and to buy spices. The ruler formally welcomed him to his Kingdom, and sent with him pilots to steer his ships to a safer anchorage to the north of the city.

The next day, Vasco had the gifts for the Lord of the Oceans rowed ashore. There were twelve bolts of striped cotton, four crimson caps, six hats, four strings of coral, a box of sugar, and two barrels each of olive oil and honey. The governor of Calicut came to inspect them. He said: "These are ridiculous. The poorest Arab merchant gives his majesty more than this. There is nothing here fit for a king. You have to give him gold."

Vasco improvised, that these gifts were not from the King of Portugal. They were his personal ones. The gold was to follow.

The governor refused to allow Vasco to return to his ship. Vasco demanded another audience with the Lord of the Oceans. The latter received him, and uttered a string of insults so extreme that his interpreter declined to translate them.

Vasco was told that it was scandalous that he had not brought anything suitable for royalty. With remarkable *sang froid*, Vasco replied that he did have with him goods to trade: wheat and wine, cast iron and copper. The Lord of the Oceans relented. He had Vasco given a horse on which to ride back to his anchorage. Vasco refused to mount it, saying it was beneath the dignity of an ambassador of the King of Portugal. He demanded and was given a palanquin.

The Arab merchants of Calicut had appreciated from the outset the threat posed to their monopoly by the arrival of the Europeans. They now made the most of Vasco's loss of face, deriding the goods as they were brought ashore. There were few customers. The Hindus however continued to receive the Portuguese enthusiastically. They came on board the ships, bringing their children with them. The Portuguese entertained them as lavishly as they could, and the partying continued late into the nights.

The Portuguese moved their goods to Calicut itself. There, too, the Arab merchants for the most part managed to prevent them from trading. A local resident, a Tunisian the Portuguese knew as Monsaide, came on board and warned Vasco that the Arab merchants had all but persuaded the Lord of the Oceans that the Portuguese were pirates and thieves, and were only waiting for an opportunity to come ashore to loot and plunder Calicut. The Arab merchants had offered the Lord of the Oceans a huge sum of money, if he would have Vasco and the Portuguese seized and beheaded. Those Portuguese who were already on shore, were prevented from rejoining their ships or removing their goods.

Vasco bided his time, until he noticed, among a group of two dozen Indians who had come on board for a Portuguese lunch, six men who were dressed as and behaved as major nobility. He took the six prisoners and then traded them with the Lord of the Oceans' factor for the freedom of the Portuguese being held captive.

Vasco sent word that he took the strongest exception to being called a thief or a pirate, and that he was about to set sail, and not return. The Lord of the Oceans summoned one of his officers, and presented him with a letter to the King of Portugal. It said that he had been pleased to receive His Majesty's noble ambassador, and that he would like to trade. If the Portuguese King sent gold, he would provide spices and jewels.

Soon afterwards, they did sail, their mission accomplished. Their journey back to Portugal was pervaded with tragedy. More than a hundred, over two thirds of them, died, mostly of fever or scurvy. For want of crew, they had to abandon two of their four ships, beaching them, then setting light to them, to prevent Arabs from being able to study their design and construction. When the first of the ships reached Lisbon with the news of the offer of a treaty, King Manuel ordered that church bells be rung throughout the country, and that another, much larger fleet, be prepared as quickly as possible, to return to Calicut, and put the treaty into effect. He wrote officially to the Archbishop of Lisbon, that the ships had brought back, "all manner of spices; cinnamon, cloves, pepper, ginger, nutmeg, balsam, amber, musk, pearls, rubies and every other kind of precious stone". It was estimated that the cargo that Vasco had managed to acquire, though small, had a market value of sixty times the cost of the voyage.

Vasco himself did not return to Lisbon for some weeks, for his older brother Paulo had caught the fever. Vasco had taken him to the Azores, in the hope that the fresh air there would revive him, but sadly it did not.

Years later, Vasco was named Viceroy of India. He was made a gift of his native town of Sines, a pension of 30,000 gold reis a year, for him and his heirs, the equivalent of 200 crusados of spices per voyage, the right to travel on ships of the royal fleet without charge and to levy rents on anchorages along the Indian coast. He was given the title of Count of Vidigueira. His sister and younger brother were also ennobled, and awarded pensions. He died in India in 1524.

CHAPTER XI

INDIA AND BEYOND

Six months after Vasco da Gama returned to Lisbon, Pedro
Álvares Cabral sailed from there in command of a fleet of thirteen
ships, with 1,200 men and provisions for them for eighteen months.
His crew of sailors, soldiers, artisans and paroled criminals also
included herbal pharmacists, barber-surgeons, physicians, nine priests,
and a master of cosmography. On the way to India, Cabral paused on
the coast of Brazil — the official account was that he was blown off
course and came across it by chance. He claimed it for Portugal.
Struck by a violent storm off the Cape of Good Hope, he lost almost
half his fleet, both ships and men, including the great sea captain
Bartolomeu Dias.

He reached Calicut in September 1500. He was received in
audience by the Lord of the Oceans. He had brought acceptable gifts:
silver, bowls and maces, inlaid with gold, and silk carpets and fine
tapestries. A ship had just arrived in the harbour from Sri Lanka, with
a cargo of five elephants. The Lord of the Oceans asked Cabral to
capture the ship and its cargo for him.

This the Portuguese did, and they promptly received permission to
begin trading. Once again, the Portuguese were harassed and
obstructed by the Moslem merchants. Cabral replied by capturing one
of their ships. The Moslems on the shore attacked the Portuguese
trading post, killing fifty men, including three of the priests. They also
took several prisoners, and seized all the Portuguese merchandise.

In reprisal, Cabral ordered and led the capture of all the Arab ships
in the harbour. All their crews who did not escape, the Portuguese
slaughtered. The Portuguese loaded the Arab cargoes on to their own

ships. They bombarded the town with their cannons, destroying many of its buildings, and then sailed south to Cochin. They were well received by the Hindu ruler, who welcomed the opportunity of diverting trade from the Moslems of Calicut.

The next expeditions from Portugal to India had an increasingly military aspect. It became a routine to pause at Calicut, to bombard the town and set fire to the ships in the harbour, on the way to trade in Cochin.

Francisco de Almeida reached Cochin in 1502, the first European to have been given the title Viceroy of India. He found that the town had been attacked by ships from Calicut, and that the Hindu ruler and the Portuguese garrison had taken refuge on an island. The ruler agreed to become a vassal of the King of Portugal, in return for protection, and he was presented with a golden crown.

Cochin was attacked again. This time, the ships from Calicut had been joined by warships from Turkey and Egypt. The latter had been paid for by the Venetians. In one of the most hard fought and decisive naval battles in history, the Portuguese won, and were never again challenged on anything approaching the same scale in the Indian Ocean. They realised however that if they were to achieve their ambition in the Orient, of seizing the spice trade from the Arabs and the Venetians, they needed a more secure base. Goa, a large island, separated from the mainland by a river, was occupied and ruled by Arab horse-traders. One of the leaders of the Hindu majority approached the Portuguese, for help in expelling them. Afonso de Albuquerque was by now the Portuguese commander in the Indian Ocean. Timoja, the Hindu emissary from Goa, promised him that if he attacked their island, the Hindu people would rise up against the Arabs and help expel them. Albuquerque had Timoja join the Portuguese fleet. They sailed into the mouth of the river and let forth a fusillade of cannonballs. The Turkish mercenaries guarding the island city leapt on to their horses, and escaped across the causeway to the mainland. From there, soon afterwards, the Moslem ruler arrived with a force the Portuguese estimated to be more than 50,000 strong. During a heavy rainfall, in the middle of the night, they captured the fort the Portuguese had hurriedly built, and moved back into the city.

Albuquerque could neither attack nor withdraw. His fleet was becalmed for three months. The winds returned, and brought with them new warships from Lisbon. They bombarded the fort, then they stormed the city. Hundreds of Moslem troops managed to escape the Portuguese swords, only to drown while trying to swim across the fast-flowing river to the mainland. The Moslems were to launch one further attack on Goa, when Albuquerque was absent. Returning with his fleet, he bombarded their positions for eight days, until they surrendered. He installed Timoja as the Hindu governor of Goa. He sent officers to the Hindu rulers of the surrounding region expressing his and the King of Portugal's respect for their religion and customs, and assuring them of Portugal's friendship.

In Goa, where the Portuguese were to remain until 1961, Albuquerque set about creating Asia's first European city. First, he had the citadel, which his cannonballs had destroyed, rebuilt, and he took up residence there. A contemporary account shows him rising before dawn every day for Mass, and every evening entertaining at least 400 captains and others to dinner. Before the meal, twenty-four elephants would be brought forward, and curtsy to him. The meal was illuminated by copper torches and accompanied by trumpets and drums. On Sundays, the Hindu nobility assembled in the square before the citadel to be greeted by him. The Portuguese military bands would play, and Hindu temple maidens dance.

Much of his days he spent on horseback, touring the construction projects. He was accompanied by four secretaries, each with paper, pens and ink wells, recording his instructions, and his reports to Lisbon. He had built and equipped a mint, which produced Portuguese coins from locally purchased gold. A shipyard came to being, making craft of up to 900 tonnes from local teak, reckoned to be the best of all ship-building materials. A darker aspect of the drive towards Goa's self-sufficiency from Portugal was the construction and commissioning of India's first munitions factory.

A new style of missionaries arrived from Portugal, members of the Society of Jesus, led by one of its co-founders, São Francisco Xavier. They studied and adopted Indian customs and languages, and took to wearing Indian clothes, and to eating Indian food. One of them, Friar João de Brito, established his own ashram in the holy city of Madurai, a Catholic guru discussing spiritual matters with Hindu priests as equals. This remarkable ecumenism was ended by fundamentalist fanatics, who murdered him. It is in his memory that Indian Jesuits today, still a major force in education, wear red sashes; and the place of his assassination is a shrine venerated by Hindus as well as by Christians.

In Goa the Jesuits built secondary schools, and provided education up to and including university level. This became Asia's first international and multi-cultural place of higher education. The announcement of the arrangements for the new academic year of 1584 were published in sixteen Asian languages. It was the Jesuits who had brought printing to Asia. In addition to teaching, they undertook research, some of it for the benefit of Europe — notably, they established a medicinal botanical garden, and through rigorous and lengthy experimentation upon themselves, identified and recorded which Indian plants had curative powers over which ailments. The translation of their researches from Portuguese into other European languages was a foundation stone of modern pharmacology.

Albuquerque pardoned the paroled criminals. He encouraged and helped them and others to establish themselves in Goa in a wide variety of crafts and small enterprises. Among other things, they established baker's shops, shoemakers', taverns, carpentry and stone-working shops and blacksmithies. Some of Lisbon's more enterprising prostitutes had had themselves smuggled on board ships, disguised as men, to go and claim their share of the new wealth in Goa. Vasco da Gama, on his second voyage, found that there were half a dozen such on board his flagship, and had them flogged, to widespread indignation and protest from his officers. Albuquerque, in Goa, encouraged Portuguese men to marry and settle down with Indian women. Some of these were already held by the Portuguese as slaves, and their newly elevated status was sometimes of little practical advantage to them. At least, however, it secured the civil and other rights of their children as Portuguese. Gross exploitation of Indian women through marriage was by no means a universal rule however. The Christian gospel, as preached by the Portuguese Jesuits, was of the equality of all men before God, and of Jesus's espousal of the cause of the poor and the outcast. This proved, unsurprisingly, extremely persuasive to members of India's lower castes. Whatever the faults of Portuguese husbands and attitudes towards women at that time, the oppression was at least markedly less than that they had suffered at the hands of their fellow Hindus. While Indian women converted to Catholicism on marriage, if their families had not done so before, São Francisco Xavier noted that many Portuguese men in Goa had taken up with enthusiasm the local custom of polygamy, and had their own harems, some of them substantial.

Today, Portugal continues to acknowledge the descendants of the Portuguese settlers as citizens, with the right to reside in Portugal; and a growing number of Goans are coming to live here, bringing with them fresh talents, skills and energy.

*　*　*

To procure the supply of spices, medicines and precious stones was, in the most literal sense, only half the battle. There remained for the Portuguese the challenge of destroying Arab power in the Indian Ocean, and so defeating the trade routes to Venice. While Afonso de Albuquerque never achieved his stated ambitions, of diverting the River Nile from Egypt, and capturing the Prophet Mohammed's tomb in Mecca, they otherwise applied themselves to this task in a very different mood from that which they showed towards the Hindus, with a ferocity that several times expressed itself in brutality.

Francisco de Almeida, the first Viceroy, was supplied by Lisbon with a fleet of twenty-two ships. Fifteen hundred of the 2,500 men on board were heavily armed and armoured soldiers. Many of the rest were there to man the breech-loading cannons. They sailed into the harbour of the Arab trading port of Kilwa, on the east coast of Africa. First, they shelled the town for several hours. Then they went ashore and fought their way through the narrow streets. Though many were wounded, the Portuguese won the town without any loss of life on their side. The Emir fled, with many of his supporters. The Portuguese stayed on, and built a fort, from the rubble of the houses and other buildings they had destroyed in the bombardment. The speed with which the Portuguese worked is astonishing. They completed the structure in sixteen days, the officers lending their hands to the manual labour. A troop of infantry was installed in the new fort, and a local African was appointed governor. The Portuguese also left two ships, to patrol outside the harbour, and drive off any Arabs who might try to approach.

The remainder of the fleet sailed up the coast, to the much greater Arab city of Mombasa. Here, they were fired on by cannon the locals had retrieved from a Portuguese shipwreck on their coast. The Portuguese responded with a terrifying bombardment of cannonballs and lighted torches, which destroyed the city. Coming ashore, the

Portuguese suffered thirty fatalities, mostly from poisoned arrows. According to the journal of one of the Portuguese officers, many times more would have died, were it not for a local who provided them with an antidote to apply to the wounds. The surviving Portuguese troops sacked and looted the ruins of the city, and took a large number of women as captives. But Almeida forbade them from loading their bounty on to the ships, and made them release all the captives, but for some children, whom he thought young enough to be convinced of the One True Faith, and to become sincere Christians. Some of these were sent back to Lisbon for their education, where they were well received, and eventually made good marriages.

On the other side of the ocean, the Lord of the Oceans, after years of successive Portuguese bombardments of Calicut, sued for peace. Those Moslem merchants who had remained there, now left. They and others re-established themselves much further south, in Malacca. Unable now to sail up the Portuguese-controlled coasts of East Africa or western India, they assembled their ships into convoys at the Maldive Islands, then together sped as fast as they could north to the Red Sea, praying not to encounter any Portuguese warships on their way. However, Tristão da Cunha was sent from Lisbon with a large fleet to the mouth of the Red Sea at Socotra, where the Portuguese built a fort commanding the straits.

The Arab captains steered their ships instead to the port of Hormuz, in southern Persia. From there, they could send the spices and other goods in camel caravans to the east coast of the Black Sea, where they could be taken by Turkish ships to Istanbul, and there sold to the Venetians. But Afonso de Albuquerque chased them to Hormuz, early in 1514. His fleet arrived outside the harbour at lunch time, but made no move until dusk, when he startled the citizens with fanfares of trumpets, and fusillades of cannon fire that lit up the evening sky. He sent a message to the ruler demanding that he acknowledge Portuguese sovereignty over his city by paying tribute. When the ruler did not reply, the Portuguese set fire to all the Arab and Persian ships in the harbour. The ruler sent out a large quantity of gold to Albuquerque's flagship. In the following days, Albuquerque had his men begin building a fort at the harbour entrance. It was now midsummer. They protested against doing hard manual labour in the intense heat. He had some of them flogged, to encourage the others.

But the entire crews of two ships deserted, sailing away beyond the horizon, and beyond effective pursuit. Albuquerque abandoned his project for the time being, and sailed back to India. On his way he sacked Aden, and destroyed and looted the towns of the coast of Oman. He returned to Hormuz later, with a team of construction workers, who built the fort, and thus cut off the trade route to Istanbul.

Albuquerque sailed on south to Malacca. This was the last bastion of the Arab merchants in Asia. When the Portuguese fleet arrived at the harbour, such was Albuquerque's reputation that the crews of many of the merchant ships anchored there fled to the shore in terror. The Sultan of Malacca wrote and had delivered to him a letter, in Arabic, proposing peace negotiations instead of a battle. Many of the townspeople were Hindus, and word had already reached them from India that the Portuguese were their allies and protectors. One of them came on board ship, and warned Albuquerque that the Sultan's plan was to string out his negotiations with the Portuguese until the monsoon struck. Then, when the Portuguese ships were battling the storm, he would attack and sink them. The Hindu told him: "The Sultan thinks of little but treachery." That night Albuquerque sent his gunships to the shore, to begin the bombardment of the city. Under the cover of the cannon fire, soldiers went on shore in small boats, and moved along the harbour front, setting light to the buildings' palm-leafed roofs.

The next night, the fleet moved still closer to the shore, and launched a much greater bombardment. One of Albuquerque's officers wrote: "We could hear in the darkness the whole city thrown into uproar, the cries and the shouts of people fleeing with their children without knowing which way to go." At dawn the Portuguese troops entered the city, meeting little resistance, until they were challenged by a group of Malay noblemen in a square outside the mosque. The Portuguese soon put them to flight. Coming into the city's main avenue, they were suddenly faced by the Sultan and the Crown Prince, together with ten courtiers, mounted on war elephants. The elephants roared and charged the Portuguese. The latter however, from experience in India, knew that an elephant, no matter how fearsome, is easily repelled by a spear thrust at one of his sensitive points — his belly, or an ear, or an eye. Thus injured, the elephants turned and fled, trampling many Malaccans in their path. The

Portuguese were guided through the city by Hindus. They had with them quantities of small Portuguese flags. Hindu and other non-Moslem merchants were given them to fix to their front doors. This gave them and their families immunity from the looting of the city, which the Portuguese enthusiastically carried out during the whole of the next day. When evening came, Albuquerque had the trumpets sounded, to announce the end of the looting. By then, the Portuguese had acquired several times more than their ships could possibly carry away. In the streets were piled jars of musk and camphor, fine Chinese porcelain, and boxes of carved sandalwood. Much of this they sold to the Hindu, Chinese and other non-Moslem merchants, to whom they had given immunity from their assault. The prices were naturally low. Nonetheless the quantities were so huge that it was reckoned that each soldier and crew member had profited, on average, by between 5,000 and 6,000 gold reis, and each officer by between 30,000 and 40,000.

When it came time for the main Portuguese force to return to India, Albuquerque had his flagship, *Flower of the Sea*, loaded with his own magnificent booty, and with even more for King Manuel I. The goods destined for the monarch included two life-size, solid silver, jewel-embedded replicas of baby elephants, four gold statues of lions filled with rare perfumes, and the throne of Malacca encrusted with jewels.

The fleet set sail across the strait, Albuquerque's ship so laden it barely floated above the water. When it reached the coastal waters of Sumatra, less than half a day's sailing, it was rocked by a small squall, and immediately sank. Albuquerque and his crew took to their life rafts, from which they were rescued and taken aboard other ships. In 1992 Sotheby's, the art auctioneers, were commissioned to value the sunken treasure at today's prices. They estimate 2.5 billion dollars. Hardly surprisingly, however, there has been intense competition to locate the wreck by satellite tracking, and a fierce international dispute as to the rightful ownership, in which Portugal plays no part, and which is principally between modern Malaysia, of which Malacca is a provincial capital, and Indonesia, of which Sumatra is a part.

Albuquerque left in Malacca a large, newly built fort, a garrison of soldiers, several warships, and a civil governor. The capture of the city state turned out to be more than just another defeat of the Moslems. Malacca was the gateway to the Far East: to the Moluccas or Spice

Islands, to China, and to Japan. Portuguese ambassadors were dispatched to Burma and to Thailand, to open diplomatic and trade relations. A growing consensus of Australian historians believe that it was Portuguese from Malacca who were the first Europeans to set foot in their country. Certainly, even today, one finds the proud descendants of Portuguese officials and merchants in Sri Lanka, Formosa and Bengal, as well as in Macao and Malacca itself.

It was in Malacca that two of the most disparate figures of the rise of Portuguese power in Asia met, and joined fortunes. The account written by Fernão Mendes Pinto, an adventurer turned merchant, of his extraordinary exploits in the Orient was first published at the beginning of the seventeenth century, at the same time as Cervantes' *Don Quixote*. The two books were as successful as one another. Over the course of a few years, Mendes Pinto's book, *Wanderings*, was translated from the Portuguese into six European languages, and went into seven editions in Spanish, two in Dutch and German, and three in English and French.

By his own account Mendes Pinto was taken prisoner off the coast of Ethiopia by the crew of a Turkish galley, who took him to the nearest port in southern Arabia where they sold him at a slave auction to a Greek Moslem. Cruelly treated, he threatened to commit suicide. His owner re-sold him to a Jewish merchant. He in turn ransomed Mendes Pinto back to his fellow Portuguese at Hormuz. There, Mendes Pinto was press-ganged into the navy. He fought in a series of sea battles against the Turks, and escaped to Malacca, where he was given the job of Portuguese ambassador to the kingdoms of Sumatra and of the Malay peninsula. In Malaya, he met up with some other Portuguese. Together, they decided to become pirates, and took to attacking Moslem ships in the Gulf of Tongking.

Mendes Pinto sailed further, to the South China Sea, as far as Korea; then, shipwrecked off the coast of China, he was arrested for vagrancy, and sentenced to one year of hard labour, helping build the Great Wall of China. Before he had completed his sentence, however, a horde of Tartars invaded China and captured him. Mendes Pinto demonstrated to them how to storm a stone fort, and in gratitude, they freed him.

Among many other assertions he made about himself, Mendes Pinto claimed to have been the first European to reach Japan. For this and other reasons he came to be regarded in Portugal, for centuries, as an entertaining liar, a quixotic figure or a Baron Munchausen. His greatest extravagance was for long thought to be his claim to have been a close companion and adviser to São Francisco Xavier, one of the founder members of the Jesuits.

Whatever his exaggeration, the Japanese have always upheld the essential truth of his account. In Japan today, Mendes Pinto is a folk hero, about whom books, plays, epic poems and films have been made. A theme park dedicated to him and other early visitors from Portugal has recently opened at the spot where he landed. He is credited with having brought from "the other end of the world" the first guns to reach Japan. A modern American historian, Professor Rebecca Catz, of the University of California at Los Angeles, has conducted a thorough re-examination of Pinto's account. She has suggested that many of the events Mendes Pinto recounted, and which have long been dismissed as fanciful, such as his becoming a mercenary general in command of the King of Burma's army, actually accord with historical fact. Furthermore, these historical facts were unknown in Europe until long after his death. So it is hard to see how he could have known about them, without having been there. The dates in his account correspond convincingly with those of recently discovered oriental records. He was derided for his account of the court of a kind of oriental pope, until it was realised, comparatively recently, that his description resembled remarkably the Dalai Lama's court in Llasa.

Mendes Pinto described boarding a Chinese junk at Guangtang in the hope of returning to Malacca. A violent storm drove it across the sea to south-western Japan. He went ashore, and hunted for wild animals to eat. The locals were astonished to see him raise a rod to his shoulder, a flash from its other end with a loud retort, and then a bird drop dead from the sky. The local governor received him, and Mendes Pinto gave him his musket. The first European to land in Japan, through his first gift, had introduced the Japanese to the gun. As the country was in civil war, the new technology was the more welcomed.

By his own and Japanese accounts, Pinto made a second visit to Japan. Just as he was ready to leave again, a young man, chased by a group of older men, rushed into his arms. Mendes Pinto pushed him on board his ship, and took him to Malacca. His name was Anjiro. During the journey, he told Mendes Pinto of the many wrongs he had done, which had forced him to flee. Mendes Pinto told Anjiro about the Catholic Sacrament of Confession and Absolution. When they landed in Malacca, Mendes Pinto took Anjiro to São Francisco Xavier.

São Francisco had moved to Malacca from Goa, but had found the Portuguese there to be leading as un-Christian a way of life as he had encountered in Goa, their sins including the taking of bribes by officials, and the maintenance of harems by merchants. São Francisco heard Anjiro recount his sins, gave him forgiveness and baptised him. Anjiro taught São Francisco essential elements of the Japanese language and good manners. São Francisco wrote to the king in Lisbon: "Your Majesty sends here regulations, which are ignored. I see what goes on here. I have no hope of Christian conduct being imposed here. I have already wasted too much time and I do not want to waste more. I am going to Japan. There I will find pagans, whose minds will be open to ideas new to them about God and humanity."

Mendes Pinto himself had meanwhile had a mystical experience. This had led him to join the Society of Jesus as a lay brother. He had given the Jesuits most of the wealth he had acquired from his sales of guns and other trade goods to the Japanese. In Mendes Pinto's ship, São Francisco with two other Jesuit fathers and Anjiro sailed to Tagoshima. They were well received by the local governor. The latter was fascinated by their accounts of "the opposite end of the world", from which they had come. In the governor's court São Francisco publicly debated theology with Buddhist monks. He wrote a catechism of Christian doctrine, adapted to a Japanese understanding, which attracted great interest.

After two years in Japan, São Francisco fell ill. Mendes Pinto took him away on his ship. Off the coast of China his condition worsened. It was illegal for Europeans to land. On a small island, eighty kilometres south of the Pearl River, the Portuguese had secretly set up a rudimentary trading post, to do business with Cantonese smugglers. By the time São Francisco was brought there, he was so ill he could no longer walk. One of the Portuguese traders carried him to his hut. There after almost three weeks, early in December 1552, he died, aged forty-six. His body, apparently embalmed by Chinese techniques unknown to Europeans, who attributed its preservation to a divine miracle, was eventually taken to Goa to be publicly exhibited in St Paul's Cathedral. His physical remains did not lie in peace. Within two years, as an act of piety, Donna Isabel de Caron bit off one of his toes. In 1615, at the request of the then Vicar General of the Society of

Jesus, São Francisco's right arm was severed below the elbow and shipped to Rome. Its skeleton can still be seen there today, in a glass case, in the Jesuit Church of Gesù. The upper part of the arm and his shoulder blade was cut off in 1619, and was sent to Nagasaki in Japan. As recently as 1859, during a special exhibition, a portion of another toe fell off, which the governor of Goa sent to descendants of his family.

Mendes Pinto returned to Portugal, and lived just across the River Tagus from Lisbon. He became chairman of the local Misericordia, then as now the country's main charitable institution, and wrote his book.

By 1582 there were forty-five European Jesuits living in Japan, and thirty Japanese had been ordained. They reported to Rome that year that there were 150,000 converts in all. Young Japanese students went to the Jesuit universities at Macao and Goa, and displayed a striking liking and aptitude for European baroque music. To Japan, trade followed the flag. Portuguese merchants settled there in such quantity that they founded and built the city of Nagasaki. Their most important contribution was to introduce the mosquito net to the Japanese, who took up its use with enthusiasm and immensely beneficial effect. They established Japan's first firearms factory, and brought cast metal work from Europe, medicines from India, and silk from China. They brought new words to the Japanese language. *Thank you*, in Portuguese *obrigado*, became *orrigato*. Bread, previously unknown to the Japanese, became known as *pan*, from the Portuguese *pão*. The Portuguese introduced their method of cooking fish in *tempura*, and this remains today Japan's favourite fast food. They showed the Japanese how to build in stone, and it was because of this that the damage inflicted on Nagasaki by the dropping of the A-bomb in 1945, though appalling, was not much more so.

The Japanese were forbidden from trading in China. Their demand for Chinese woven silk was so voracious, and the potential trade so hugely profitable, that the Mandarins legalised sales to the Portuguese, in the early sixteenth century. They granted the Portuguese in effect a perpetual lease of the peninsula of Macao, in the estuary of the Pearl River, connected to the mainland by a causeway. Before many years, the island's main beach was lined with substantial Portuguese villas. On the hill were two churches and the Jesuit monastery. The trade with Japan was mostly in well-armed government ships. The profits were private; and as well as enjoying immense wealth, the merchants of Macao also enjoyed self-government, electing from among themselves the Senate, which was virtually independent of Lisbon. As in Goa, so in Macao inter-marriage between the Portuguese and other races was the norm. The community took to adopting girl babies abandoned by their Cantonese peasant parents. They were brought up as Portuguese, and mostly married when they became adults. They were provided dowries by the Misericordia, which would sometimes, in lieu, find the husband-to-be good employment in the government service or in a merchant house.

The Canton province prospered from the sales of its silk. Some of the African slaves brought to Macao by the Portuguese as personal servants, escaped into China and were given asylum. Eventually they became so many, that they had their own suburb in the provincial capital, and earned good livings as interpreters and traders for European merchants other than the Portuguese.

Through Macao to China, as to India, South-east Asia and Japan, the Portuguese brought new foods. The recipe for filo pastry, perhaps introduced to Iberia from North Africa — still the culinary home of the deep-fried pastry-wrapped parcel, the brik — during the Islamic period, led to the introduction of the samosa, as standard a snack in Portugal as the pasty in Cornwall. It evolved into the dumpling and the spring roll in southern China and Thailand. To the Chinese mainland, they also introduced the sweet potato, which became a dietary staple in the Canton province, and the peanut, from which to extract cooking oil. Other new ingredients, which had a major impact on Chinese diet and recipes, included green beans, bean sprouts, lettuce and watercress, which the Chinese still call "the Western Ocean vegetable" — "Western Ocean" being the Chinese term for Portugal. From other parts of their maritime empire the Portuguese brought pineapples, guavas and papayas. They introduced the recipe for shrimp paste, the production of which became a major industry, enriching Guangtang province's previously poor coastal villages, and which is still a widely used condiment there in soups, stir-fries, and casseroles.

The most dramatic of all these innovations, was the introduction by the Portuguese, from Brazil, of the chilli, which became, and remains a dominant flavour in the cooking of much of Asia, from the fiercely spiced kebabs of Kashmir, and Thai tomyum and red and green "curry", to the sambal of Malaysia, and the renowned cuisine of

Sezuan. Of these dishes, among the most fiery is vindaloo, from Goa. The term is a contraction from the Portuguese for "garlic wine", in which the meat is marinated, with chilli, in barrels, before cooking.

Sauces dominated by the flavour of chilli are known in much of the world, as "curry", and are widely assumed to have originated in India. The word itself is derived from the Hindi "kuri", which means "sauce".

But having eaten *en famille* in homes in various regions of India, over many years, the lack of chilli as the major flavour of most dishes has been consistent, and in contrast to other Asian countries. As Madhur Jaffrey, the Indian film star, BBC television cookery instructor and New York restaurateur, remarked: "The word 'curry' is as degrading to India's cuisine as *chop suey* was to China's."

Partly because of the climate, Indian cooking is based on fresher ingredients than are common in Europe or north America, flavoured by freshly ground spices. British culinary historians have tended to concur that curry was invented for British civil servants in India, by their cooks, on grounds of economy: stale spices could be masked inexpensively, by adding dried and pulverised chillies. The mixture became a thriving export from India to England, and by the nineteenth century, was part of the national diet.

David Burton, in his book *The Raj At Table,* wrote that curry could not have been invented without the Portuguese. They had ceded Bombay to the English, and were numerous in Bengal, by the time Britons established the East India Company there. Although curry has largely been replaced in Britain by more (if not fully authentic) Indian flavours, it remains a mainstream dish in Portugal. Jumbo packages of curry powder sell briskly in the supermarkets. High-class restaurants feature on their menus *Caril a Indiana,* usually of chicken or prawn. The same curry sauce is featured by restaurants in France, for sole or lobster. While no dish resembling it is to be found in India, it is strikingly similar to the curried chicken and prawns eaten by the southern Chinese, and to the curry a company in Japan sought, in 1999, to patent internationally, as a Japanese invention.

From China the Portuguese took to Europe, tea — it was introduced to England by Catherine of Bragança, on her marriage to King Charles II. After successful breeding trials by the Jesuits on their experimental farm in Macao, Chinese boars were sent to Portugal, resulting in the leaner and more tender pork which remains a striking feature of Portuguese produce. They took the small orange fruit we now know as the tangerine because the Portuguese planted the trees in Tangier, when it was their colony, and they brought what we know as the satsuma from the province of that name in Japan. The oranges today grown in the Algarve, which some think to be the most delicious in Europe, were transplanted from south China. From the same region also came to Europe for the first time, celery and rhubarb. The latter was marketed as a laxative, and the seemingly insatiable demand for it led the south Chinese to believe Europe to be the continent of constipation.

CHAPTER XII

THE GOLDEN AGE IN LISBON;
DISASTER ABROAD

What money could buy, Lisbon bought. Bankers, merchants, boutique owners, jewellers, dressmakers, tailors, hatters and boot makers came from Belgium, England, France, Germany and Italy, to seek a share of Portugal's new and already fabled wealth.

As King Manuel's own fortunes increased, so did the size of his royal court. The new nobility dressed in the finest silks and linens. Damião de Góis, the royal chronicler, noted that Tristão da Cunha, discoverer of the island still named after him, rode around town wearing a hat entirely covered in large pearls. The King dressed in new clothes every day. Those that he had worn once, he distributed among his courtiers, twice a year. The new nobility rode around town in ornate carriages. The King himself moved around his capital in a procession led by a rhinoceros and then four elephants. The latter had been trained to entertain the crowds, by curtsying, and by sucking up water from horse troughs with their trunks, and spraying everyone nearby. After the elephants, came a Persian horse carrying a hunting leopard, a gift from the Sultan of Hormuz. The royal carriage was escorted by mounted noblemen and by trumpeters and drummers. King Manuel was addicted to music. He had himself serenaded as he went to bed, both for the afternoon siesta and at night. While he read documents in his office in the Casa da India, a chamber orchestra played. Even on Fridays, when he fasted on bread and water, and spent the best hours of the day in the criminal court listening to the pleas of mitigation of the newly convicted, and their sentencing, he did so to the accompaniment of clavichord and flute. In the afternoons, he liked to go boating on the River Tagus, to quote Góis, "in a small galley with an awning, all upholstered with silk, taking musicians along, and any official he was dealing with".

"For his chamber music and for his chapel," Góis noted, "he collected famous performers from all parts of Europe. These he paid lavishly, and also gave them many favours, so he had the best musicians, and the best choir of any king in the world." In the evenings, he often gave parties, with not only musicians in attendance, but comedians, who satirised members of the nobility and the bishops of the Church with impunity. His master of ceremonies was Gil Vicente, still regarded as the greatest of Portuguese dramatists. While it would be invidious to seek to compare him to his contemporary, William Shakespeare, his style is as lively; and he enjoyed and made full use of a freedom of expression and of topic which, in England at that time, would probably have led to his beheading. His first recorded work was of a nativity play in which, for the first time in the long tradition in Europe, the shepherds and kings had distinctive and comic characters, clearly based on contemporaries. Material which had been the preserve of the jesters, he now developed into full-scale plays. He portrayed noblemen who kept their wives virtual prisoners in their homes, while themselves going out on the town, fornicating, if not with all, with a lot of sundry. King Manuel's favourites of Vicente's dramatic caricatures were of priests who preached morality from the pulpit but practised blackmail and extortion.

King Manuel had built a huge and opulent opera house, and a new royal palace, on the hill overlooking Belém, on the waterfront immediately to the west of Lisbon. His agents recruited the finest architects, stonemasons and other skilled artisans that they could find in Castile, Italy and France. Three of the most outstanding were Portuguese: Mateus Fernandes, and Diogo de Arruda and his son Francisco. But perhaps the most distinguished of them all was Diogo de Boitac, from Languedoc in France. Together they developed the exuberant late renaissance style that became known as Manueline. No new building methods evolved; the technique remained gothic. Classical statuary and decoration, not to mention restraint, were superseded by the mystical symbols of the Order of Christ (by then the name of the Knights Templar), of which King Manuel was the Grand Master. These were joined by carvings depicting nature, of birds, wild animals and flowers, often placed in biblical scenes.

Manuel commissioned the rebuilding of the Knights Templar's great castle-monastery at Tomar, and the construction of a remarkable three-nave church in Setubal and of the Pantheon of his royal dynasty, in the cathedral at Batalha. In Belém, beneath his palace, he had built the tower, in what was then the middle of the river, commemorating the first voyage of Vasco da Gama. Behind it, across a large garden, he commissioned the Jerónimos, the monastery of Santo Jerónimo. This national shrine remains one of the most remarkable buildings in southern Europe. The work was begun by Boitac, and continued after his death by Diogo de Torralva, a Spanish architect who had been trained in Italy. The building was financed by a special tax on oriental spices, of five per cent. Many of the masons who built it came from India. In the church, which occupies a more central position in the ritual life of Portugal than Lisbon Cathedral, the great pillars are fashioned like the trunks of palm trees, the vaulted roofs seemingly their leaves. The cloister, on two levels, now commemorates not only Vasco da Gama, but some of Portugal's more recent great, including the twentieth-century poet Fernando Pessoa. In the era of the spice trade, the Jerónimos monks ran, among other activities, a school for children brought from Africa and Asia. Some were princes, others prisoners of war and even slaves. Whatever their origins, or the tragic circumstances of their coming there, most grew up to prosper as members of the elite. The ethic of racial harmony was not kept to the colonies, but was an integral part of the spirit of Lisbon itself.

Still the money poured in. The Casa da India's counting house now occupied the ground floor of the royal palace. The royal chronicler recorded that he often saw foreign merchants come with bags of gold in order to buy spices, only to be told by the clerks that they had already taken in more coins than they would be able to count that day, and to please come back tomorrow. The Medicis continued to be the Portuguese monarch's main bankers. In Rome, Giovanni de Medici, son of Lorenzo the Magnificent, was elected Pope, and crowned as Leo X. King Manuel's bank manager had become the spiritual leader of Catholics, not only in Europe, but in Portuguese Africa, Asia and America. Giovanni was thirty-seven, and not yet ordained a priest, an omission that was made good a few weeks later. King Manuel sent Tristão da Cunha with some gifts.

Tristão da Cunha, his family, friends and attendants landed near Florence. The new masters of the spice trade went in procession

152

through Italy in flamboyant style, preceded by an elephant carrying a great chest filled with presents, then musicians, and then the noble visitors, scattering gold coins into the crowds that flocked to see them. As they approached the Eternal City, the cardinals rode out to greet them. The Portuguese were escorted to the Castel Sant' Angelo. There the new Pope awaited them. The main gift to him was a set of pontifical robes. The chronicler wrote: "All the vestments were woven with gold thread and so covered with precious stones and pearls that only in a few places could you see the cloth of gold. The stones and pearls were knotted in the shape of a pomegranate. In some places the gold fabric had been embroidered in silk with a face of our Saviour and of the saints and the apostles. All these were outlined with uncut rubies. The raw materials were precious, but the workmanship the more so."

King Manuel also sent by sea to the new Pope a rhinoceros. It was shipwrecked off the coast of France, where it drowned, and was washed up on a beach west of Marseilles. It was stuffed and embalmed, and became the model for Albrecht Dürer's famous drawing. Several of Portugal's noble families set up their own residences in Rome, in what is still known as the Portuguese quarter, near the Piazza Navona. The Fonseca family's palace on the Piazza della Minerva was on such a scale, that it is now a 190-room, five-star hotel.

Looking back, slightly dazed, on all this opulence and showing off, it is easy to overlook the contribution of the Portuguese then to the advance of knowledge. The export from Portugal of maps and globes was illegal, and carried severe penalties. This encouraged a thriving trade in smuggling, and the defection of some Lisbon cartographers abroad for huge transfer fees. Books by Portuguese travellers, both Jesuits and secular, were widely translated and avidly read throughout Europe, providing the first knowledge of the world beyond. It was an age of major technical innovation, from the breach-loading cannon and ship's compass, developed by João de Castro, to the prefabrication of stone buildings. In mathematics, Pedro Nunes of Lisbon produced a major new treatise on algebra, which won him a reputation throughout Europe.

Perhaps the greatest innovation was in medicine. We have seen already how the Portuguese Jesuits, almost from their earliest times in Asia, studied and experimented with the medicinal herbs they found there; and how the Japanese continue to recall with gratitude the introduction of the mosquito net. The Portuguese were the first Europeans to identify the mosquito as the carrier of malaria. The famous ancient Greek physician Hypocrites spent his life surrounded by people contracting the fever, and often dying of it, without discerning its cause. Later on, the British in Africa failed to heed the warnings of their Portuguese neighbours, on the grounds that they lacked a scientific basis. They declared that the Portuguese must have a natural immunity, as a result of interbreeding with Africans. The English continued to sleep unprotected from insects and to hunt for wild duck in stagnant marshlands, and succumbed to the disease.

Garcia de Orta, a Portuguese physician in Goa, spent much of his career in scientific dialogue with Indian and Persian physicians. However, he took nothing for granted, and empirically tested every hypothesis and every drug. His *Compendium of Drugs*, first published in Goa in 1563, was a landmark in scientific medicine. In it, he poured scorn on the professional dependence of European physicians on the ancient Greek texts. It was partly because of the tremendous stir his book created, that so many European monarchs took to retaining Portuguese physicians, including, as we shall see, Queen Elizabeth I of England.

In their perception of their own cultural standing at that time, the Portuguese saw themselves as being as backward in the humanities, as they were advanced in their science and technology. As well as sending students to Rome and to Florence, King Manuel purchased in Paris a substantial college near the university, for the use of Portuguese students. He recruited scholars to become fellows at Coimbra, from Salamanca, Paris, and Antwerp and from as far away as Oxford and Edinburgh. Latin replaced Portuguese as the official language in court. A contemporary writer complained that children of noble birth were now fluent in written as well as spoken Latin, whilst barely able to converse in their own language. A certain earnestness set in, so that the Portuguese satires and comedies of Gil Vicente and his artistic successors gave way to leaden productions of Latin translations of ancient Greek tragedies.

King Manuel died of fever just before Christmas in 1521, at the age of fifty-two. Having come to the throne as King of Portugal and the Algarve, he died, "Lord of the Navigation, Conquest and Commerce of Ethiopia, Arabia, Persia, and India". In the rest of Europe he had been better known as "The Grocer King". During his reign, the Portuguese had come to be not only admired by the Dutch, the English, the French and, above all, the Spanish, but envied. With the great monarch dead, they began to watch like vultures, to see what fate would befall Portugal, and more pertinently, her empire.

Manuel had been widowed twice and at the time of his death was engaged to be married a third time, to Princess Leonore, the sister of the Spanish Emperor. The Senate in Lisbon urged their new monarch, King João III, then aged nineteen, to marry her in place of his father, so as, at the least, Portugal did not have to return the huge dowry she had brought with her. João refused. He not only returned Princess Leonor and her dowry, but sent his sister Isabel with her, to marry King Charles. He paid the Spanish throne an unprecedented dowry of 900,000 gold dobras. As extra measure, he also gave to Spain 350,000 crusados, in compensation for the Portuguese discovering and monopolising the trade of the Spice Islands before the Spanish got there.

At home, King João inherited a huge royal court, swollen by those whom his father had newly ennobled, by hundreds of retainers he had recruited on fixed salaries and pensions, and even by peasants, who had waylaid Manuel on his tours of the countryside, told him hard-luck stories, and been promised, on going to Lisbon, royal sinecures. The countryside, still more depopulated by plague, lay mostly fallow. Food was being imported in huge quantities. Meanwhile the oriental spice trade had fallen on hard times. Just as the Portuguese, as Catholics, had held that to steal and plunder from Moslems, so far from being immoral, was pleasing to God, so a Protestant ethic grew up in northern Europe, that acts of piracy against Portuguese Catholic cargoes was a divinely blest venture. Huguenot buccaneers from the ports of western France infested the Azores, the cross-roads between the South and North Atlantic. During João's reign they captured over 300 Portuguese ships. Selling the spices and precious stones in competition with the Portuguese, they brought down market prices to a level at which the trade became barely profitable to the Portuguese themselves.

What profits there still were, came almost entirely into private hands, while the Portuguese state remained burdened with the expense of a large, if increasingly ineffectual, navy. Virtually everyone in Portugal with private wealth had been exempted by King Manuel from paying taxes. King João, finding himself unable to levy them, began to sell bonds in the financial market in Antwerp, and then began meeting the interest payments through the issuance of still further bonds. The Royal Treasurer wrote to him: "So many reasons for despair appear before me." Portugal's credit rating sank to such a low level that the bankers in Antwerp demanded an interest rate of twenty-five per cent a year. By the time King João died, in 1557, Portuguese bonds had become what is known in financial markets today as "distressed paper", changing hands when there were buyers at all, at five per cent of their face value.

King João III's immediate heir, also named João, had died before him, like so many of the family, of plague, at the age of sixteen. He had been married at the age of fourteen to a Spanish princess. She, less than a month after her husband's death, gave birth to their son, Sebastião.

He was three years old when he inherited the throne, and was with his mother in Spain. She hurried with him to Lisbon. Here it was agreed that his grandmother should act as Regent, and in 1562 she was succeeded by his great-uncle, Cardinal Henrique, Archbishop of Lisbon, Évora and Braga. The Lisbon Senate vetoed the notion that the King's Spanish mother should have charge of a Portuguese monarch's formation. They appointed a Jesuit to be his tutor, instructing the priest to "educate his majesty in the customs of old Portugal. Have him dress like a Portuguese, eat like a Portuguese, ride in the Portuguese style, speak Portuguese, have all his acts be Portuguese."

The Lisbon Senate also had Sebastião kept isolated from the royal court, so that he could incur no debts or other favours to be repaid, and installed him in a medieval palace on the other side of town. He was a sickly child, who developed an obsessional determination to overcome his illness through arduous physical exercise. This consisted of military drill and combat training. He grew to see himself as "Christ's Field Marshal against Islam". He assumed the powers of the monarchy in 1568, on his fourteenth birthday. Within months he had quarrelled and sacked the ministers whom his great-uncle, the Cardinal, had chosen for him, and appointed in their place others nearer to his own age. The royal chronicle records that he went with them to the mausoleum of the royal house of Avis, in the monastery at Alcobaça. He ordered that the tombs of his ancestors be opened, so that he could revere their bones. He went from there to Évora, to witness, in the main square, the public burning of seventeen suspected heretics. This, it is said, gave him the inspiration to go and conquer heretical Morocco for Christ. Some of the money he required to do this, he raised by selling immunities from being burnt at the stake, to Jews and others at risk of being so. He borrowed more from Conrad Roth, a German banker, against the security of the anticipated profits from looting. To claim his share, Roth sent to Lisbon, to sail with King Sebastião, 2,600 Germans. Then Sir Thomas Stukeley, an English adventurer, called at Lisbon, on his way back from Rome to Ireland. He had with him a fleet of ships carrying foot soldiers, bowmen, and artillery, entrusted to him by the Pope, with which to lead a Catholic Irish uprising against the English Protestant monarchy. His arrival in Lisbon was seen by the King as a gift from God.

By the age of twenty-four, Sebastião had amassed his invasion force. The send-off was festive. In all, 24,000 people sailed for Morocco in 500 ships. They included four regiments from the Alentejo, 2,000 Portuguese mercenaries, 1,000 Andalusian free booters, there against the express orders of their King, 1,500 cavalry and 1,000 carts with mules and carters, with which to carry away the booty for the greater glory of God. Even when the invasion force reached the Moroccan coast, at Arzila, the party atmosphere continued. For they had also brought along more than 6,000 camp followers, ranging in rank from landed duchesses to Lisbon prostitutes, as well as footmen, butlers, valets and priests.

In Arzila, they were warned that the Emir was waiting with a huge force, to engage them if they went further south. Led by King Sebastião, they marched south. It was by now August 1578. After five days, exhausted, and almost out of food and water in the blazing summer heat, they found themselves facing a Moslem army, fresh, well fed and supplied and ready for battle. The Moslem infantry outnumbered King Sebastião's two to one, their cavalry ten to one. They had in addition 7,000 bowmen, and ranks of cannon. Within a few hours, 15,000 of Sebastião's party had been killed, including Sebastian himself and Sir Thomas Stukeley. The Moslems captured 8,000 more, including most of the camp followers, whom they sold into slavery. Less than 100 managed to escape to Tangier and to sail from there back to Portugal.

Cardinal Henrique, Sebastião great-uncle, was next in line, and assumed the throne. He sent a petition to the Pope in Rome, for a dispensation to marry; for, despite his advanced age, unless he was able to produce an heir, he would be the last of the great Portuguese royal dynasty of the house of Avis. Before the Pope finished his deliberations, the Cardinal died. King Filipe II, the new King of Spain, despatched a small army to Lisbon under the Duke of Alba. Its defenceless citizens quickly surrendered. Portugal had become a domain of Spain.

CHAPTER XIII

THE COMING OF THE INQUISITION; THE DEPARTURE OF THE JEWS

Before the end of the fifteenth century, Portugal had become the only country in Europe in which Jews were not persecuted. They had been expelled from England in the thirteenth century, and from France in the fourteenth, and then from Germany, Poland and Russia. In Switzerland, hundreds of them were burnt at the stake. In several of the city-states of Italy, they were permitted to live, but only in compounds or ghettos beyond the city walls. They were forbidden from practising the more lucrative trades and professions, denied political and civil rights, and taxed penally. The exception to this was a notable one: the Pope was then still the temporal ruler of Rome, and here he provided "the people of Jesus" with the right to reside, and his protection.

The Jews in Portugal were known as Sephardic, meaning "western". They believed that they were descended from the aristocracy who had been enslaved during the Babylonian captivity. As we saw in Chapter I, there are several references in the Old Testament to Tarshish, which they believed, and many believe today, to be the south of Atlantic Iberia. It is likely that there were permanent Jewish residents here by the time new refugees arrived from Israel after the fall of Jerusalem, and the destruction of the second Temple by the Romans, in AD 72. The first written evidence of the presence of Jews is an edict of AD 300. It forbade Christian peasants from having rabbis, instead of priests, bless their fields and marry them. That the bishops felt it necessary to issue such a ban is ample, if negative, demonstration of the acceptance by Christians then not only of Jews as neighbours, but of the equality of their religion.

During the centuries which followed, the benefits the Jews brought to the Christian majority in Portugal included the technique of printing. The first book here was produced by Samuel Gascon in Faro in 1487, and the first in Lisbon by Rabbi Eliezer, in 1489. They were prominent in most fields of scholarship, including medicine, and mathematics and astronomy, without which the discoveries beyond Europe could not have been achieved. The chief rabbis were prominent in the royal court since the reign of Don Dinis in the late thirteenth and early fourteenth centuries. The only notable point of friction between them and the archbishops and priors in the court, was their practice of astrology. King Duarte, to the protest of the Cardinal, even delayed his coronation because the Portuguese Chief Rabbi of his time advised him that the conjunction of the planets was unfavourable. Portuguese Kings frequently employed Jews as their ambassadors abroad, because of their good manners and linguistic skills, and particularly in Moslem countries, where they were more welcome and more trusted than Christians. In many parts of the world, including northern Europe and Asia, Portugal was often assumed to be a Jewish nation.

The Jews were not merely permitted, but encouraged, to work as goldsmiths and jewellers. The guilds that regulated these crafts were run by committees of Christians and Jews in equal numbers. The Christian authorities acknowledged that the Jews had a different tradition of family and communal law, and they were permitted their own judges.

While they kept to their dietary laws, and worshipped in their synagogues, the Jews supplanted Hebrew with Portuguese as their liturgical language. They lived, dressed and conducted themselves virtually indistinguishably from their Christian fellow citizens. A fair proportion had aristocratic titles conferred on them. Christian and Jewish friends customarily visited one another on religious holidays with gifts — often baskets of fruit and decorated eggs, the Jews calling on the Christians at Christmas and Easter, and the Christians on the Jews at Hanukkah and Passover.

This atmosphere of security, and of being valued, enabled the Jews of Portugal to develop their culture and sophistication to a height unknown to Jews elsewhere. Lisbon's Jewish Academy produced generations not only of distinguished physicians, botanists, geographers, mathematicians and lawyers and theologians, but pioneering authors of new forms of fiction and of poetry, which were later to influence the work of non-Jewish writers, particularly in Holland and Germany.

The disruption of this creative and civilised environment, and the replacement of tolerance and respect by severe persecution, was without question the worst of all the ill effects that Portugal suffered from the growing influence there of Spain, and then its period of Spanish rule. Portugal's own "Babylonian captivity" under three Spanish kings was to last only sixty years. Jews were eventually to be welcomed back, after the liberal revolution of 1834. But the flight of so many of its Jews from Spanish-directed oppression, with their knowledge and their international network, to Holland and then to England, became an essential inspiration for and dynamic of the creation of the Dutch and English empires, at the direct expense of Portugal's.

In Spain, under the rule of the Catholic monarchs Fernando and Isabel, the Jews there, after centuries of relative peace and prosperity, came under intense pressure to convert to the royal faith. Rather than face reprisals, some did so because they had no particular religious feelings either way. Others recalled the council of Maimonides, the great Jewish theologian. During an earlier period of attempted forced conversions by Moslem fanatics, he had taught that it was valid to opt for life, particularly if one had family responsibilities, by professing one faith with one's voice while nurturing another in one's heart. Whatever the motives, and there was a variety of them, the converts found themselves, in 1478, confronted by a worse threat than if they had remained Jewish religiously. This was the year in which the Inquisition was set up, for the stated purpose of investigating the sincerity of their profession of Christianity. Over the next eight years, 700 converts to Christianity were to be burnt at the stake for allegedly showing insufficient sincerity. By a deep irony, those who had remained Jews were immune from the torture chamber and death by burning.

In 1480 the order went out that Jews could no longer live among Christians, but must move to segregated ghettos. Then, in 1492, a year more widely known for Columbus's first expedition, the Jews of Spain were given notice that within four months, they must either convert, and risk the Inquisition, be summarily executed, or leave the country. Most chose to seek refuge in Portugal. This included many who had nominally converted. Some historians have criticised King João II, then on the Portuguese throne, for what they see as his less than generous welcome. Only 600 of the families that fled from Spain were given the right of permanent residence, for a once-only payment of 10,000 crusados a family. The remainder were issued, at six border posts set up for the purpose, transit visas for a fee of one crusado a month, valid for up to eight months, by which time they were expected to have found a home elsewhere. Some 60,000 Spanish Jews were admitted into Portugal. Rabbi David Altabé, President of the American Society of Sephardic Studies is inclined to exonerate João and his fellow Christians. "Many of the Jews of Portugal," he wrote, "had reservations about accepting the Spanish exiles. It was they who recommended to the King that the Spanish Jews be allowed only a temporary stay."

The leaders of the Jewish community in Lisbon feared that the large and sudden influx of Spanish Jews, if all were allowed to remain permanently, would unbalance the city's social equilibrium, and create potentially dangerous resentment among their non-Jewish neighbours.

Some of the refugees chartered ships to take them from Lisbon. They found themselves at the mercy of captains who threatened to abandon them on desert shores, if they did not surrender their remaining wealth. It was said that some sailors believed that Jews carried their gold and jewels in their stomachs, and they slit them open in a search for them. In the winter of 1493, Rabbi Juddah Chagyat took his congregation of 250 on board a ship he had chartered. They sailed for four months, from port to port, only to be turned away everywhere for fear that they would bring with them the Lisbon plague. They were captured by pirates who took them to Malaga and ransomed them to fanatical priests, who had the Jews denied food or water until they converted. One hundred succumbed and fifty preferred to starve to death. The surviving 100 escaped to Morocco, where they were kidnapped by Berbers, and then sold to Jews living in Fez, who freed them. The great majority remained in Lisbon when their time limit expired, and were placed in captivity.

One of King Manuel I's first acts on coming to the throne, was to order the release of all these Jews. One of his next moves, however, was to seek the hand in marriage of Princess Isabel, daughter of Fernando and Isabel. His hope was that, thereby, he and his heirs would succeed to the throne of Spain, as well as of Portugal. Fernando and Isabel were inclined towards this, not least because Portugal then, though barely a fifth the size of Spain, was by countless times the richer. His future in-laws did insist that before the marriage took place, he rid Portugal of every one of its Jews. This was a standard condition of the Catholic monarchs in marrying their children into foreign royalty. As a pre-condition of another of their daughters, Catarina, marrying the future King Henry VIII of England, they obtained a written undertaking from his father, King Henry VII, that any Jews found in England be either put to death or exiled. As Jews had been forbidden from residing in England for the past century and a half, this was no more than a token gesture.

The predicament facing King Manuel was altogether real. One of the last things he wished to do, was to rid the country of so many of its most valuable citizens. The solution he chose was a somewhat fantastical one. First, he ordered all Jews who had not converted to Catholicism by the end of Easter Sunday 1497 to leave the country immediately. Second, he issued an order prohibiting any Jews from leaving. Third, on the morning of that Easter Sunday, he had all known Jews rounded up and herded into the churches, where they were baptised en masse, the holy water being sprinkled over them almost randomly. Some resisted. A few were hidden from the vigilantes by sympathetic Christian friends. A number were said to have committed suicide. Parents who tried to prevent their children from being baptised, had them taken from them and sent to monasteries and convents to be educated at the King's expense. Some of these were then shipped to populate the islands of São Tomé and Principe, and establish a sugar industry there. From Easter Monday 1497, by King Manuel's decree all Jews in the country were now officially known as New Christians. Thus he satisfied the Catholic monarchs and he married their daughter.

The new Queen, Isabel, on coming to live in Lisbon, was not so easily assuaged as her parents. At her insistence, the Pope was petitioned to authorise the establishment of the Inquisition in Portugal, to investigate and deal with heretics. The Pope sympathetically received a delegation of Jews from Portugal, and refused his consent over four years. Meanwhile, Dominican friars had followed Queen Isabel from Spain, and, under her protection, began preaching anti-semitism. Among their accusations was that Jews, themselves immune to the plague, infected Christians with it as a means of genocide. Two

Dominicans, during a procession of the Host in a Lisbon street, suddenly accused two Jewish bystanders of showing disrespect. What followed had become all too familiar in Seville, Toledo, Barcelona and elsewhere in Spain, before the expulsions, but was until that day unprecedented in Portugal. In the priest-led riots, Jews were slaughtered, their homes wrecked and their property burnt.

It took King Manuel three days to re-establish order. Of those arrested, he had sixty executed, including the priests. Lesser offenders were publicly flogged. He shut down the Dominican monastery in Lisbon, as well as the Guild Hall, some of whose members had supported the priests. Most importantly, as a gesture of his regret to the New Christians, he placed a ban on the Inquisition inquiring into their true beliefs for a period of twenty years. By its charter, the Inquisition was not solely directed at Jews, but also had the task of rooting out Lutherans and Moslems. But the Reformation sweeping northern Europe had entirely passed Portugal by, so that Lisbon contained no Protestants. The few Moslems that there were, the Inquisition dared not move against, for fear of reprisals against Catholic missionaries in Moslem North Africa.

Lisbon's Jews, both Portuguese and Spanish, adapted to the role of New Christians. Some became sincere Catholics. Some remained uncompromisingly Jewish, in all but the most minimal outward obeisance to Christianity. A large number practised the two religions alongside one another. Rabbi David Altabé has stated that members of many New Christian families became ordained as priests. In the churches they presided over masses, attended by their relatives and other New Christians. Then, in the privacy of their family homes, they would conduct Jewish services and perform marriages. Some of these priests achieved positions of prestige and prominence in the Church hierarchy. A curiosity from this era are communion chalices, made for these priests by New Christian silversmiths. The cup can be unwound or lifted off, to reveal, hidden in the thick stem, miniature Judaic candlesticks, prayer shawl, and biblical scroll. There are more living survivals of this dualist tradition to be found in Portugal today. Successive generations of the now famous Jewish community of Belmonte, in north-eastern Portugal, maintained their Judaic faith, and a form of rites they evolved themselves in secret, for almost 500 years. In Lisbon, there are church-going Catholic families of Jewish descent who also now openly at home observe the Jewish festivals.

To Portugal's old Catholic aristocratic families, many of whom had fallen on hard times financially, a benefit of the Jews' change of status to becoming New Christians was that they were freed from religious obstacles of inter-marriage and the resulting sharing of wealth. So many of these "old" families married their children to those of New Christian merchants and professional men, that there is hardly a noble lineage in Portugal today, which does not pride itself on its partly Jewish ancestry.

King Manuel died in 1521. His guarantee of protection of the New Christians from the attentions of the Inquisition expired eleven years later. The Pope, however, remained firmly on the side of the New Christians. From Rome came a series of amnesties forgiving without penalty all the Jews in Portugal for any lapses of faith, covert practice of Judaism or any other heresy. Nonetheless, the Holy Office of the Inquisition was re-founded, at the instigation of Spanish Dominicans, in 1547. Again and again, its ambition to persecute New Christians was frustrated both by papal amnesties, and the refusal of the monarchy and of parliament to fund its activities. Then, with Portugal falling under Spanish rule in 1580, the Inquisition was empowered by King Filipe to finance itself by keeping and auctioning the property it confiscated from those it convicted of heresy. By now more than half of the wealthiest ranks of Lisbon's merchant bankers were New Christians. Antonio José Saraiva, a leading twentieth-century historian, described the Inquisition as "a vehicle for distributing money and other property to its numerous personnel — a form of pillage as takes place in war, all be it more bureaucratic".

In 1995, a touring exhibition came from England to Portugal, purporting to show the instruments of the Holy Office's torture chamber. Its exhibits included a chair, with large iron spikes jutting from its seat, to which victims were supposedly strapped, and the "iron maiden", a coffin into which a suspect was allegedly placed live, when — it was claimed — the spiked lid would be lowered on to him. Equally fanciful are the film sequences of *auto-de-fé*, showing the king and noblemen, the bishops and the vulgar mob, watching heretics tied to stakes, engulfed in flames. The main instrument of torture used by the Inquisition was a rope and a pulley. Nobody was executed at *autos-de-fé*.

The real horror of the Inquisition was minutely recorded by clerks in its employ; for it was, among other things, a meticulously bureaucratic body. The Chief Inquisitor had on his large staff, aristocrats, priests and men of letters, to sit with him in judgement, and also prosecutors, jailers, torturers and bailiffs, and notaries to record faithfully everything the others said and did. The latter's tasks included the keeping of detailed accounts of the behaviour of inmates awaiting trial in the Inquisition prison. One could be convicted for leaving pork uneaten on one's plate, or passing up a meal on a Jewish fast day.

Not all the Inquisition's victims were Jews. Homosexuals were hunted down ruthlessly, even if they were priests, and particularly if they belonged to the Inquisition's main opponents, the Society of Jesus. A second offence, perhaps while incarcerated in the Inquisition's prison, led to a sentence of death — by burning for the unrepentant, and by strangulation before being thrown on the fire, for those who did recant. Most of the priests executed by order of the Inquisition had been found guilty of a very different category of offence, known as "quietism". They taught that one did not need to have a priest to act as one's intermediary with God. One could learn to pray to Him, and to listen to Him directly. Today, particularly since the proclamation of the Second Vatican Council in 1975 of the Church as the "People of God", this is orthodox Catholic teaching. It was then punishable by death.

The great majority of those arrested, tortured and otherwise punished by the Inquisitors were New Christians, and most of them were women. For the Inquisition showed an awareness that the home is the centre of Jewish religious observance, and the head of a Jewish home is the wife and mother. It was they who kept the Jewish faith alive, not least by teaching it to their children. The Talmud was unknown to them. From their studies of the Pentateuch (the Old Testament), they developed a distinctly Portuguese Jewish theology that their objective in life was personal salvation by God, and that this could be achieved by following the Law of Moses. This was known to the Inquisition as "judaising".

To ferret out New Christians engaging in "judaising", the Inquisition employed large numbers of amateur snoopers, known as *familiares*. Hardly a street in Lisbon, nor country village, was without at least one. It was their task to collect in gossip and rumour from their neighbourhood. If a suspicion developed — for example, that a family did not eat meat and cheese at the same meal, or feasted on Jewish festival days — the *familiar* went to the Holy Office, and made a formal statement of accusation. If this interested the Inquisitor, a warrant was issued. Bailiffs, accompanied by a notary, went to the home of the accused and arrested her, or less usually him. While the prisoner was being taken to the Inquisition's own jail, the notary remained behind, and made an inventory of the family's possessions, including any outstanding moneys owed to them, which the Inquisition would itself collect.

In the interrogation room, the prisoner was not told of what he or she had been accused, or the identity of her or his accuser. The accused was obliged to volunteer the nature of the sin which had lead to her or his arrest. If the answer was judged to be wrong, or there was no confession at all, the accused was taken to the torture chamber. If the Inquisition's physician thought the accused too frail or infirm to undergo the rope torture, she or he was placed on the rack. Otherwise, her arms were tied at her wrists behind her back, with a rope which extended over a pulley attached to the ceiling. The torturers pulled sharply on the other end of the rope with such force that the prisoner left the ground. The rope was then suddenly released, and then gripped again by the torturers, to break the prisoner's fall just before her feet reached the ground. This wrenched the arms from the shoulder sockets. Few could endure more than three pulls, though there are records of some younger ones failing to break, even after six. It was rare for anyone, once arrested, to be found innocent and thus released, for at least three years. During this period, the torture would be repeated. There were acquittals, on the grounds that under torture the suspect cried out for help from Christ or from the Virgin Mary; but they were few. Another means of being released was convincingly to denounce your accuser (if you could figure out his identity) of being a "judaiser" himself. This more often had the result that a prisoner would implicate under torture everyone whom she thought might bear a grudge against her, in the hope that one of them would turn out to be the accuser. This more often caused, of course, ever increasing waves of arrests.

Most of those arrested did not see the light of day again for at least ten years, when they were brought before the *auto-de-fé*. These were held in Coimbra and Évora, as well as Lisbon. They were held only rarely, because of the expense. This included the erection of a large, ornately canopied platform in the main square, to accommodate the royal family and other dignitaries, and to provide lavish refreshments for them. A Capuchin friar recorded that of the eighty-six prisoners at an *auto-de-fé* in Coimbra, one was a bigamist and one a blasphemer. Three were priests who had taught that anyone could have direct spiritual contact with God, without the mediumship of the Church. The remaining eighty-one were New Christians, convicted of "judaising". Of the New Christians, most were sentenced to a further term in prison. A few were banished to Africa or South America and a few were allowed to return home, but obliged to wear penitential gowns with yellow flames painted on them. Seven had been sentenced to death. One of these had died already, and was carried to the *auto-da-fé* in a coffin with flames painted on it. The ceremony took place in an amphitheatre off the main square, in the presence of foreign guests among the dignitaries. The monk noted a group of Englishwomen, apparently drunk, laughing and jeering at the prisoners. The ceremony began at six a.m., and the day was spent listening to the penitents among the prisoners reciting their confessions. The seven who had not repented, including the dead one in the coffin, were handed over to the secular authorities. They were taken by the state executioners to the killing field on the edge of town, tied to stakes, and burnt at midnight. Any who at the last moment were willing to show contrition, by kissing a crucifix, were strangled first.

The Rev. Michael Geddes, Anglican chaplain to the English merchants of Lisbon and their families, attended an *auto-de-fé* in the capital. He wrote that it was led by Dominicans, "in black cloaks without sleeves, and bare foot, with a wax candle in their hand. Next come the penitents, who have narrowly escaped being burnt. Over their black cloaks, flames are painted, with their points turned downwards, to signify their having been saved. Then, came heretics who had renounced their wrong doing, and so entitled to be strangled before being put on the fire. Then came the unrepentant, the negative and the relapsed, with flames upon their habits pointed upwards. Then came those who professed doctrines contrary to those of the Roman Catholic Church, who, besides flames pointing upwards on their habits, had their portraits painted upon their breasts, surrounded by images of dogs, serpents, and devils, all with open mouths."

Dr Geddes estimated the crowd of onlookers to be as large as 12,000. In addition the king, the nobles, the bishops and men of letters sat comfortably on a stage, listening to the confessions of sexual and doctrinal wrongdoings.

This took the whole of the first day and the morning of the second. The cost of the ceremony was recorded by the Inquisition's notary as 1,370,516 reis, the major items being salaries, materials and refreshments. Over the first half century of the Inquisition in Portugal, 108 people were executed. In later years, the numbers would have become far greater, were it not for Father António Vieira. This Jesuit priest devoted a large part of his adult life to opposing the Inquisition. At one stage in his campaign, the chief inquisitor of Coimbra had him arrested, and imprisoned him for two years. After securing his release, Father António continued to devote himself to the protection of New Christians from persecution. He recruited several other influential priests to the cause, including the royal chaplain. When, despite this, he found himself outnumbered and outmanoeuvred in Lisbon, he went to Rome and petitioned the Pope. The latter refused to see him for more than four years. Father António patiently stood his ground, until the Pope finally received him and issued an edict of protection.

Some of the New Christians who were sentenced by the Inquisition to banishment to Brazil found this less than a punishment. Other New Christians escaped there after receiving tip-offs that they had been denounced as judaisers. Still others smuggled themselves and their families out of Portugal to South America, before any move against them was contemplated.

In Brazil, they went to Recife. The city was in the grip of a diamond boom. The stones were found in the surrounding countryside simply by digging through the soil, or sieving the mud beneath waterfalls. The banished and fugitive New Christians occupied themselves in the export of these diamonds. They set up a diamond sales office in New Amsterdam and built the first synagogue there more than a century before the English arrived, and renamed it New York.

So many Jews fled from Portugal to Rome, that the leaders of the established Jewish community there protested to the Pope that the influx would cause disruption to the city. They urged him to deny them entry. The Pope responded by welcoming the refugees from Portugal, and expelling the Jews already resident to beyond the city walls. After camping out in the fields for a while, they apologised, paid a fine, and were allowed to return.

Jews from Portugal were welcomed, more than anywhere else, in Turkey. The Sultan threatened to have anyone who harmed the refugees from Portugal, executed. They were to be helped in any way necessary to settle into their new home. The Sultan even offered to send ships to rescue them. A letter had been smuggled to Lisbon from Rabbi Isaac Sarfati of Constantinople, "Turkey is a land where nothing is lacking, and where all shall be well with you. Is it not better to live under Moslems than under Christians? Here every man may dwell at peace beneath his own vine and his own fig tree." The new migrants brought with them to Turkey, tobacco, which quickly became one of its main export crops. Jews began the sale of Turkish tobacco overseas, a trade they continued until the Nazi holocaust. They introduced modern techniques of weaving textiles, and of manufacturing munitions. As elsewhere, they introduced printing. As they had only Hebrew type fonts, they published works in Portuguese and Turkish, transliterated into Hebrew characters.

Generations of sultans continued their protection and encouragement. When the Catholic citizens of Ancona, the Italian port on the Adriatic, began persecuting their Jewish community, the Sultan forbade any ships from Ancona to dock in Turkey, or for any Turkish ships to call in at Ancona. Such was the economic might of Turkey then in the east Mediterranean, that Ancona suffered a financial collapse from which it never recovered.

The New Christian merchants and bankers who left Lisbon mostly migrated to Antwerp, then the major trading city and port in northern Europe. Like Portugal, it had also fallen under Spanish rule. The practice of Catholicism was compulsory, and that of Judaism forbidden. The essential differences were that there was no Inquisition, and a royal guarantee for New Christians living there, of immunity from religious investigation. Portugal's Spanish rulers had already expelled the Dutch and the English merchants from Lisbon. Antwerp now replaced Lisbon as the European centre of trading in spices and precious stones from the Portuguese empire. The most prominent of the New Christian merchant banking families who re-settled in Antwerp from Lisbon, were the Mendes. They were able to enter into direct commercial relations from Antwerp with the Portuguese colonies of Africa and Asia, in part because they had relatives spread throughout them. Moses Mendes was a merchant in Formosa. Alvaro Mendes, a jeweller, was in Goa, where he was the government's assessor of precious stones. Graça Mendes, who ran a bank with her nephew Josef Nasi, was a confidante of the Sultan of

Turkey, and also banker to the King of England, despite the fact that Jews were banned from that country. Three generations later, it was the Mendes family who paid the expenses for the virtually penniless King William IV to ascend to the English throne. In one of the first acts of his reign, parliament ended legal persecution of Jews.

Diogo Mendes, the head of the family in Antwerp, was said to have achieved a virtual monopoly of the trade in spices, medicines and precious stones, extending around the Baltic, as well as to Germany, eastern Europe and England. He had rendered Lisbon and Cadiz, once the wealthiest of ports, mere backwaters, just as the Portuguese had done to Venice in the days of Vasco da Gama. Perhaps for this reason, in 1564 the Duke of Alba, the Spanish governor, cancelled the New Christians' immunity from persecution, and the Inquisition came to town.

Amsterdam, to the north, was now in the hands of Dutch Protestants, after their long war against the Spanish Catholic occupiers. Jews moved there from Antwerp. They met for worship at the residence of the Moroccan ambassador, himself a religious Jew. Their language of worship was not Hebrew, but Ladino, a Portuguese-Spanish dialect. Overhearing their prayers, Dutch neighbours suspected them to be Spanish secret agents. They called the guard, who arrested the congregation. Their rabbi, Josef Tirdo, did not speak Dutch, and pleaded their case before the judges in Latin. He put it to them that so far from being agents of Spain, they were as much the victims of its religious intolerance as had been the Protestants of Holland. He promised that if his congregation were allowed to stay in Amsterdam they would bring great wealth to the city.

The new nation, after years of fighting for its independence, was impoverished, and without natural resources to exploit. The first Jews, having been allowed to settle there in peace, were joined by many more, so that already by 1620 Amsterdam had four synagogues. Portuguese Jews in Turkey sent to their cousins in Holland, as a gift to their Protestant protectors, the first tulip bulbs to reach that country. The Jews introduced the diamond trade, and the skill of cutting precious stones, for which Holland also remains world famous. From Cuba they brought tobacco, and founded the Dutch cigar industry. From the West Indies they brought chocolate, establishing the Dutch chocolate industry. Thus Portuguese Jews brought prosperity to Protestant Holland.

In their new freedom, many Jews who settled in Amsterdam undertook instruction in Judaism and openly resumed the practice of the faith of their ancestors. Some reacted against it. During the persecutions in Portugal, they had formed their own concept of Judaism from their study of the only Jewish text available to them, the Pentateuch (the Old Testament). Now they encountered, for the first time, the Talmud. It seemed to these dissidents to have more to do with a medieval intolerance and pedantry, than with the revelations of Abraham and the Law of Moses, and they left their synagogues. Among the dissenters was the great philosopher Spinoza, who was actually expelled from his synagogue for heresy, before he could resign. A few, despite the forced conversions of their families, and their persecution by the institutional church in Portugal, had become sincere Catholics, and continued their practice of this faith in Holland. The most famous of these was Erasmus.

All these were at least united with their Protestant neighbours in the belief that to steal from Spanish-occupied Portugal was no sin. Their jointly financed fleet of ships attacked and captured the cargoes of more than 100 Portuguese merchant vessels a year. Then came the remarkable episode of Linshoten's map, which enabled Holland to become northern Europe's first imperial power.

Linshoten, a young and clearly well-educated Dutchman, left Amsterdam in 1576, and travelled overland to Lisbon. There, by means unknown, he met Frey de Fonseca, who had just been appointed Archbishop of Asia and East Africa, based in Goa. The new Archbishop appointed Linshoten as his secretary, and they sailed together for India.

In the ten or more years which Linshoten spent in Archbishop Frey's service, he kept his own, secret record of everything he could find out about Portugal's oriental empire. From Fernão Vaz Dourado, the government cartographer in Goa, he purloined copies of the official maps, showing the Portuguese routes from Europe, and between the trading cities of their seaborne empire, including the coasts of Africa and India, China, Japan, the East Indies and the West Indies. He added detailed descriptions, instructions and advice for captains sailing these routes. He collected together invaluable information about the annual weather pattern and tide tables. He gathered, partly from his own travels with the Archbishop, and more from the accounts missionaries gave him, detailed descriptions of

172

every trading city in the Portuguese empire. Each one included an account of the local people and their customs, of the climate and health conditions, of the commodities and manufactured goods on sale — their quantity, quality and price.

His compilation was a masterpiece of accuracy and detail. How he detached himself from the Archbishop's circle, and made his way back to Holland, is not known. In Amsterdam, in 1596, twenty years after he had set out, he published his records. Almost immediately Captain Cornelius Hoofman sailed with a Dutch fleet for Java, where he established Holland's first foothold in Asia. Over the following five years he sent forty ships back to Amsterdam, loaded with spices. In 1602 the Dutch East India Company was founded, and quickly became immensely profitable.

During the last, decadent years of the reign of the Aviz dynasty in Portugal, and also under Spanish rule, the Portuguese merchant fleet had lost more than its competitive edge. The ships now being built in the Portuguese yards were much too large, too unwieldy, and too unstable. It was as though the navigations were now directed by madness. In some fleets bound for Asia, more than half the ships capsized before they could reach their destination. The crews were often, by those days, composed largely of slaves, under-fed, in ill health, poorly motivated, and anxious to find a harbour on the way from which they could escape. The Portuguese military navy had been virtually destroyed off the west coast of England by Sir Francis Drake, where they had been part of the Spanish Armada which had sailed from Lisbon.

The Dutch designed and built lighter, slenderer, swifter, more stable ships. By 1619 they had built a fortress and harbour at Java, from which they raided the Portuguese ships on the trade routes between Goa and Macao and Nagasaki. They expelled the Portuguese by force from Ceylon, Formosa, the Spice Islands, Malacca and much of the Malabar coast. Given the verve and efficiency of the Dutch, combined with the detail and accuracy of their information, the surprise was not that the Dutch succeeded so well, but that the Portuguese presence in Asia survived at all.

When the Dutch finally reached Japan, they made little headway, as the Portuguese and Spanish Jesuits were so firmly entrenched there. Their success at making conversions, particularly among the aristocracy, naturally unsettled the Buddhist abbots. Father Forez SJ wrote: "They had noted that the Fathers were devoting most of their efforts to the conversion of men of noble birth. Believing that their pretext of saving souls was merely a devise for the conquest of Japan, they had done their best to rouse suspicions."

In a Bull of 1585, the Pope declared Japan to be a monopoly of the Portuguese Jesuits, under the *padroados*. Spanish Franciscans were given a much less attractive exclusivity, of the Philippines. The latter began a campaign of poaching on Jesuit territory of Japan. On arrival, they presented themselves not as missionaries, but ambassadors. They were allowed to proceed to Kyoto, the capital, on condition they engaged in no proselytising work, a condition they promptly violated. The suspicions of the royal court were further aroused. Then in 1596, a Spanish galleon went aground on the Japanese coast. Its cargo included 600,000 silver coins. The captain somehow made his escape, but the pilot was captured. Hoping to divert attention from himself, he produced a map of the Portuguese and Spanish empires. He explained how so many countries had been subjected: "They begin by sending in priests who induce the people to embrace our religion. When these have made considerable progress, they send in troops who meet up with the converts, and there's little difficulty in accomplishing the rest."

Almost immediately, the Spanish Franciscans, together with three Japanese Jesuits and seventeen more Japanese Christians, were executed by crucifixion. All foreign priests were ordered to be deported. Forty-seven hid in the Portuguese enclave at Nagasaki, and many who had been expelled, returned. The Japanese rulers were at first remarkably tolerant of this defiance, or at least too distracted by their civil wars to act firmly. Any Christian who renounced his faith, was restored to honour and granted a pension. Few took the offer, and found themselves the victims of a terror that at least equalled that of the Inquisitions in Europe. The Jesuits estimated that 200,000 Japanese converts received punishments that stopped short of execution. More than 1,400 were crucified. In a striking parallel with the Jews in Portugal who secretly maintained their faith despite Church persecution, the Church that the Portuguese Jesuits had founded in Japan went underground for over two centuries, emerging into the open again with the proclamation of religious tolerance in 1867. Like the Jews in Portugal, they had no books but had maintained their observance, from memory and innovation, of baptism, of prayer and of the Eucharist.

Back in Portugal the mayor and councillors of Tomar, in the eastern part of the country, received a letter stating that King Filipe II of Spain was coming to their town. They were to receive and entertain him as the King of Portugal. The mayor replied that as the only townspeople in Tomar to have any amount of money were Jews, and all their property had been seized by the Inquisition, they had no funds for a royal reception. Tomar's synagogue became a warehouse. It remained so for more than 400 years, until the 1990s. It has now been lovingly restored and returned to the Jews. At Passover 1994, members of Bevis Marks, London's oldest synagogue, built by Portuguese Jewish exiles, came to Tomar, met with local Jews, and restored it to religious use.

CHAPTER XIV

FREEDOM REGAINED

The defeat of the Spanish Armada in 1588 off Plymouth, by Sir Francis Drake, remains one of the best-known events in the history of England. Its sequel, by far the largest military operation of the reign of Queen Elizabeth I, is rarely mentioned.

On 18th April 1589, an English fleet of 150 ships, carrying 18,500 armed men, sailed south from Plymouth. In the view of Queen Elizabeth I, their mission was to seek out and destroy the remnants of the Spanish Armada, in the Atlantic ports of northern Spain. However, the Queen was financially broke. She had over-spent her allowance from parliament of 250,000 pounds a year, fighting the Spanish at sea and, on land, in the Netherlands. Parliament declined to vote her more. So of the ships that sailed, in by far the largest military venture of her great reign, only eight were of her royal navy. The rest were financed privately.

This force was under the command of Drake, and Sir John "Blackjack" Norris, the general. Norris had 20,000 pounds of his own invested in the venture — as against Queen Elizabeth's 17,000 pounds — and had raised several times more from his friends in the army. Drake had put up 2,000 pounds of his own, a further 6,000 pounds from his naval colleagues, and 15,000 pounds from his admirers in the City of London. Further funds had been raised from city corporations and wealthy individuals around England. Their view of the expedition's purpose was very different from the Queen's, and it was theirs which prevailed.

Sailing with Sir Francis on his flagship was D. António, the Prior of Crato, an illegitimate son of a younger brother of King João III of

Portugal. It was Drake's and Norris's plan to expel the Spanish from Portugal, install D. António on the throne, and make their fortunes, and those of England, by taking over the Portuguese empire and its trade. There had been some scruples as to whether it was proper for English Protestants to support a Catholic would-be monarch; but puritan mystics whom Drake consulted, assured him that any damage inflicted upon the Catholic Kings of Spain, by whatever means, was pleasing to God.

As a gesture to Queen Elizabeth, Norris and Drake sailed the fleet first to the Spanish port of La Coruña. They found a single galleon in the harbour, which they set alight. On landing, they found the lower town undefended. The soldiers and sailors ransacked the place. They found quantities of wine and became extremely drunk. In this condition, they found in a mansion a lot of fancy old clothes, belonging to a noble family. These they took and wore, and were attacked by fever-carrying fleas. Hung over and diseased, they re-embarked on their ships and sailed on southwards.

They reached Peniche, a fishing town north of Lisbon, on the afternoon of 16th May. The Earl of Essex leapt into the sea, the water coming up to his shoulders, and led the first wave of 2,000 men ashore. He wrote later that he "killed a Spaniard hand to hand", but there was little resistance. The Count of Fuentes, the Spanish commander of the local garrison, had retreated with his 5,000 soldiers at the first sight of the English fleet, and the Portuguese commander of the castle presented the English with his keys. About the only casualties were men on board a ship who drowned when it was smashed to pieces against the rocks by the heavy seas. Before the first evening, Norris had landed with his main force, and taken the town.

Two days later the English began their march on Lisbon, ninety-two kilometres away. Drake stood on a hillside, waving them goodbye. He then boarded his ship, and sailed with his fleet around the Cabo da Roca, to Cascais and the estuary of the River Tagus.

From Peniche, Norris wrote to the Privy Council in London — his report is conserved by the Navy Records Society. His force had already been reduced, mainly by desertion and shipwreck, to 8,526. Of these 2,791 were still sick from the disease they had contracted from the old clothes in La Coruña. Those who could not march towards Lisbon, were carried. The Earl of Essex lent the use of his private carriage, which he had had shipped from England. Some were strapped to the back of pack mules. Some were carried by local peasants, hired for the task, on stretchers made of sheets stretched between pikes. As this bedraggled force advanced, so the Count of Fuentes retreated, trying to keep a day's march between him and them. This was no great challenge, as the English were advancing by barely more than ten kilometres a day.

When eventually they reached the northern suburbs of Lisbon, they found the area had been deserted by all but the elderly, the infirm and a single beggar, calling out to them, with palm outstretched: "long live King António". The English found that the retreating citizens had set fire to the granaries, and taken the remaining food and other provisions with them. Strangely they had left behind in their homes large quantities of jewellery and other valuables. The English soldiers had not been paid and they spent their first afternoon in the suburbs, looting. Next morning, they attacked the Church of Santo António, dedicated to Lisbon's patron saint, which was strategically invaluable as it was set into the city's wall. These walls were much higher than the English had expected, and they had brought with them no weapons or equipment suitable for undermining or for scaling them. They entered the church through the sacristy, so as simply to walk down the nave and out of the front door into Lisbon itself. But they were met by a fresh and determined force of Spanish soldiers, ready and waiting for them. Feeling tired after a while, the English withdrew, had lunch, and settled down for a siesta. While they slept, the Spanish suddenly attacked them with a fusillade of "bullets as fast as hailstones". Three officers and 46 men were killed outright, before Norris and Essex brought up reinforcements and drove the Spanish back through the city gates.

D. António promised Norris that they would be joined by a force of at least 3,000 armed Portuguese loyalists the next day. The only people to materialise were six bare-foot friars and an aristocratic lady, who presented the would-be king with a basket of cherries and plums. They brought with them word that those few men who had declared themselves for D. António had been beheaded by the Spanish. Norris decided to cut his losses, and to move his men to Cascais, less than a fifth the distance a retreat to Peniche would have involved.

Sir Francis Drake was already installed in Cascais, with his troops and his heavy artillery. On his way there, he had spotted a fleet of 60 ships from Hamburg, and he had pirated them, and their cargoes of food, and masts and cables and other spare parts for ships. The people of Cascais received the English warmly, with gifts of bread, fruit, spring water and wine. Drake reported back to London that Cascais was "a most sweet town and cleanly kept". After his troops had been there a week, he was recording that they had turned it into "a place most loathsome".

Arriving in Cascais, Norris installed D. António in the castle. But for all the civility of the Portuguese, they were war-weary, their ranks of fighting men were severely depleted, and fewer than 200 of them volunteered to join the English forces. Drake, leaving one third of the English behind, as they were still too sick to fight, advanced with the rest towards the Spanish-held fort of St Julian's, on the north shore of the Tagus estuary. Spanish reinforcements arrived at St Julian's from Lisbon to help hold the fort. The Earl of Essex sent a messenger to the fort, to challenge any Spanish officer to a duel at noon the next day. He would be recognisable, he said, by a red scarf tied around his left arm, and extra feathers in his hat. At noon, the Spanish launched a massed attack. The English fell back. They were by now so deeply demoralised that Norris and Drake decided to abandon the entire campaign. Drake wrote: "if God will bless us from Heaven with some reasonable booty for our soldiers and mariners", all might be well again. So he set off for the Azores, hoping that he and his men could find Spanish galleons there, and plunder their cargoes of South American silver.

Norris sailed almost directly home, pausing only at Bayonne, in south-western France, to drop off D. António into exile and obscurity. He reached Plymouth to find that Drake had already arrived there, empty handed.

Seven years later, the Earl of Essex, together with Sir Francis Drake, Sir Walter Raleigh and others, were sailing along the south coast of the Algarve. They had just sacked Cadiz, and their ships were now heavily laden with booty of a plenitude which had evaded the English soldiers and mariners for so long. Anxious though they were to return home and sell their spoils, the others conceded to the Earl of Essex's insistence that they call in at Faro, to see if there were not some more worth looting. The soldiers were disembarked. After wrecking the tuna fisheries in the harbour, Essex led them to the town. This had been abandoned already by its citizens. The newest and finest mansion in Faro was the Bishop's palace. Essex moved in, while the soldiers roamed the surrounding countryside, burning villages but finding nothing of any value beyond some cows and pigs. The Bishop of the Algarve, D. Jerónimo Osório, had only recently moved his see from the inland town of Silves to the coast. His scholarship in the humanities, theology and Latin history and literature was renowned throughout Catholic Europe. His library was one of the most valuable in private hands anywhere. For want of anything better to plunder, the Earl of Essex had the Bishop's books loaded on board ship, and taken to England. There, he gave them to Sir Thomas Bodley, founder of Oxford University's Bodleian Library. This thus became perhaps the only major university library in the western world to have, as its core, a collection of stolen books.

The Portuguese were not to regain their independence from Spain for a further 60 years. This at first did not seem to them to matter greatly. King Filipe II of Spain, on becoming King Filipe I of Portugal as well, was scrupulous in his dealings. He more or less endorsed the role of parliament, and rarely visited Lisbon. He presented the Portuguese capital with what many still rate as among the dozen finest paintings in the world, Hieronymus Bosch's triptych, *The Temptation of St Anthony*. His grandson, Filipe III of Portugal and IV of Spain, showed a contrary attitude. He never set foot in Portugal, and saw it as an aberration that the Portuguese should be allowed privileges denied to other nations which had come under the Spanish crown. Andalucia and Catalonia, for example, were ruled from Castile, and in an authoritarian manner, by his Prime Minister, the Duke of Olivares.

This style of monarchy resulted in widespread oppression throughout Iberia. The Catalans were the first to rebel, rising up against the Spanish crown with arms supplied by Cardinal Richelieu of France. Filipe ordered the Portuguese to raise an army of 1,000, to go to Catalonia to help quell the uprising. Almost immediately afterwards, Cardinal Richelieu sent a secret agent to Lisbon, offering arms to use in a Portuguese uprising against Spain. A group of noblemen visited the Duke of Bragança. The latter, descended from an illegitimate branch of the royal house of Avis, was by birth the most plausible pretender to a newly independent Portuguese throne — but not a born leader. He lived in his pleasant country palace at Vila Viçosa, in the midst of Alentejo. He was dedicated to hunting wild boar, and had a huge walled hunting park behind his palace. The Duke was also a keen and talented amateur composer of sacred music. *Adeste Fidelis* was attributed to him — though it seems to have been plagiarised from an English composer.

When the noblemen proposed that the moment had come to rise against Spain, not least because the latter had no spare troops, the Duke refused to have anything to do with it. It was too risky. Then his wife, Luísa, an Andalucian aristocrat, heard of the scheme, and declared: "I would rather be Queen for a day, than Duchess for life."

At nine o'clock in the morning on 1st December 1640, a group of armed aristocrats, with their servants also armed, gathered in the Terreiro do Paço, and rushed together up the steps of the palace. Miguel de Vasconcelos, the most senior Portuguese official, and regarded by his attackers as the nations leading traitor, was shot dead almost immediately, and his body thrown out of the window. The Duchess of Mantua, acting Spanish governor for Portugal, called for help. None came. She was arrested and taken to a rural convent, where she was kept in confinement by loyalist Portuguese nuns. Several leading pro-Spanish dignitaries were also arrested. Four aristocrats were beheaded, and six commoners hanged. The Archbishop of Braga, branded as a collaborator with the Spanish, died in prison. The chief inquisitor was imprisoned on a similar charge but was eventually released, as a result of pressure from Rome. All these events were concealed from the Duke of Bragança, from fear of his virtually total lack of ambition. The coup succeeded, however, and a fortnight later, on a platform in the open air, in the Terreiro do Paço, he was acclaimed King João IV.

Among the tributes paid to the new King was a book by Brother Bernardo de Brito, *Monarquia Lusitana*. With the benefit of hindsight, at least, its obsequiousnesss seems to stray into sacrilege. In the context of the time, this was clearly not so. Bernardo stated that God had designed Portugal, even before He had had the idea of creating the Earth. King João had been anointed by God. His destiny was to become Emperor of Emperors, presiding over the new Kingdom of God on Earth.

It was not so much João's reign, as that of his wife, now Queen Luísa. This forceful woman, after fifteen years as the power beside the throne, became, on her husband's death in 1556, the Regent. This she remained even after their son, Afonso, became titular King. For Afonso VI suffered from a severe mental deficiency, which caused him to eat from the floor, throw tantrums and go out to Lisbon taverns, where he would get drunk, brawl and reputedly, on occasion, kill people in fights with impunity. He was induced to renounce the throne, and despatched to exile first in Sintra, then in the Azores.

The challenges facing Queen Luísa were extraordinary. Portugal had effectively no army. Its navy had been all but destroyed, as part of the Spanish Armada. The treasury was almost empty. In the event, the French sent no help, except for a minor princess, who was married first to Afonso, and then to his younger brother and successor, King Pedro II. The Dutch, asked for aid, instead began attacking Portuguese merchant shipping, and captured Malacca.

Under Spanish pressure, Pope Urban VII refused to recognise Portugal as anything but a province of Spain. Portuguese ambassadors, sent to Rome, had to travel there circuitously, by ship from Lisbon to Bordeaux, and then overland, to avoid passing through Spain. When the Bishop of Lamego arrived in Rome, the Pope refused to receive him. A commission of cardinals declared his ambassadorial credentials to be invalid, as he was representing a state which did not legally exist. He was attacked by Spanish agents in the street, who killed two of his servants. Lisbon then sent the prior of a major monastery to plead the Portuguese case in Rome. By this time seventeen out of eighteen dioceses were vacant, as Rome refused to appoint new bishops on the deaths of the previous ones. The prior was denied an audience. He too was attacked in the street by Spanish agents, who killed one of his servants.

Though the Pope was against her, Queen Luísa had on her side another priest, of humble rank but extraordinary ability, Father Daniel O'Daly. A native of Kerry in Ireland and a Dominican friar, he had come to Lisbon to found a seminary where young men from England and Ireland could study for the priesthood and be ordained beyond the reach of Protestant persecution. Father O'Daly and the Queen first met through his petitioning her for a licence to open his English College. Their mutual attraction seems to have been immediate, and it was not long before the Queen appointed him her confessor. Soon afterwards, she also appointed him to her council of ministers, to be in charge of foreign affairs, and he became his adopted country's leading international statesman.

He saw as Portugal's most urgent priority, the recruiting of a powerful military ally. The key to achieving this was to offer in marriage Queen Luísa's daughter, Catarina of Bragança, her dowry to consist of Portuguese colonies. He travelled to France, to the court of King Louis XIV, to whom he put the proposal. The Sun King denied him. He was not going to devalue his own throne by marrying into a new and insecure dynasty, of a nation unrecognised by Rome. He was forbidden from offering military aid for Portugal against Spain, by the recently signed Treaty of the Pyrenees. But he had sympathy for Father O'Daly's cause, and showed it in practical ways. He promised that if King Charles II, newly installed on the throne of England, married Catarina, the French would buy from England the Channel port of Dunkirk for 370,000 pounds, this money to be spent on providing British troops to defend Portugal.

Father O'Daly sent from Lisbon to London an English Dominican, Father Barlow. Among Father Barlow's achievements was the invention of the repeater watch. When two buttons were pressed in sequence, it chimed out the hour and the minutes, making it possible to tell the time in the dark. These watches are still made as curiosities and sold for 27,500 dollars each, and are known as "Le Portuguisier". Father Barlow gave one to King Charles, who was fascinated by it and invited the priest to move from the Portuguese embassy into an apartment to be his own in the royal palace, Somerset House. The Spanish ambassador, getting wind of what was afoot, offered to pay a dowry of double whatever the Portuguese put up, if Charles married any princess except Catarina of Bragança. This was received with scorn in court, where it was well known that the Spanish Hapsburg monarchs had virtually bankrupted themselves through wars. The deal struck by Father Barlow on behalf of the Portuguese was that on marrying Catarina of Bragança, Charles would receive the Portuguese colonies of Tangier and Bombay, and 350,000 pounds in cash. Father Barlow had had the authority from Lisbon to clinch the deal if need be by throwing in the island of Madeira. This proved to be unnecessary. Without this extra concession he also won a licence for his fellow Dominicans to recruit mercenaries in Celtic areas of Britain, to go to Portugal and help defend it from the Spanish.

While not much interested at first in Bombay — it was to be three years before the English sent out officials and soldiers to take possession — many influential people in London believed that by acquiring Tangier, England would be enabled to dominate the Mediterranean, commercially and militarily. The Earl of Sandwich became chairman of the Tangier Committee, and Samuel Pepys, the diarist, its treasurer.

Early in 1662 Sandwich sailed to Tangier, and its Portuguese governor handed over its government to the English. He sailed on to Lisbon, to collect Princess Catarina. Her family had only been able to raise a little more than half the dowry agreed, but England was not in a financial position where it could afford to hold out for all or nothing. Sandwich settled for an IOU to cover the amount outstanding. A splendid tapestry, hanging today in the residence of the Portuguese ambassador in London, depicts the English fleet setting sail from Lisbon to England, carrying the Princess. Large crowds greeted her enthusiastically when she arrived in Portsmouth. John Evelyn, in his diary, noted that she was small and with a slightly protruding lower jaw, but otherwise acceptably pretty. The King, on his first sight of her, however, is reported to have remarked: "You have brought me a bat."

They were married hurriedly in Portsmouth Cathedral, and retired to a bedroom. Here Catarina, now the Queen of England, refused to consummate the marriage, as the wedding had been a Church of England one. A Catholic priest was summoned to the room, where he conducted a nuptial mass witnessed by four Portuguese noblemen and three Portuguese ladies-in-waiting, but no English. After this, Queen Catarina consented to go to bed with the King.

The royal couple, who spoke not a word of the other's language, and conversed in Spanish, sailed along the south coast and then up the Thames to London, where they were greeted by still larger and more enthusiastic crowds; but the new Queen's popularity, at least in the royal court, was short lived. Samuel Pepys recorded how taken aback the courtiers were by the Portuguese ladies-in-waiting kissing everyone on the cheek at first meeting. The Queen's personal physician, Doctor Mendes, denounced the water as unfit to drink, and later published a pamphlet recommending the consumption of water from Tunbridge Wells. The new Queen had brought her own cooks with her, and insisted on eating only Portuguese food. She refused to wear English dress, in favour of the archaic-looking clothes of the Portuguese court.

King Charles, for his part, continued to consort openly with Lady Castlemayne. The royal mistress's title had been arranged by the King, by making a commoner, in return for his marrying her, a lord. Under this transparent cover, the new Lord Castlemayne stood in as the father of the six children Lady Castlemayne had borne His Majesty in as many years, with the King being their godfather. Charles insisted that his wife appoint Lady Castlemayne Mistress of The Queen's Bedchamber. Catarina refused adamantly. Charles threatened to send all her Portuguese ladies-in-waiting back to Lisbon unless she conceded, which she then did. Pepys recorded a court anecdote: Lady Castlemayne came into the queen's dressing room, where Her Majesty's hair was being braided in the then Portuguese fashion. Lady Castlemayne remarked on how much patience she must have to undergo such a procedure. The Queen is said to have replied: "This is the least of the demands on my patience." Soon afterwards, Pepys's diary entry for Lord's Day, 10th June 1665, was this: "The Queen, in ordinary talk before the ladies in her drawing room, did say to my Lady Castlemayne that she feared the king did take cold by staying so late abroad at her house. Lady Castlemayne answered, before them all, that he did not stay so late abroad with her, for he went betimes thence (though he doth not before one, two, or three in the morning), but must stay somewhere else.

"The king then coming in, and overhearing, did whisper in Lady Castlemayne's ear, and told her she was a bold impertinent woman and bid her begone out of the court and not come again until he sent for her ... She went to a lodging in the Pell Mell, and kept there two or three days." After three days, she wrote to the King to ask if she could return to remove her things. The King replied that she must first come and identify them. She came. The King was waiting for her. She threatened to publish his love letters to her. Both relented and became again, in Pepys's expression, "all friends".

To Pepys, this was very bad news for the royal exchequer. For the Portuguese were now using the King's adultery, and slights to the Portuguese at court, as a reason for further delaying the money still owed for the dowry, and, as Pepys said: "I do not think the City will lend a farthing." To make matters worse, the Portuguese gift of Tangier, so far from proving the financial jackpot Pepys and others had expected, was costing England 55,000 pounds a year, in maintaining a garrison with virtually no commercial reward.

Eventually, the King broke with Lady Castlemayne, in favour of Louise de Kéroualle, Duchess of Portsmouth, who remained his lover for the rest of his life. The Queen maintained a separate, Portuguese household in Somerset House. After dinner one night, Pepys was taken by a friend in court to see the Queen's bedchamber: "She had nothing but some pretty, pious pictures and books of devotion. And her Holy Water at her head as she sleeps." She spent much of her time at Mass and in prayer, in confession, and in reading homilies. She otherwise occupied herself with playing cards.

As Charles II's biographer, Professor John Miller, has remarked, "the marriage was a personal and political tragedy". From the King's rare visits, the Queen became pregnant four times, and miscarried on each occasion. On the fourth, the King ordained that she had not been pregnant in the first place and that she was barren. There were moves in court and in parliament to have the King divorce her. These failed, in part because it would have involved returning what dowry had been received. Puritan politicians sought to have her charged with involvement in "papist conspiracies" against the crown. The King, honourably enough, denounced the accusations as obvious nonsense. After his death, the manufacturing of malicious rumours against the Queen increased, and she returned to Lisbon. About her only lasting contribution to English life had been the innovation of afternoon tea with cakes.

The fortunes of Portugal had been transformed in her absence. Her half-witted brother, King Afonso VI, had been forced to go into exile in the Azores. Her second brother, King Pedro II — on coming to the throne —, had married his brother's wife. Meanwhile the mother of the three of them, Queen Luísa, had remained the effective monarch.

Father O'Daly, the Queen's chaplain and Minister of State, had returned from Britain with two regiments of infantry and two of cavalry, and ten warships. When the Spanish invaded in 1665, and advanced towards Vila Viçosa, the home of the Bragança family, they were met by a Portuguese force, supported by English and German troops, under the command of Schomberg. On the first day, 17th June, 4,000 Spanish soldiers were killed and 6,000 taken prisoner; 3,500 Spanish horses were also captured. This became known as the Battle of Montes Claros.

Not long afterwards, apparently to the surprise of everyone in Lisbon, Portuguese settlers in Brazil rose in rebellion against the country's Dutch colonial rulers, threw them out, and took power for themselves. Soon these settlers began sending tobacco to Lisbon, in amounts which grew to twenty-eight shiploads a year. By the 1680s tobacco tax had become the Braganças' biggest source of revenue, for its import and re-export was a state monopoly, of which the royal mark-up was twenty per cent. The craze for tobacco swept across Europe. While the London merchants supplied northern Europe with tobacco grown by English planters in Virginia, the merchants of Lisbon sold the tobacco from north-eastern Brazil to Spain, Italy and France. It was marketed, not as a pleasant social habit, or even as a pleasure, but as a drug, which delivered a quick exhilarating buzz to the brain. The preferred means of taking it was as a powder (snuff). This, one pinched between thumb and forefinger and snorted into one's nostrils. The membrane of the nostrils fed the nicotine directly into the bloodstream, which delivered it to the brain in seven to nine seconds. In Portugal itself, the craving for this stimulant became so widespread that judges in Évora appealed to Lisbon to introduce legislation to enable them to tackle the epidemic of tobacco-related crime. To obtain money to support the tobacco habit, a large number of addicts had taken to mugging and burglary. The judges' plea fell on deaf ears in the capital, for the monarchy itself was prominent among those becoming wealthy from the craze. In contrast, criminal legislation was introduced with severe penalties for anyone trading in tobacco, other than with the state monopoly. It was also made illegal to grow tobacco in Portugal itself. A large anti-black-market police force was recruited, which raided premises throughout the country in search of illicit tobacco. Members of many noble families were apprehended, fined and sometimes imprisoned, for growing their own supplies in their vegetable-gardens. In 1676, the police raided the monastery of São Benedito in Lisbon. They confiscated, from the priests, grinding machines, sieves and four sacks of snuff. Priests had immunity from prosecution, but their abbot was deported. In 1700, a police raid on the convent of Santa Ana, in Viana do Castelo, found records showing that the sisters were selling up to 120 kilos a day of tobacco, which they grew on the convent's farms.

The craze spread to Goa where its grip became such that by 1680 the Portuguese and the Indians there were paying Lisbon ten sacks of diamonds a year to sustain their habit. The inferior grades of leaf were marinated in molasses, and shipped to West Africa, as chewing tobacco, which was bartered for slaves. The slaves were shipped to Brazil, to help create new and bigger tobacco farms.

Tobacco was but the overture of the wealth that Brazil was to deliver to the Braganças, their royal court and the merchants of Lisbon. There was a flow from the Atlantic ports of South America to Portugal of sugar, hides, medicinal herbs, diamonds, and the darkly glowing red hardwood after which Brazil itself was named. There was also a large trade in silver, smuggled from Spanish South America, via Brazil and Lisbon, to London. This was greatly in demand there, because it was the coin most in demand in Asia, and therefore the currency essential to the British to commercially develop their empire there.

Then, in 1694, Bartolomeu Bueno de Siqueira discovered gold in the Itaverava hills, inland from São Paulo. Having inherited a fortune, Siqueira had gambled it away. He had determined to replace his lost wealth, in his own words, "by work rather than by gambling". He recruited a band of Indians, who led him to a stream, where they panned some gold dust, and returned with it triumphantly to the city. Colonel Salvador Furtado de Mendonça quickly followed in his footsteps, and soon had his men pan one and a half ounces of gold from the streams. On his way back to the city he was met by Captain Manuel Garcia Velho. The captain persuaded the colonel to exchange the gold for his pick of the two most beautiful native women in the captain's entourage of slaves. The colonel chose a twenty-four-year old woman, and her eleven or twelve-year-old daughter. The colonel had them baptised, and settled down with them in Patangui, where they lived together for the next forty years. Meanwhile, Captain Garcia Velho went down in history as the first man to extract a commercial quantity of gold from the Brazilian interior.

There followed America's first ever great gold rush. A century and a half before any such happening in the USA, Europeans trekked to the interior. Brazilians of Portuguese descent were joined by thousands more, arriving on every ship from Lisbon. Their common destination was the area known today as Minas Gerais. The forest undergrowth was trampled down. Those of the local natives who did not escape were enslaved, and set to work panning every stream and rivulet. A series of camps sprung up along the banks, which soon grew into three substantial towns. Written records of this epic of greed are very few, not least because most who took part were illiterate. It is clear, however, that many, perhaps most, of the prospectors found what they had come to look for.

Other Europeans made fortunes, by driving beef cattle, and carting other food to the region, selling it for ten or fifty times its value elsewhere. Crime prospered no less. It was commonplace for a prospector to lose all the gold he had found, and possibly with it his life, before he could get it to the Assay Office. Hostility between the Brazilian-born Portuguese, and the new migrants from Lisbon, was intense. Each side felt it to be less than criminal to kill one of the other, for his gold. Those who had come from São Paulo often rounded up, in the suburbs on their way, native peasants, to become their forced, unpaid labourers. This was illegal. The government official charged with the protection of the "Indians", protested first to the governor, and then to the King in Portugal. Receiving no reply, and denied militiamen to impose the rule of law, he resigned. His successor also protested, to no immediate avail. When the King of Portugal eventually did try to intervene in defence of the Indians, both officials rounded on him for seeking to interfere in Brazil's internal affairs. By then, it was possibly too late. These suburban, horticulturist Indians lacked the physique to survive the harsh conditions of gold hunting in the rain forests, and died in huge numbers. They were replaced by slaves shipped from Guinea and elsewhere in Africa. A large amount of the gold discovered was smuggled out of the country, to avoid paying the twenty per cent sales tax imposed by the Portuguese monarchy.

Despite this, the Braganças had little of which to complain. By 1699, 18,000 ounces of gold were officially imported to Portugal. By 1720, this had increased to 900,000 ounces. King João V's share amounted to an annual income more than thirty times greater than that of the entire revenues of the King of England.

King João V had other major sources of money. While a glut of diamonds, pouring into Europe from Asia and South America, had created a slump in prices, demand for tobacco continued to soar. The Braganças were no longer to be spurned in the diplomatic game of dynastic marriages; and the Austrian empire's Princess Maria Anna won the hand of João V.

He cultivated an extravagance in his court in Lisbon which other European monarchs could either envy or deride as vulgarly ostentatious, but not emulate. The arrival of a foreign ambassador, the departure of a Bragança cousin abroad, the feast of Corpus Christi, the christening of a new-born Bragança — all were an unending series

189

of reasons for parties. These required the building of pavilions, theatres, triumphal arches, temporary bridges across the river, and light shows.

The Braganças largesse extended to the Vatican. The Archbishop of Lisbon was named by the Pope, and still remains, Patriarch, one of only three Catholic bishops throughout the world to hold the title. King João V took, as one of his mistresses, the Abbess of Odivelas Convent, Paula da Silva, and had a child by her, which he and the royal family acknowledged as his. To celebrate the birth, convents in Alentejo, the Braganças' home territory, created a series of desserts for children, including "angel's wings", "bacon of heaven" and "breasts of nuns".

Domenico Scarlatti, Director of Music at St Peter's in Rome, was recruited to Lisbon to take over the royal chapel, together with his finest soloists and choristers. A great new grand opera house was built, then the magnificent aqueduct of Alcântara. The Chapel of São João Baptista, now in the Church of São Roque, was made from *lápis-lazuli* in Italy, assembled there, blessed by the Pope, disassembled, and brought to Lisbon.

In 1717, in thanks for the birth of an heir to the Bragança throne, João V commissioned the design and construction of a palace in Mafra, about as far north from Lisbon as the Escorial was from Madrid, but larger. The plan was further enlarged in 1733. As a result, it has the longest corridor of any palace in Europe, including Versailles. The best-known contemporary Portuguese novel in English translation, *Memorial do Convento*, by José Saramago, describes the suffering and death of the Portuguese forced labourers, as though they were equivalent to the Egyptian slaves who had built the pyramids. After the palace was completed, a large part of it was used as a monastery. The monks collected an outstanding library of classical manuscripts, and their chapel, with six organs, was renowned as a centre for liturgical music. The Bragança royal family spent their last night on Portuguese soil there in 1910, immediately before they were deported to England, and exiled in Twickenham, Middlesex, on the proclamation of the republic.

Another result of the Braganças' now fabulous wealth was a fundamental change in Portuguese politics, some would say their abolition. As in other European countries, the kings of Portugal had summoned sessions of parliament, in order to raise taxes. By tradition and practice, the king conceded new rights and privileges to the groups of whose representatives parliament was composed: the nobility, the Church, and the commoners, the municipalities and the trade guilds. With more money than they knew how to spend as it was, the Braganças were not to call another parliament for the next 120 years.

CHAPTER XV

POMBAL AND THE KING: A DUET
IN MEGALOMANIA

The huge wave struck the islands of the Caribbean on the evening of All Saints' Day, 1st November 1755. Early in the afternoon it had hurled itself around the coast of Britain. In Germany Goethe, then aged six, felt the earth shake, and experienced a sense of shock that he was to remember for the rest of his life. The ground also shook beneath Voltaire, the great French author and philosopher, in his exile in Switzerland, and inspired his satirical novel *Candide*, still his most popular work.

The great Lisbon earthquake was and remains the most violent in the recorded history of Europe. Its epicentre was in the ocean, to the south-west of Cape St Vincent. Its tremors swept devastatingly through the Algarve and the Alentejo, and first reached the capital at nine-thirty in the morning. In each of Lisbon's fifty-six churches, Mass was about halfway through. The churches were unusually crowded: the observance of All Saints' Day was obligatory for the entire population. The candles lit by the altars and in the side chapels were exceptionally numerous, because of the festival. The ground shook violently for two minutes. In that first shock, all but five of the city's churches were destroyed. A second tremor followed, sending up huge clouds of dust covering Lisbon, suffocating to death many who had survived the collapse of the buildings. Then the huge tidal wave came racing up the estuary of the Tagus and flooding the lower part of the city, drowning many who had survived the dust cloud. On Lisbon's seven hills, thousands of candles, though dislodged, stayed alight, and set off uncountable major fires, some of which burnt for six days, cremating the living trapped beneath fallen masonry, as well as the dead.

The severe tremors continued long into the day. By the time the waters receded and the fires had been extinguished, 17,000 of the city's 20,000 buildings had been destroyed. They included six out of seven homes, the Cardinal's palace, the Holy Office of the Inquisition, and the House of India, the headquarters of the Portuguese empire. Also lost to posterity were the Royal Chapel, where Scarlatti had been Master of the King's Music and had composed some of his finest work, the Opera House, the grandest in Europe, opened only a few months before, royal and noble palaces along with their contents, some of Europe's finest works of art, and libraries. The town jail remained standing, but the jolts shattered its locks and bolts. Convicts poured out and found that, among the warehouses which had been destroyed, were those containing weapons and ammunition. A rampage of looting spread through the ruined streets.

Out of a population of 240,000, probably more than one in ten lost their lives. Two thirds of them were not killed immediately, from the tremors themselves, but afterwards, from collapsing masonry, flood, fire or murder, and from infected wounds. Many accounts of the suffering of the survivors were written by members of the large foreign community: three dozen in English alone and others in French, German, Italian, and Spanish.

From makeshift open-air pulpits, priests proclaimed that earthquake, flood and fire were but a small foretaste of the wrath of God to come, for those who did not repent. Some asked why, then, had God spared the prison and the brothel district, while destroying virtually all the churches, with the faithful packed in them? The country's most eminent sinner, King José I, with his reputation for adultery and theatrical entertainment, had himself been spared. For that morning, instead of being at work in the royal palace, he had ridden out of town with his entourage, to amuse himself at Belém. It is said that he asked his youngest minister, the future Marquês de Pombal what he should do, and received the reply: "Bury the dead. Feed the living. Rebuild the city." Instead of returning to Lisbon, the King ordered marquees to be brought out to Belém. He, his family and the royal court installed themselves in them, while he sent his young minister to the capital.

Sebastião de Carvalho e Melo, the future Marquês de Pombal, was thus launched on a career which was to make him Portugal's most famous prime minister of all time, and a leading politician in Europe of his generation. He is still the centre of controversy among historians. The Jesuits, whose Order he caused to be suppressed for over a century, have sometimes seemed inexhaustible in their quest for historical revenge through character assassination. His apologists see him at the vanguard of the Enlightenment, whose brutality was not out of keeping with the time in which he lived. They also deny that he in effect usurped the monarchy, claiming him to be the loyal servant of a shy but decisive King. He has often been called "an enlightened despot" as though there could be such a person, and there has been much talk of Pombal as a "conundrum". This is not the consensus of modern Portuguese scholars.

So far from seeing the disaster as an act of divine retribution, Pombal saw it as a huge political opportunity. He wrote and published a manifesto entitled: *The Advantages That The King of Portugal Can Obtain from the Earthquake of 1755*. In it, he said: "There are occasions when a river can only establish its true and natural course as a result of flooding. Similarly there are instances when, to establish an ideal state, it is necessary that the State be partially annihilated. After this phenomenon, a new clarity emerges."

His own residence, outside the city walls, had been spared. After the disaster, however, he did not return there for eight days and nights. He spent the time in his carriage, moving around the city, making his assessments, and issuing his written orders, which bore the royal seal. More than 220 of them have survived. Able-bodied men, who had not yet fled the city with their families were now prohibited from leaving, and directed to rescue work and fire-fighting. There was acute awareness of the risk of a major outbreak of plague. Pombal obtained the consent of the Cardinal to dispense with individual last rites and funerals. Soldiers were detailed to remove the corpses, weigh them with stones, and throw them into the river. All the merchant ships in the harbour with cargoes of food were commandeered. Shopkeepers were ordered not to increase the prices of food, on pain of severe punishment. In each of Lisbon's eight districts, he had public gallows erected. He appointed judges, with powers to condemn looters, profiteers and other criminals to death, and to have them executed immediately and on the spot.

By the time a semblance of order had been restored, Pombal had become – with the connivance of King José — the dictator of Portugal, which he was to remain for the next twenty-two years. Of

194

the other two ministers of state, one had died, and the other, Pombal had exiled to an island off the coast of Estremadura, where he too died. It has been a source of speculation since, as to how Pombal achieved such immense power, not to mention admiration. In part, he did so by his precocious understanding of propaganda as a political tool. He wrote, and had published under other people's names, not only advocacy of his policies, and ferocious attacks on his and the King's enemies, but glowing biographies of himself. Thus the legend survived until recently, that as ambassador in London he collected and avidly studied a major library of works of contemporary English philosophy, theory of mercantilism and imperial trade. In fact, after being there for six years, he was still complaining that English was a language completely beyond the grasp of the Portuguese like himself. When an English newspaper published an article about him, he had to ask an Anglo-Portuguese acquaintance to translate it for him. Similarly he is credited with master-minding the rebuilding of Lisbon, virtually alone, because the only account of it which he permitted to be published was his own.

Rumour among the Portuguese nobility of his time was that his first step to power was becoming an archivist in the state records office, where confidential genealogical data about the royal family and the aristocracy was kept — it was alleged that he had used this later to blackmail his way up from the ranks. There is little question that his two wives were shrewdly chosen from the point of view of his career. The son of a squire, he eloped with the daughter of a prominent aristocratic family, and gained their rank by marriage. After she died, he married an Austrian countess. The Queen Mother of Portugal, Mariana von Hapsburg, had been raised in Vienna, and was lonely and homesick. She quickly took the future Marquesa de Pombal as a companion, and showed a notable interest in helping her friend's husband advance in position and wealth.

Much of his success can surely be attributed to his ruthlessness, in pursuit of his goals. Yet, he was also scrupulously loyal, in wielding it on behalf of King José, when the latter wished it. This was evidenced in the Távora case. King José was riding in his carriage, to spend an evening with his mistress, the young Marquesa de Távora. The affair enraged the noble family into which she had married. At the first gate to the Távora estate, a shot was fired at the King, injuring his right arm. He immediately turned back — which was lucky for him; for at the second gate a group of armed men, headed by the Duke of Aveiro, who aspired to succeed him, was waiting to finish him off.

Pombal had by now taken over the Inquisition, from the Church, by royal decree, to use against his and King José's personal enemies. He had the Inquisition arrest and torture the male members of the Távora family, and then send them to trial. However, the judge initially dismissed the case. He said he did not believe the prosecution's claim that the male members of the Távora family had not known at the time of their attempted assassination of the King, of the Marquesa's adultery with him, remarking in court: "It is such common knowledge."

Under threat from Pombal, the judge changed his mind and declared them guilty. Several of them were executed the next day. The rest spent the next twenty years in underground cells. The dowager Marquesa was ordered by Pombal to witness the execution of her husband and her two sons, before being executed herself. Her daughter, now the king's ex-mistress was confined to a convent for the rest of her life.

On Pombal's orders, the family's palace was demolished, and its ornate gardens strewn with salt. All representations of the family's coat of arms were destroyed throughout the country, being chipped off walls when necessary.

Pombal had by this time developed the notion that, as he was the King's loyal minister, any disobedience towards or criticism of him, his actions or his decrees, was an attack on the King himself, and thus treason. This was supported by the King himself, in putting his seal on virtually all of Pombal's decrees. As Louis XIV had said, "The State is me", so Pombal held that, "The Monarchy is me". He now used this concept to crush the common people into subservience, as soon as a year after he came to power.

In 1756, he sold, on behalf of the King, to a small cartel of merchants, the royal monopoly right to sell wine in Portugal's second city, Porto. A large number of tavern keepers and other retailers were thrown out of business. At the same time, the price of wine shot up. There were protests in the streets, and 478 of the demonstrators were arrested. The judge sympathised with their case, and found them innocent. The King sacked the judge, and Pombal confiscated his property. Those arrested were re-tried. Of the 478, 13 men and five women were hanged. The remainder were flogged and imprisoned, or deported to central Africa, and their property was confiscated — possibly to Pombal's personal profit. He then sent five regiments of infantry to Porto, to occupy the city. Its citizens were made not only to lodge and feed the solders in their own homes, at their own expense, but also to pay them their wages, on behalf of the King.

Nobody was more energetic in crediting Pombal with the reconstruction of Lisbon, than Pombal himself. It was certainly he who made it a state enterprise, or monopoly. But the overall design, novel to Europe then, was that of the pioneering town planner, Manuel da Maia. Inspired by the modern cities he had seen in South America, the essence of his design was a huge square on the waterfront, with the new royal palace set back, facing the river. Another feature, which deeply impressed visitors from elsewhere in Europe, was the — for those times — great width of the streets. Almost as remarkable, they were straight and formed together a grid. The style of building which has become known as Pombaline was actually that of the great architect Eugénio dos Santos. Pombal's aesthetic contribution was to insist on absolute uniformity. His regulations prescribing this even forbade the placing of a vase of flowers on a windowsill, or the displaying of one's coat of arms by one's doorway.

After studying the designs, Altenburg, a leading member of Lisbon's German merchant community, went to King José, and offered to help finance the project, by organising an international bond syndicate. The King suggested he go to Pombal to discuss this. Altenburg replied that he would not, as Pombal was dishonest. It seems that the King passed on the remark to Pombal. The latter had the German seized and forcibly put on board a boat to Angola, where he died of disease.

The great days of the Brazilian gold boom were almost over. A steep head tax charged for every man working in the mines had made it profitable only to exploit the richest seams, and had priced prospecting almost out of existence. Brazil was still shipping huge quantities of sugar and tobacco to Portugal, but there was now intense competition from suppliers of these commodities in the Dutch, English and French colonies in the Caribbean, forcing prices down. This depleted the flow of excise duties into the royal coffers severely. So, to finance the rebuilding of Lisbon, Pombal resorted to a four per cent tax on all retail sales in the city. This had the effect of depressing business, and slowing the pace of building, so that the reconstruction of Lisbon was not completed until years after the dictator's death.

When the first shops and apartments became ready for occupation, there were virtually no takers. The people preferred to remain in the shanty towns that had sprung up from the ruins of other parts of Lisbon. They preferred the absence of rent, the sense of community, and the relatively free and unregulated lifestyle. Declaring the shanty towns to be illegal, as they had grown up without royal consent, Pombal sent in soldiers to destroy the shacks, and drive their inhabitants into the new housing.

The great square, originally known as the Terreiro do Paço — the Terrace of the Palace — Pombal renamed the Praça do Comércio, or Commerce Square. (It has recently been finely restored.) Pombal had a huge equestrian statue of King José placed in the centre of the square. He personally led three days of homage to the statue, and celebrations of it. The one person of note, who did not attend, was the King himself. José was gravely ill, and so confined to a bed by the window of a room on the side of the square, so he could watch, unseen, the troops, the nobility, the officials and the townspeoples pay their elaborate obeisances to the statue of him. It seems the King was able to see little. After the ceremonies, Pombal wrote him a lengthy letter extolling the virtues and achievements of his reign – while making it clear how many of them were thanks to Pombal.

In seeking to redevelop Portugal as a leading centre of international commerce, Pombal became convinced that the English, though he had grown to dislike them heartily over his six years in London, had found the key. It was a powerful middle class, which devoted itself to business. This class, in Lisbon, was then dominated by English, Dutch and German merchants. Of the Portuguese themselves, the majority of merchants lived under the severe disadvantage of being Jewish, officially known as New Christians. Pombal saw in them the means of regaining Portuguese ascendancy over the foreigners in commerce. He abolished all the official discrimination under which they had suffered. In taking over the Holy Office of the Inquisition, in the name of the King, Pombal had ordered the destruction of all the files containing accusations against Jews. He sent emissaries to Portuguese Jewish communities in exile elsewhere in Europe, inviting them back.

A famous anecdote, no doubt promoted by Pombal himself, is still told to children in Portugal, to describe the still-prevailing attitude towards Jews.

One day King José told Pombal that he had decided to decree, at the instigation of the Cardinal Patriarch, that all Jews be made to identify themselves as such, by wearing white caps. When he next went to the King, Pombal brought with him three examples of the proposed headgear, explaining: "One for Your Majesty, one for the Cardinal, and one for myself."

Another part of Pombal's plan for Portugal's commercial recovery was to set up trading cartels, roughly on the lines of England's East India Company. The most lasting of them was the Upper Douro Wine Cultivation Company. The export of port wine, particularly to England, had increased many times, making it one of the country's major economic activities. This had been helped by a preferential duty levied on it by the English, of a third less than those charged on French wines. The practice of adding brandy to the wine before it had completed its natural fermentation was introduced — it seems by Dominican friars from Jerez de la Fronteira — in the 1730s. The resulting sweet, more alcoholic wine both travelled better, and better suited the English palate. Then the supply became a commercially disastrous glut of increasingly inferior quality wine. The price decreased. By midway through the eighteenth century the price had fallen by nine times.

Pombal's new company, as the monopoly middleman in the wine trade, was able to raise prices for the growers of the grapes in the Douro valley, because the English merchants of Porto had no other source. At the same time, the area became the first demarcated wine-growing region in the world. There was one exemption to the new requirements that all port-wine grapes be grown in the Douro, which was that of Pombal's own estates near Lisbon. The elder trees, whose berries had been used illegally to darken and flavour the wine, were uprooted and burnt. Chemical fertilisers were banned. Unhealthy vines were replaced by new ones. To further improve quality, the growers were required to specialise in either red or white wines, not both.

That the Jesuits declared the new wine to be unfit for use in Communion was to be expected. The Society of Jesus had been the most determined, bold and powerful opponent of Pombal and his dictatorship, from the very beginning of his rise to power. Its priests were, over generations, the confessors to royalty, and were believed thereby to exercise great influence over the affairs of state. They included many of Portugal's most popular preachers. They dominated secondary education, both in Portugal and in its empire overseas.

In the Portuguese empire, the Jesuits had come a long way since the lone, pioneering ventures of São Francisco Xavier. In Brazil, 600 Jesuit priests owned and operated huge sugar cane plantations — one alone near Rio de Janeiro was of 40,000 hectares, cultivated by 1,000 indentured labourers. They had seventeen factories to refine the sugar. This was but small stuff compared with their activities in the interior, the subject of Robert Bolt's classic film *The Mission*. In the border country of Portuguese Brazil and Spanish Paraguay, they had what was in effect an independent state. Here, native South Americans were offered, in return for their conversion, protection against marauding conquistadors and European bandits. The Jesuits accommodated them in fortified villages, and organised their farming.

The conflict between the Jesuits and Pombal erupted when the Portuguese dictator re-negotiated the borders between Portuguese and Spanish South America, to bring an end to the smuggling of precious metals and jewels, for the purposes of avoiding customs duties. Pombal ordered the Jesuits and their converts out of the area. Portuguese and Spanish troops who came to expel them forcibly, were repeatedly driven back over a long period by the ferocious and impassioned resistance of the native Americans.

Characteristically, Pombal's first move against the Jesuits was to write, and have published under another name, a denunciation of them. His pamphlet declared that before the Jesuits came to Portugal, it was a religious, prosperous and powerful nation. Under their subversion, it had sunk into sexual immorality and an overall decline in its military power, in navigation and in commerce.

Then Pombal acted. Accusing the Jesuits of plotting against King José, he had all their communal houses surrounded by troops, and then searched for evidence of treason. None was found. Nonetheless Pombal had ten eminent Jesuit priests arrested, and tortured. These were the last people in Portugal to be submitted to the *auto-de-fé*. The Cardinal Patriarch issued a pastoral letter forbidding Catholics from all contact with priests belonging to the order. Then all the remaining Jesuits in Portugal and its colonies were expelled, and all their property was confiscated. Much of the latter, he appropriated for himself.

Foreign priests were deported back to their countries of origin. Those who were Portuguese were shipped to Rome.

Not yet content, Pombal launched from Lisbon a huge international propaganda and diplomatic campaign against the Jesuits. He wrote diatribes against them, which he had translated into and published in French, German and Spanish. His thrust was that the Society of Jesus was the main obstacle to the advance of enlightenment and progress, science and technology, reason and objectivity. This was calculated to strike a chord in a Europe fascinated by the new philosophies of Descartes, Pascal and Voltaire.

There was, as Pombal sensed, a rising feeling abroad, that the Jesuits had become too powerful, politically and economically, and too dominant a force in education and scholarship. The Society was expelled from France in 1764, five years after their banishment from Portugal. In 1767, they were also thrown out of Spain and its empire. Pombal now wrote to Pope Clement XIII in Rome, demanding that he "extinguish" the Jesuit order. Otherwise, he would orchestrate a joint military invasion of Rome by Portuguese, Spanish and French troops. Its purpose would be to remove Clement from the throne of St Peter, and replace him with a new Pope who would do what Pombal ordered him to do.

Clement declined. Pombal expelled the Vatican's ambassador from Lisbon, and declared that he was preparing the establishment of an independent national Church, on the lines of the Church of England. Clement XIII died in 1772. Within a year, his successor, Clement XIV, issued a Bull abolishing the Jesuits; it was not rescinded until early in the nineteenth century. On the resumption of diplomatic relations with Rome, Pombal welcomed to Lisbon the new Pope's envoy. The latter brought with him the news that Pombal's brother Paulo, a priest, was now to be a cardinal, and a gift of relics: the entire bodies of two saints, in glass-panelled coffins.

The Jesuits had dominated Portuguese education, including its leading higher institution, the University of Coimbra. They had also run the only network of secondary schools, two dozen of them in Portugal itself, and more than sixty of them in the islands and the colonies overseas. More than 20,000 boys were being schooled by them in Portugal at any time, and successive generations of alumni of Jesuit institutions had grown up to become the educated core of Portuguese society.

Pombal threw himself into the task of uprooting Jesuit influence from the very subsoil of Portuguese society. He wrote, and published anonymously, a tirade claiming that Jesuit education had turned Portugal into a nation of European savages, and had debased them spiritually and morally, as well as intellectually. The King appointed him Inspector of Reform of Coimbra University.

There is no question that the Jesuits, today noted for their advanced scholarship, were then reactionary in Portugal to the extent that they denied the value of research, as human knowledge was already complete, and by and large forbade questioning and debate, as it could cause only confusion and error. The only valid philosophical model was to be found in the works of Aristotle, and developed by Thomas Aquinas. The sole key to scientific understanding was the writings of Aquinas. Not only the publication, but the import of books containing the new thinking elsewhere in Europe, on philosophy and science and in other fields, had been forbidden at the Jesuits' behest. Students prepared for admission to Coimbra by the Dominicans and other more intellectually liberal orders, had to conceal at interview any deviance from Jesuit-defined orthodoxy, to gain a place.

In Coimbra, Pombal's goal was to transform it into a university more advanced than Oxford or Cambridge and, however briefly, he succeeded in several respects. He founded there the university press, with the immediate task of publishing significant works of scholarship which had been banned.

He dismissed the entire faculty of medicine, including its thirteen professors. He recruited, in their place, academic physicians and surgeons from the universities of Bologna and Padua. The study of anatomy by dissecting human corpses had been illegal. Pombal changed the law, and imported from London an anatomical theatre, and anatomical instructors. He added a hospital, laboratories and a botanical research garden.

In other faculties, for every Jesuit-appointee he sacked, Pombal recruited two professors from abroad — of architecture and engineering from England, of Greek from Ireland, of astronomy, physics, chemistry and mathematics from Italy.

He then turned his attention to primary and secondary schooling. His plan to innovate state involvement in and direction of a programme of mass education aroused attention from the rest of Europe, and alarm. Voltaire, who had mocked Portugal for its naivety, now asked: "Who will cultivate the fields, husband the animals, maintain the roads?"

The dictator introduced an education tax, a levy on sales of wine and brandy. During his regime, he spent this on the creation of 440 primary schools and 358 secondary schools throughout the country. He countered accusations that he had built a new educational hegemony, as uniform as that of the Jesuits, by claiming to promote private schools, particularly run by religious orders. At the same time, he set up a board of examiners, to judge the competence of teachers. The standards were rigorous, which caused such a shortage of licensed teachers in state schools, that some never opened, and many depended on under-qualified "monitors". Priests and monks working as teachers in Church schools who flunked the board's exams, were not merely barred, but even deported to slave colonies.

At the same time, Pombal required parish priests, in their presbyteries, to school the sons of peasants and manual workers in the elements of Christian doctrine, with an emphasis on loyalty and obedience to the King.

The School for Nobles, built by Pombal in Lisbon to train 100 young aristocrats a year as army officers and/or diplomats, opened with only twenty-four students, and the numbers declined from there. A problem was, as at the university, that there were far too few Portuguese lecturers competent to teach the subjects on Pombal's syllabus. He recruited them from abroad, again mostly from Italy; but almost all of them left, defeated by social resistance to themselves as the bringers of Pombal's discomforting revolution.

King José I, Pombal's junior by 14 years, died in 1777. Pombal had tried to prevent his daughter, Princess Maria Francisca, from succeeding the King, as she was mentally unstable, and maintained a court whose members were unruly. He had written to her: "There is nobody else with sufficient knowledge and vision to replace me." But when he arrived at the palace immediately after José had died, the Cardinal came out of the bedroom where the royal corpse lay and said: "You have no more business here."

The new Queen, the first woman to rule Portugal, exiled Pombal to his country estates by the village of that name, after which he had chosen his title but which he had never before visited.

News of Queen Maria Francisca's leniency was greeted with widespread protest. A large number of accusations were laid against

Pombal to the courts. Many were of acts of violence against persons. These were often incurred in the course of extortion. One of the means by which he had accumulated immense wealth was to force a nobleman to sell him his country estates for a tenth of their value, and then sell them to another nobleman for ten times their value. To achieve such deals, he threatened, and on occasion resorted to torture, imprisonment or banishment. The children of those who resisted his business tactics were locked up in remote monasteries.

In Europe generally, the time of Pombal had been one of energetic construction of roads and canals. The stimulation of internal trade was seen in London, Berlin, Paris and Madrid as the way towards progress and broader prosperity. Pombal had built no roads, and one canal. This connected his palace outside Lisbon with the navigation channel of the River Tagus. While his personal wealth had become the most fabulous of any politician of the western world, he had deprived the military of the funds they needed. The gravely depleted state of the army and navy he left behind was to have disastrous consequences for Portugal.

The Queen sent two judges to question Pombal. They reported back, privately, that he had documents showing the late King's authorisation, for virtually everything of which he had been accused. Publicly, it was said – as truthfully — that he was clearly too near death for a trial to be possible, let alone for any punishment to be inflicted. A judicial commission was established to deal with Pombal's atrocities. Among the prisoners released from the political jails was the Bishop of Coimbra, who had been incarcerated for ten years for preaching against the study of the French humanist philosophers. Other victims were also exonerated, and their possessions and status returned to them.

For Pombal, it had not been enough that he should be allowed to die in peace. He did so while writing a lengthy refutation of all the charges against him. He had been, he insisted, completely innocent, except when his obedience to Queen Maria's father had caused him to err.

CHAPTER XVI

PLAYGROUND OF THE GREAT POWERS

The coachman whipped his horses into a canter. From the passenger compartment, Queen Maria de Bragança's lady-in-waiting was said to have called out to him: "Not so fast! People will think we're running away."

The Queen sat beside her, bound and gagged. From the beginning of her reign she had been tormented by visions of her father burning in hell, for his complicity with Pombal, in challenging the Church. The foreign academics, technicians and other experts he had recruited, she had had sent home. Qualified lay teachers had been dismissed from the schools, and replaced, if at all, by often barely literate friars.

Now aged 57, she had been declared insane. Dr Willis, the London physician famous for treating the "madness" of King George III of England, had been called to Lisbon; but having examined Maria, had declared her to be beyond treatment. Her son Prince João, who ruled as Regent in her place, was taking her with him, on his flight to Brazil. Napoleon's army was marching on Lisbon. The Braganças, their officials, courtiers and over 1,000 others were hurrying to the harbour to board ships destined for Rio de Janeiro. A military escort had been provided by England's royal navy. In return, João had agreed to allow England to take over from Portugal, Brazil's extraordinarily profitable trade with Europe.

Maria had been overshadowed by the threat from France. No less than other European royal families, the Braganças had been terrified by the French revolution, and the fear that it could be exported to their country. She had imposed a rigid censorship, forbidding publication in Portuguese newspapers of anything about France, and

205

banned the import of foreign newspapers. Foreign visitors now had to be vouched for by a local resident before they could land. If they so much as discussed the events in Paris, in a café in Lisbon, they were liable to immediate arrest and deportation.

Then Napoleon had seized power, and by 1807 his armies had conquered virtually all of southern Europe, except for Portugal. The latter now provided Napoleon's arch enemy, England, with her only access to the continent. Napoleon sent General Junot to Lisbon, with an order to Prince João to close all Portuguese ports to English shipping, to confiscate all English property in Portugal, and to imprison or expel all English citizens. For João to have complied would have meant the economic ruin of his country. What prosperity it had both in the towns and in the country, depended greatly on its privileged access to the English market. The presence of large English merchant communities in Lisbon and Porto was essential to these exports. On learning of João's refusal, Napoleon drew up a plan to eradicate Portugal as a state. The north was to become a colony of France, and the south was to be absorbed into Spain. He sent Junot back to Lisbon, this time as a military commander leading a force of 30,000 men. Talleyrand, the French Foreign Minister, gave the Portuguese ambassador in Paris advice to pass on to Prince João. It was that the Braganças had no future in Europe, and should try their luck in the New World. There, in Brazil, they could create a "new empire of the first order," said Talleyrand, "far away from the revolutionary disturbances of the old world".

Just before he abandoned his subjects, the Prince Regent issued them with his final orders. The French troops were to be received without resistance. Members of the Portuguese military were to remain at their posts, but only to maintain an orderly peace, and not to oppose. Junot and his soldiers were to be received as a "force that will unify us Portuguese with the rest of Europe".

Many of Lisbon's leading citizens were in fact pleased to see the back of the Braganças and their autocratic style of ruling. Not only would armed resistance have been futile; the army had been starved of funds, and the soldiers were virtually untrained. Portuguese intellectuals, at least, saw Junot as a liberator more than as a conqueror, the bearer to this extremity of Europe of the new age of the French Enlightenment. Their main forum was the Regeneration Lodge, a Masonic group at the vanguard of opposition to the Braganças and an excessively powerful and wealthy clergy. As Junot approached the gates of Lisbon, members of the Regeneration Lodge rode out to welcome him, and escort him in his triumphal entry.

At first Junot lived up to expectations. Almost immediately upon reaching Lisbon, he proclaimed the dawn of a new era for Portugal. He announced a programme of liberal reforms: the creation of an efficient government administration, the introduction of financial propriety in public life, and exile for aristocrats who had violated the civil rights of others. There was to be universal and free education, and a huge public works programme, to build the roads and the canals the country needed if it was to develop economically, and which the Braganças had failed to commission.

The honeymoon had hardly begun when, in an act of astonishing insensitivity, Junot ruined it. He had his French troops stage a victory parade in the heart of the capital. Above the tower of São Jorge's castle, he had the Portuguese flag lowered and the French one raised. He stood on the ramparts and called for three cheers for Napoleon. The crowd remained silent.

That evening, Junot held a victory banquet in São Jorge's castle. Thousands of people gathered outside, and chanted: "Long live Portugal. Death to the French."

Junot ordered the police to move in on them and open fire, shooting to kill. They refused. Junot then presented a decree from Napoleon appointing him "Sole governor of Portugal". What was left of the Portuguese army — about 9,000 men — he had rounded up, and forced-marched across Spain to France. From there they were sent, as "the Portuguese Legion", to take part in Napoleon's disastrous attempt to conquer Russia. A delegation of noblemen and bishops went to Napoleon, then in Bayonne, to protest. The self-proclaimed Emperor received them. He said he was puzzled as to why they should want to remain Portuguese, when they could become French or Spanish. They refused his demand that they sign a formal surrender, so he had them arrested and jailed. After three years, they gave in and signed his "peace treaty", and were released.

Back in Lisbon, Junot had had himself made Duke of Abrantes, and it was widely thought that he would soon declare himself King. He had been joined by two Marshals of France, Soult and Massena, and France's mastery over Portugal now seemed complete. The French troops were spread across the country and were carrying out a systematic plan of extortion, looting and vandalism. The wealthy, at knife point, handed over their gold coins and jewels, and signed statements that they had done so voluntarily. In the churches, the French troops smashed with impartiality Romanesque, medieval, gothic, renaissance and baroque statues and ornaments. They gathered up the silver and gold communion vessels, some of them masterpieces made by the great Italian artisans, and melted them down. They smashed open tombs, to take the rings and other jewels with which the dead had been interred. Then they stripped the country mansions of their old-master paintings, tapestries and exquisite furnishings. Among the most ironic instances of their vandalism was their wrecking of the abbey of Alcobaça, built soon after the creation of the Portuguese nation by French Cistercian monks, and possibly the finest surviving example of that pure and elegant French style of architecture. At the monastery of Alcantara, French troops ransacked its invaluable library, seizing volumes at random, and ripping pages from them to use in the making of cartridges. The monastery's kitchen had been reputed as one of the finest in the country. A young French officer picked up a page that had been torn from the monks' recipe book. It was for pheasant, boned and then stuffed with foie gras, and cooked with truffles in port wine. He sent it to his mother, a countess, who passed it on to the great chef Escoffier. In his own classic recipe book Escoffier remarked: "It is perhaps the only good thing the French gained from that disastrous campaign."

While the French soldiers thus stripped Portugal of its artistic heritage, Junot had hired Spanish soldiers to impose order on the citizens of Porto. It seemed that he neglected to pay them. The Spanish soldiers mutinied, walking together out of the city, abandoning it to its own people. When they reached Lisbon, and were waiting at the quayside at the Praça do Comércio for ships to take them home, they were attacked by French soldiers. There was a fierce battle between the two occupying armies. Its outcome, as well as heavy casualties on both sides, was the virtual collapse of military control in Lisbon.

The news, from English spies in Portugal, quickly reached London. The Prime Minister, the Duke of Portland, saw the opportunity to end Napoleon's five-year blockade of the British Isles. In a move which was to prove the beginning of the end of France's domination of Europe, and the downfall of Napoleon, Portland sent a fast ship to

Porto with a letter of encouragement to the mayor and the people, together with a substantial sum of money with which to buy arms and equipment. Soon afterwards, a young British military commander, Sir Arthur Wellesley (later created the first Duke of Wellington), landed in the Mondego estuary with 8,000 men. It was August 1808. Partly through the surprise of their attack, and partly through Wellington's precocious skill as a tactician, he and his Irish troops defeated the French in two short but decisive battles, after which the latter begged for a cease-fire.

The terms of the French surrender, which Wellington signed, not only allowed the French to leave with all their arms and equipment. They were also permitted to take their loot home with them. Furthermore, the British provided the ships which took the French and their swag back to France. Wellington himself set sail for England. It seems that he had not reckoned on the presence of English journalists in Portugal. He reached Portsmouth to find the newspapers already carrying lengthy reports of his odd magnanimity, together with indignant editorials. One said: "Every British heart must sicken with this breakdown of our country's honour." Progressing to London, he found the intensity of public opinion against him to be such that he retreated to his family's estate in Ireland. The newspapers still did not let up in their campaign. Eventually, the government gave in to it, and had Wellington and his fellow officers tried before a court martial in Chelsea Barracks. Wellington pleaded that he was not responsible for the treaty's contents. He had had only the haziest impression of what it meant. He had signed it merely because his superiors had ordered him to do so. All the accused were acquitted. Portugal's loss of its art treasures was permanent, and has never been compensated for by the French or the British. It is, understandably, still a cause of bitterness in Portugal. It seems as though, to the English establishment then, Portugal's loss of her artistic heritage was a virtually irrelevant side issue. Lord Canning was to remark: "We go to Portugal to plant the standard of England on the well known heights of Lisbon. Where that standard is planted, foreign dominion shall not come."

Wellington was sent back to Portugal in 1809. In addition to his army, he had with him a young, tough Irish Protestant general, William Carr (later to be known as Lord Beresford), and a letter from King João in Rio de Janeiro, obtained from him by the English despite his unease, and under duress, appointing Beresford the commander of the Portuguese army. The French general, Soult, had recently attacked and re-taken Porto, apparently with the intention of proclaiming a new monarchy, with himself as its King. Wellington attacked Soult and his army. They retreated back over the Spanish border. Wellington and his men chased after them, until they reached France.

Then he and Beresford began to prepare for a further French attack, which they were both convinced was coming, and on a much larger scale than before. Beresford set about recruiting and training a Portuguese army. Part of the folklore from that time is that, as Beresford and his fellow British officers kept declaring that, to them, all Portuguese looked the same, the latter took them at their word. On pay day, they would each present themselves several times for their wages. It became known as "counting for the English".

Wellington set about fortifying Lisbon. It was a huge task, but carried out in effective secrecy. His scheme became known as the Linhas of Torres Vedras, a country town to the north-east of the capital. This was the logical route for the French to follow. Wellington spent two weeks on horseback, surveying the area. Then he issued his engineers with a twenty-one point plan, and recruited — by force if need be — every peasant in the vicinity to help in the preparations.

Rivers were diverted, creating impassable swamps. Trenches were dug, deep and wide, and filled with thorns. Steep slopes were cut vertically, into unscaleable cliffs. There were man-traps, and palisades of pointed staves. Stone walls were built, five metres thick and thirteen metres high. There were 600 gun emplacements, and 152 stone forts. The Lines of Torres Vedras extended for eighty kilometres. Each of the army posts along it was linked by a nine-stage semaphore signalling system, so that orders and messages could be passed from one end to the other in seven minutes — an unprecedented speed for the time. Behind the Lines, manned by 30,000 Portuguese militia and home guardsmen, was what was now a huge citadel of 700 square kilometres. It had ample fresh water, grazing for animals, orchards of fruit, gardens of vegetables, granaries full of wheat and maize, and plentiful fish in the sea.

The far side of the Lines had been turned, as much as it could be, into a desert. Any food growing there which could not be taken into the citadel, was burned or otherwise destroyed. Virtually anything which could provide shelter to the French when they arrived, was removed. Trees were felled. Peasants were made to destroy their own barns and homes. Wellington set up his headquarters to the south of this, at the top of a hill 300 metres high, and waited.

The summer passed. Then in October Marshal Massena arrived at the head of his army, of 65,000 French and 10,000 Spanish soldiers. Massena had his forces halt. Alone, he rode towards the Lines, coming within range of the English cannons. He later remarked that he had been overcome by astonishment: "the whole foreground was filled with guns and Englishmen and Portuguese". From an observation post, a warning shot was fired at him. Massena raised his hat, and galloped away. Over the next three days, Wellington watched Massena concentrate his troops near to the fortress at Sobral. They attacked. The English fought them off, with a loss of 150 men. The next day Massena approached again, riding towards a range of 120 cannons. Again a warning shot was fired, and he withdrew. Wellington was under growing pressure from his officers to launch an all-out attack. He replied: "I could lick those fellows any day, but it would cost me 10,000 lives. As this is the last army England has got, we must take care of it."

A strange kind of siege developed. It was one in which the besieged enjoyed plentiful food and wine and entertainment. Some there described it as almost a party atmosphere. Meanwhile, the siege party outside suffered increasingly from hunger, from water which had been polluted, and from the onset of winter. Men began to die of malnutrition and disease in ever larger numbers. Massena saw his army thus reduced by 30,000 men to 45,000, and retreated under cover of night. Wellington and his army pursued them across Portugal, then through Spain and into France, and did not stop until he had driven them to Toulouse. The apparently impregnable power of Napoleon had been broken, and the stage set for the battle of Waterloo.

The Portuguese themselves awoke after the victory to find that the country was now no more their own than it had been under the French. With Wellington gone, Lord Beresford had been proclaimed head of a council of regents. Portugal was now under the rule of an English military dictator. He proved arrogant and brutal. Portuguese who took issue with him over the conduct of their country's affairs were imprisoned or executed. His particular target became the Masons of Lisbon's Regeneration Lodge, a group of intellectual liberals bent on liberty and progress. A revolt against Beresford erupted in Porto, in

August 1820. Beresford took a ship to Rio, to consult with the King. Sailing back across the Atlantic, he tried to land at Lisbon; but he was prevented from leaving his ship. He went on to England, where it was felt that his cause was not worth the sending of another army.

The following January, there were elections. Parliament met in Lisbon, and appointed a ruling council. A *coup d'état* in Brazil caused King João to return, reluctantly, to Portugal to reclaim his European throne. This was at the price of his swearing loyalty to liberal principles. A constitution enshrining these was proclaimed in 1822.

When João died five years later, his eldest son and heir, Pedro, had already proclaimed himself Emperor of Brazil, and had no desire to move to Lisbon. He named his seven-year-old daughter, Maria da Glória, the Queen of Portugal, and appointed as her Regent his younger brother, Miguel, then aged 24.

Miguel had been living in the imperial court in Vienna. This was the centre of the Holy Alliance of Austria, Prussia and Russia. Its aim was to stamp out liberalism and insist on the divine right of monarchs to rule absolutely. While he was still in Vienna, Miguel was sent from Portugal a copy of the constitution. This he showed to Metternich, who advised him to ignore it. In Lisbon Cathedral, Miguel made a public display of mocking the constitution. It was said that he had sworn to honour it, not on a bible, but on a popular novel, titled *Os Burros (The Donkeys)*. Miguel's Spanish mother, Carlota Joaquina, who came with him, was still more ferociously anti-democratic. She surrounded her son with the most reactionary advisers she could find, and had a list drawn up of real and imagined enemies. Several thousand of them were arrested, 150 were executed, and the rest imprisoned or banished.

A group of liberals, including several leading army officers, escaped to Galicia, and thence to England. There they were not particularly welcome, and were accommodated in an abandoned warehouse in Plymouth. However, with the help of Spanish Jewish refugees in London, they managed to borrow 2,000,000 pounds in the City of London, albeit at a usurious rate of interest, fourteen per cent.

By 1832, Emperor Pedro I of Brazil had proved to his subjects to be so obnoxious, that they forced him to abdicate and threw him out of the country. The only part of the Portuguese empire whose governor still professed loyalty to Pedro as monarch was the island of Terceira, in the Azores. There, Pedro was met by the dissident liberals from England. This improbable coalition sailed for Porto. Miguel's troops there were taken completely by surprise, and fled. A long siege of the city began, with Pedro and the liberals inside it. Conditions in the town deteriorated, but the citizens remained true to their tradition of upholding freedom and democracy. The besiegers fared much worse. An epidemic of cholera spread through their camps. Survivors deserted en masse, and went on a marauding campaign of looting and vandalism up the valley of the River Douro, before deciding to march south, to sack Coimbra.

The liberal Duke of Terceira sailed with the English naval captain, Charles Napier, and 2,500 volunteers, and landed with them in the Algarve. From there they began a march on Lisbon. Napier, as he rounded Cape St Vincent, chanced upon Miguel's navy, capturing five boats, and scoring a major blow to the absolutists' morale. As the Duke of Terceira and his men reached the south shore of the River Tagus, facing Lisbon, Napier sailed up the estuary with his fleet and bombarded the city. Miguel was in the north, attempting to re-capture Porto. His supporters in Lisbon fled up river, to Santarém. The battle that took place there was terrible in terms of human suffering and loss, and of damage to the city and to the farms around. Defeated by the liberals at last, Miguel returned south, and retreated to Évora, where he made his last and hopeless stand. At the village of Évora Monte, he signed a surrender and abdication. He was then put on a boat to Genoa. Arriving there, he declared the documents to be invalid, as he had signed them under duress, and that he was still King of Portugal. He proceeded back to Vienna, and little more was ever heard of him again.

Pedro came to Lisbon, where he became his daughter's Regent. After his death, she became Queen Maria da Glória, aged fifteen. The first parliamentary elections of her reign resulted in a newly liberal regime. But the price the Portuguese had paid for their liberty had been the devastation of much of their country, a post-civil-war bitterness that divided families, an empty treasury and a massive burden of foreign debt. In an attempt to pay this off, Pedro arranged for the abolition of all the religious orders, and the confiscation and sale of all the convents and monasteries, their lands and other properties. The sheer quantity of properties put up for auction depressed the prices, so very little money was raised. No buyers could be found for some of the finest monasteries, including several masterpieces of Cistercian architecture, which fell into disrepair and decay. Many of those who bought the farmland at bargain prices lacked the agronomic skills of the monks, and production declined.

Under the monks at Alcobaça, the tenant farmers had lived decent lives, and paid very low rents. The monks provided them with technical expertise, and lent them money in drought years. With the expulsion of the religious orders, these men found themselves to be indentured or casual labours, working — when there was work — for pittances, for absentee landlords. At the same time, as the great liberal anti-cleric Almeida Garrett remarked, a new landed class arose, whose members turned out to be far more rapacious and harmful to society than the monks and nuns they had replaced.

CHAPTER XVII

THE FALL OF THE HOUSE OF BRAGANÇA

"What a transition to come from Spain into Portugal. It was as if flying from the Middle Ages into modern times," wrote Hans Christian Andersen, after a lengthy visit to the country in 1865.

Before he won lasting fame as a writer of stories for children, Andersen was the best-known and most internationally admired travel writer of his day. His books were translated into the main European languages, and his reputation was such, that when he visited England, he stayed as the honoured guest of Mr and Mrs Charles Dickens, and Queen Victoria and Prince Albert invited him to stay with them at Osborne in the Isle of Wight. In Portugal, Queen Maria da Glória had died, while giving birth to her tenth child, in 1853. Andersen was received in the Palacio das Necessidades in Lisbon by her widower, Prince Albert's cousin Ferdinand, Duke of Saxe-Coburg and Gotha. King Fernando, as he was now known, had ruled Portugal as Regent, and had recently passed on the monarchy to his son Luis. Luis's inheritance from him was a new style of kingship, of presiding over a democratic constitution and an elected government. So successful and popular had Fernando been in this, that the governments of Spain and Greece begged him to become their sovereign as well — invitations that caused alarm in Portugal itself.

By the time Luis became King, there was little visible trace of the terrible damage that had been inflicted by the long civil war. Hans Christian Andersen, crossing the border from a disordered and backward Spain, remarked on the modernity of the railway, the punctuality of its trains, the comfort of the carriage, the excellent quality of the meals, the fresh-painted tidiness of the villages and

215

towns he passed through, and, above all, the courtesy of the people — both his fellow passengers and the railway staff.

Arriving in Lisbon, he found tram-ways, and tree-lined boulevards lighted by gas at night, peopled by well-dressed citizens promenading. As he toured the capital, then travelled to Coimbra, Sintra and Setubal, he remarked on the vitality apparent in virtually every activity from agriculture to the arts.

Portugal had become the most advanced society in southern Europe. Alexandre Herculano, a close friend of King Fernando, is still renowned today for his ground-breaking historical writings. In the absence of censorship, for virtually the first time since the state came into being, Herculano de-mythologised the story of its origins, replacing the legends with evidence and objectivity.

His friend and colleague, João Arroio, though these days often overlooked, was a great educational reformer. As minister,he introduced a novel method – devised by João de Deus — of teaching young children to read and write their grammatically tortuous language. In the decade before Andersen's visit, the number of schools for boys had almost doubled, to 2,000. Every significant provincial city had a lyceum, preparing pupils for university. Education for girls still lagged. Nonetheless the number of girls' schools had been increased by six times, to 350. In Lisbon and Porto polytechnics had been founded, teaching a new generation architecture, medicine, engineering, pharmacology and the natural sciences.

Almeida Garrett, Herculano's comrade in arms on the liberal side in the civil war, who had been imprisoned under the old regime for practising freedom of speech, supervised the conversion of the defunct Holy Office of the Inquisition into a National Theatre and school of drama. The nation had had only one notable playwright, Gil Vicente. In the spirit of his time, Garrett wrote the rest of the National Theatre's repertoire himself. He and fellow writers pioneered a new, fresh and direct style in poetry and prose. They founded the Grémio Literário, the Literary Guild, which became a major intellectual force far beyond the realms of authorship, promoting liberalism in the Church as well as in politics, and sponsoring debate and innovation in fields ranging from photography to agronomy.

Industry had grown rapidly. The use of machinery had increased by 600 per cent, and the use of engines in factories had increased by 900 per cent. The country had become the world's largest processor

216

of cork, which it still is. Textiles, ceramics and glass were also being exported in substantial quantities. The goods were carried in Portuguese-built steamships. The merchants of Lisbon communicated with their customers in Britain and Brazil by means of undersea telegraph cables, one of which, from the western suburbs of Lisbon to Cornwall, is still in use. Major public works projects, including the building of a national network of roads, led to the recruitment of, among other foreign experts, Eiffel, the great French engineer, whose steel bridges and Lisbon elevator remain national landmarks. Such projects were financed by an efficient system of raising and collecting taxes. These had also been applied to reducing the previously crippling national debt, resulting in a doubling of the valuation of Portuguese government bonds on the London Stock Exchange and the Paris Bourse.

The exuberant mood of the age was displayed in its architecture. You can see today the flamboyant mock-Arabism of Lisbon's Rossio railway station, and its bullring on Campo Pequeno. King Fernando revived the Manueline style in the vast hunting lodge he had built for his sons at Buçaco, now a luxury hotel. His gothic Pena Palace still towers on its mountaintop above Sintra. It has been likened by some to a Walt Disney film set. At the time, it was seen more as a symbol of the spirit of romanticism, which attracted to Sintra artists, writers and composers from the rest of Europe, as well as Portugal's greatest novelist, Eça de Queirós.

Public parks were created, and decorated by a new, naturalistic school of sculptors. Painters prospered, and their works were not the preserve of the rich. Modern methods of reproduction made their prints available at reasonable cost, and these were to be found on the walls of most homes.

In civil rights, above all, Portugal had become a model for the rest of the world. It became possible, if still cumbersome, for non-Catholics to marry, and to register their children's births. Women had rights to own property. Slavery was outlawed throughout the Portuguese empire. So were the death penalty, penal labour, and long-term solitary confinement. The concept of prison as a place of punishment gave way to that of reform and rehabilitation. In particular, the inmates were taught skills, by means of which they could earn a decent living after their release. Women were taught to make Arraiolos carpets, which today fetch over 150 dollars a square

217

metre. Men learnt a variety of crafts, and the jail in Coimbra became a centre for some of the finest book-binding. Other prisons sold their inmates' products in shops, patronised by the bourgeoisie after church on Sundays.

This ambience of peace, enlightenment and progress became rudely disrupted by the winds of conflict between factory owners and their workers, blowing in from abroad, when Portugal found itself caught up in the internationalisation of this terrible strife. It began in Lancashire, in the north of England. Workers in the textile mills there were among the first in the western world to organise themselves into trade unions, and to foster adult education in night schools, enabling them to read the new socialist tracts. This led to their demands for adequate wages, a six-day week and other minimal rights, such as not being dismissed on account of temporary illness. The owners of the mills responded, in part, by investing in textile plants in northern Portugal, and transferring production there. The Portuguese workers came to respond to the oppressive conditions in a similar way to those of the English before them. They staged strikes. By this time textile-manufacturing machines had become so sophisticated, and thus so simple to operate, that a child could work one. That is exactly what happened. The mill owners sacked the grown-up men, and hired their children. Both the state tobacco monopoly and the English owners of the cork-processing plants in the Alentejo followed suit.

Across the Atlantic, strikes also broke out in the textile mills of New England. Their owners dismissed the American workers, and sent recruiting agents to Portugal, to hire and ship replacements from there. One of New England's surviving community of Portuguese textile workers is Fall River, near Cambridge, Massachusetts. Professor Pedro da Cunha, who spent two years among them in the 1980s, found a surviving, still prevalent fear of education as a path to calamity.

As elsewhere in the second half of the nineteenth century, the industrial revolution had brought as much new misery as benefit to Portugal. The next blow came with a mutiny in the Brazilian navy. Portuguese warships happened to be in Rio de Janeiro harbour at the time. The officers and crew sympathised with the mutineers, and allowed more than 600 of them on board; they then carried them to the safety of Buenos Aires. The Brazilian government angrily severed economic relations with Portugal. This was not only a serious blow to the merchant prosperity of Lisbon and Porto. Many poorer families depended for their living on the remittances of their sons working as migrant labourers in Brazil, and these funds were now blocked. In a ruinous game of economic dominoes, the banking system became weakened in its turn, and the government's tax revenues fell steeply. These factors were compounded by a general recession in the industrialised world, caused by a glut of manufactured goods produced by people paid too poorly to sustain the market for them, unable as they were to afford to buy them.

King Carlos I succeeded his father in 1889. He was a prolific water-colourist (pictures by him of seascapes still come up for sale in Lisbon auction rooms). His love of the sea also involved a weakness for expensive yachts, which the government reluctantly bought for him. But for all his shortcomings, including an ineffectualness which could turn into a tantrum, there was no premonition of the crisis which was to bring the Bragança dynasty to a sudden and violent end.

At the time of Carlos's succession to the throne, the prospects for Portugal seemed unusually bright again. Instead of contesting one another for power in Europe, the continent's major nation states were engaged in a race to claim a share in Africa, which had been all but ignored by them since the outlawing of the slave trade. Now missionaries and other explorers were bringing back tales of vast wealth: rich deposits of copper and gold, diamonds which could be picked from the surface of the earth, herds of elephants that could provide apparently infinite supplies of ivory.

In this fabulous new game, the Portuguese were uniquely well positioned. For they, alone, had never turned their backs on Africa. Their continuing presence there after 400 years was recognised by France, in a treaty giving the latter leave to exploit West Africa, with the exception of Portuguese Guinea. The Germans, in laying claim to south-west Africa, acknowledged Portugal's ownership of Angola immediately to the north. The British, too, at first assented to Portugal's role as the European power in central Africa. They were, after all, the oldest of allies, and the continent was large enough to share.

By the closing years of the nineteenth century, colonialism, in the sense that it came to mean in Africa, had not come into being. The Portuguese did not so much rule Angola and Mozambique, on the west and east coasts of central Africa respectively, as treat with them.

They had built ports and European settlements on the coast, and installed governors and small garrisons of soldiers. Some of the land behind the coast was farmed, by individual Portuguese families and by plantation companies, producing coffee and tobacco. Otherwise, the African nations of the interior of central Africa were left largely unmolested. Between Angola and Mozambique lived the peaceable Mashonas, and immediately to their south was the Kingdom of the Matabeles. These people were prosperous from their trade, through East Africa, with India and China. Their fortified capital, Zimbabwe, after which the current central African nation is named, was an outstanding feat of architecture and engineering — one of the greatest but least-known wonders of the world. The Portuguese established diplomatic and trade relations. In the 1880s, a plan took shape, with the agreement of the Matabeles, to establish a series of Portuguese staging posts right across central Africa, to stimulate trade and development. In the east, the Portuguese began to mine copper and gold.

Back in Lisbon, Henrique Barros Gomes, Minister for the Colonies, stood before parliament, and unrolled a map on which the whole of central Africa — what is today Zambia, Zimbabwe and Malawi, as well as Angola and Mozambique — had been tinted pink. This, he said, represented Portugal's territory, as agreed in several European treaties and at the great conference in Berlin chaired by Bismarck. Amid the exaltations, troops were sent out to protect the claims, and the Geographical Society was founded, to raise capital through public subscription to develop and exploit the territories.

When the challenge came, it was not inspired by any government, but by the free-booting son of a rural English vicar, Cecil Rhodes. He left grammar school at seventeen, to join his older brother on the latter's small cotton farm in Natal. The brother also had three diamond claims, which Cecil took over. By the age of twenty, he was a rich man. He went to Oxford, where he was accepted as an undergraduate by Oriel College in 1873, graduating eight years later. He remained hypnotised by the wealth of Africa, and was determined that it should be his. He formed the British South Africa Company as his vehicle. On its behalf, he claimed the territory south of the Zambese, which the Portuguese had painted pink on their maps, and already clsimed as theirs. He armed and trained tribesmen in southern Mozambique and sent them into battle against the Portuguese, without, of course, telling them that this was to be no war of independence, but one of conquest for the British South Africa Company. Outnumbered, and with sometimes astonishing bravery, the Portuguese defeated them.

Rhodes returned to England, and launched a huge propaganda campaign against Portugal and the Portuguese. He courted with particular ardour the Protestant missionary societies, one of whose explorers, David Livingstone, was credited with having discovered central Africa, in the place of earlier Portuguese travellers. The Portuguese were Catholics. After centuries of suppression, Catholicism had only recently become fully legalised in England again. It was still widely regarded with suspicion, a fundamentally un-English and sinister superstition, run by Italians. The souls of the noble savages of central Africa had to be protected from Machiavellian southern European priests. Furthermore, the Portuguese were not imposing law and order in the region, making it unsafe for British entrepreneurs and missionaries alike. The solution was obviously to expel the Portuguese, whom Rhodes termed "a lazy, incompetent, half-caste race of bastards", and have the territory taken over by the British South Africa Company, whose officers would guarantee the safety of Protestant evangelists. So great was the fervour that the British government — though without prospect of benefit to the national interest or the taxpayer — capitulated to it.

On 1st June 1890, the British ambassador in Lisbon presented to the Foreign Ministry an ultimatum. Portugal was to withdraw its troops from central Africa immediately. If Portugal refused, the British ambassador would be recalled to London, and the two countries would be in a state of war. King Carlos had been on the throne for less than a year. Cabinet ministers brought the British message to him and there was an emergency meeting. The outcome was to suggest to the British that the matter be put to international arbitration. The British refused. The Portuguese ambassador in London signed a humiliating agreement that Portugal would withdraw from the interior of central Africa. In Lisbon, the government fell. The streets were filled with anti-English rioters.

The press became ever more vitriolic towards the British, and the intensity of public hostility towards them increased. Teófilo Braga, Professor of Literature at the ancient university of Coimbra, who was to become the first republican President of Portugal, wrote what

221

quickly became a famous pamphlet naming the main causes of Portugal's problems to be *The Braganças and the English Alliance*. It is not difficult, even today, to find a surviving sense of humiliation and resentment in Portugal over what is felt to be an injustice for which the British have yet to apologise.

King Carlos went to parliament, to declare its dissolution, and made a speech announcing a new era. He appointed João Franco, his closest confidant and political adviser, prime minister and "President of the Movement for Renewal and Liberty" – who was to rule by decree. His brief was to eradicate the anti-monarchist sentiment, that now gripped the country. Opposition newspapers were shut down. Demonstrators were brutally attacked by riot police. The King and his family took refuge in their relatively modest palace, on their isolated hunting estate at Vila Viçosa, in the Alentejo, south of the River Tagus.

On 31st January 1908, the King signed, at Franco's insistence, a decree empowering the dictator to expel from the country, without trial, anyone whom he considered hostile to the regime. Immediately afterwards, two republican leaders, João Chagas and António de Almeida, were put on board a ship in Lisbon harbour. Franco then told the King that it was now safe for him and the royal family to return to Lisbon. On the next day, 1st February, Carlos, Queen Amelia, and the Crown Prince, Luis Filipe, travelled in their private train to the south bank of the Tagus. From there they went by boat across the river to the landing at the Praça do Comércio. They were greeted by Franco, and their second son, Manuel. They boarded two open horse-drawn carriages, and set off through a hostile crowd. A young man jumped on to the running board of the first carriage, containing the King and the Queen, pulled out a pistol and shot the King dead. Another gunman fired a carbine and killed the Crown Prince, but his bullets only grazed the arm of his younger brother, Manuel.

The assassins were themselves shot dead, on the spot — one of them by Captain Francisco Figueira, of the royal guard, who fled the country soon afterwards, for fear of reprisal, to return only after more than 40 years, on a brief and surreptitious visit.

Franco also left the country, after resigning on the evening of the killings., and was never heard from again. Manuel was proclaimed King. He was 18 years old, and, as a contemporary Portuguese historian remarked, "not so much an heir as an orphan". As the younger son, he had been given no training in the performance of the monarchy. He appointed and dismissed a succession of governments, and the country went into a drift. From around Europe, and from across the Atlantic, foreign correspondents from newspapers and from news agencies began to gather in Lisbon, to be in place for the revolution virtually no one doubted to be inevitable.

In October 1910, the series of events in which the monarchy was toppled in Portugal was a curious prologue to the overthrow of the Romanov dynasty in St Petersburg in October 1917. On the evening of 4th October, King Manuel, having dined with the President of the newly republican Brazil, was in his palace in Lisbon, playing bridge with his mother and two courtiers. Suddenly, they found themselves under bombardment. The palace was being shelled by the revolutionary officers and crew of a Portuguese battleship, moored in the River Tagus. They summoned a chauffeur. He drove them to the palace at Mafra, in the hills to the north-west of the capital. Next morning, they were driven to the nearby fishing port of Ericeira. They boarded the royal yacht, whose captain took them to Gibraltar. From there they were taken by a British royal yacht, the *Victoria and Albert*, to England. Manuel spent the remainder of his life in a mansion in the London suburb of Twickenham, dedicated to collecting and meticulously cataloguing antiquarian Portuguese books.

Back in Lisbon the next morning, groups of republicans marched on and took control of the royal palace and the headquarters of the army and of the police. The officers in command of some military units ordered their men to disband, and went into hiding. People filled the streets. They were joined by large numbers of soldiers and sailors who had deserted with their arms. One military barracks remained held by monarchists. Home-made bombs were thrown over the walls into it, causing heavy casualties. Other monarchist units continued to hold out, and to exchange fire with the majority of mutineers.

At this moment, a group of German businessmen had just arrived at Rossio railway station, on an official visit. The square outside was filled with monarchist troops, and the adjoining Restauradores was occupied by republican revolutionaries. The leader of the German business delegation tied a white handkerchief to his umbrella, and led his party through the streets. The republicans took him to be an official, proclaiming the regime's surrender. The revolutionaries marched to the town hall, jumped on to the veranda, and hoisted the republican flag. Nobody fought for the King: most troops, including the strong and well-armed municipal guard, remained in their barracks. Thus the monarchy fell, never to be restored.

CHAPTER XVIII

THE SLIDE TO DICTATORSHIP

In the 15 years that followed the abolition of the monarchy, Portugal went through seven general elections, eight presidents and 45 governments. One of the latter lasted for less than a day. All but one of the presidents failed to serve his full term of four years.

By the mid-1920s, there seemed no remaining doubt in many people's minds that democracy had failed, that it had somehow cut the country adrift from its own self-interests. Some of the republicans' innovations were enlightened. Radical improvements in education included the creation of new universities in Lisbon and in Porto, conducting research and teaching courses addressed to contemporary needs, and the separation of Church and state, resulting not only in freedom of worship for non-Catholics, but freedom of expression, and a lessening of discrimination on religious grounds, including in employment.

Yet women remained without the right to vote, to administer their own property, or to leave the country without their father's or husband's permission. A Portuguese woman, on marrying a foreigner, still automatically forfeited her citizenship, and with it, her inheritance.

The republicans' most telling failing, perhaps, was not to impose an effective tax on inherited wealth generally, to finance economic and social development. For the governing class was still drawn from the richest families, in a nation whose poverty still, to paraphrase Portugal's first patron saint, James, cried out for relief.

The right of labour to organise, negotiate collectively with employers, and even to strike, had been in place for more than a century — since 1822, well in advance of much of the developed world. The long-pent-up grievances and demands of much of the population, in the major cities now led to strikes, so extensive and bitter as to permanently damage significant sections of industry. The anarchy spread from the factories into the streets. Then the rioting spread from the streets into parliament, where deputies abandoned debate in favour of fist-fights.

But there was more behind the turmoil than simple popular discontent. There were those, coming from the country into the towns in search of better-paid work, who remained loyal to the monarchy. A group of aristocrats plotted the return of the King from his exile. The republicans had also adopted and tried to make major capital out of the radical Portuguese tradition of anti-clericism. The Portuguese had, as they still do, a marked lack of blind subservience to ecclesiastical authority. Over the centuries, kings and statesmen had declined to bow to the Pope's command, when they saw it to conflict with the national interest. Pompous and self-important clergymen had been permitted targets for ridicule as far back as the reign of King João II. When the republicans outlawed the religious orders, they were setting no precedent — for the Jesuits, it was their third expulsion from Portugal. The difference this time was the declared objective. When they had been thrown out before, it was on grounds of excessive political, social and economic power, by rulers who nonetheless counted themselves Catholics. Now Afonso Costa, a republican leader, proclaimed the objective to be the "entire eradication of religion in Portugal within two generations". It was now sometimes an act of courage even to attend Mass. The expulsions of priests meant that there were far fewer Masses anyway. The Irish Dominicans were allowed to remain, because of their school, the first to offer a scholastic education to girls, and so as to pastor to English-speaking foreign Catholics. Their church in Lisbon, Corpo Santo, became crammed with Portuguese worshippers.

Had the republicans confined their onslaught to the hierarchy, they might have suffered little harm. In taking aim at the faith — in their terms, the superstition — itself, they showed a fundamental misunderstanding of the attitude of the faithful. It was because of their unquestioning loyalty and devotion to Catholicism, that they thought themselves entitled to criticise the bishops and others whom they felt had strayed from its path. The notion that they found the Church itself a burden on their lives, was the opposite of the truth. It

226

was the Church which provided virtually all the secondary education, many of the hospitals and almost all of the social welfare and care for the needy. It also provided most of the colour and spectacle, celebration and entertainment, and was the force that bound villages into communities. It now became, therefore, the main point around which opposition to the republicans rallied.

The claims of three children that, while they were guarding their families' sheep, on a hillside near Fátima, the Virgin Mary had appeared to them, were at first met with suspicion by the Patriarch and the Church hierarchy. I am among the many who have experienced the powerful spiritual atmosphere of Fátima. Nonetheless, it seems hard to deny that in reversing their previously sceptical attitude to this popular shrine, the bishops were aware of its political expediency. It attracted much larger crowds than anywhere else in Portugal. In so doing, Fátima enabled the bishops to evidence a still massive popular following for Catholicism, and thus, they implied, against the republican regime.

The next blow against the government in Lisbon was struck from colonial Africa. In 1923, newspapers in Lisbon reported that huge quantities of false banknotes were flooding into the country. The source was soon identified as the Lisbon branch of the recently formed Bank of Angola and Metropolis (the latter word being the name given to the area of the country reserved for European settlement). The sole founder of the bank, and the man behind the fraud, had by then left Africa, for a luxurious life in Paris. His name was Alves dos Reis.

Like many intelligent lower-class Portuguese of his generation, frustrated in their careers by the still rigid social barriers to advancement, Reis had gone to Angola in search of recognition and prosperity. After a spell with the railway company, he attempted several business ventures, unsuccessfully. He raised another round of venture capital, and sailed to England. There he went to the head office of the famous banknote printers, Waterlows, and presented letters of introduction for himself as the representative of the Bank of Portugal. Business was slack. The sales manager accepted his credentials without further checks. Reis's order was for two million pounds' worth of 500 escudo notes.

These were printed, bundled, wrapped, and delivered to Reis in London. He took them to Lisbon, and put them into circulation through the bank which he had started for the purpose. Waterlows defended themselves by claiming that a letter of enquiry they had sent to the governor of the Bank of Portugal was intercepted by criminal collaborators of Reis. An international tribunal nonetheless found Waterlows lacking in their duty of care, and ordered the firm to pay compensation. Portuguese banknotes have since been printed in France.

It was not long after the fraud was discovered, that the Portuguese realised it was far worse than if the notes had been faked. Reis's were genuine. He had also used serial numbers issued by the Bank of Portugal itself, and which were on notes already in circulation. There was no way of distinguishing between those issued by the Bank of Portugal and those issued by Reis. The Bank of Portugal ended up redeeming both, and exchanging good notes for the fraudulent ones, along with the genuine ones.

The total sum of money lost was not great. The Bank of Portugal probably suffered a loss of no more than one million pounds. The question raised by the incident then was: how chaotic does the financial management of a nation have to be for such a scam to be possible? It was the same chaos which had caused, over the preceding five years, the escudo to collapse in value from 7.50 to the pound to 127.40.

Thus the national debt increased from a modest 400 million escudos, to a staggering eight billion. Among the outstanding bills, was one from the British government for 80 million pounds to be paid in foreign currency. This was the cost of the munitions and other supplies provided to the Portuguese military expedition in France in World War I. Portugal had entered the war at Britain's insistence, as "oldest ally". The venture had been disastrous. Many of the Portuguese soldiers had succumbed to dysentery and other diseases of the trenches, and a large proportion of them had died. The Germans had had little difficulty in routing the remnants. Now the Portuguese were expected to pay the costs of incurring this disaster, into which they had been cajoled, against reason, by the British.

As a result, to their intense resentment, Portuguese army officers joined the swelling ranks of employees of the state whose salaries were deeply in arrears. As Catholics — albeit of their own kind — they already felt less than loyal, to the atheistic regime. The talk in the officers' messes was of a New Order arising in Europe. If the fascists could take control of and sort out Italy, and the Nazis do so the more in Germany, why not in Portugal?

On 28th May 1926, General Manuel Gomes da Costa issued a proclamation to the nation. He had recently retired from the army, and was living in the country near Braga, the northern cathedral city. He was a man whose reputation for eccentricity was equalled only by that of his vanity. He had recently joined a small, secretive, extreme left-wing party, but had been taken, nonetheless, by right-wing officers to the Braga barracks, from where to assert his political leadership. In his broadcast, he said: "The situation in this country has become intolerable to men of honour ... Come with me to save Portugal, to victory or to death. To arms Portuguese!"

In the manner of Mussolini's march on Rome four years before, Gomes da Costa marched on Lisbon. It was the army's fourth attempt in two years to seize power. This time, the republican government collapsed without resistance. The President and several ministers went into exile abroad. The general announced that he had abolished parliament, and that he had appointed a fellow general and a naval commander to run the country with him. It took less than eight weeks for the other officers in the junta to conclude that General Comes da Costa was too stupid and incompetent by far. They promoted him to marshal, and exiled him to the Azores.

General António Carmona was named the new President. He was from a long line of career cavalry officers, and had served as a member of a court martial which had refused to convict a group of army officers who had attempted a previous coup. An admirer of Mussolini, he promoted the marching of young men through the streets in black shirts, and enthusiastically engaged in the oratory of the New Order, speaking of "the divine mission" of "a greater Portugal". He was to remain President of Portugal for twenty-five years, until his death in 1951, in a regime which he described oddly as "a dictatorship without a dictator".

Soon after his accession, however, Carmona found that the financial condition of Portugal was even worse than he and others had supposed. The deficit, as shown in the previous government's budget, turned out to be one fiftieth of the real one. On behalf of the British government, Winston Churchill wrote off almost three quarters of the outstanding war debt. Carmona and his colleagues then applied to the

229

League of Nations for help. Their initial request was for a strikingly modest loan of 12 million pounds, to finance a less than controversial project to modernise Portugal's three major ports. The security they offered was unquestionably sound: a charge on the state's monopoly cigarette industry.

The League of Nations offered to lend the money, but imposed the unusual and un-trusting condition that it be repaid through customs dues on tobacco imports, to be collected not by the government, but by League of Nations officials to be sent from Switzerland for the purpose. The insult was intended. For the only other nations on which such terms had been imposed by the League were those on the losing side in World War I. Portugal was alone among the allies to be treated so humiliatingly. Carmona's rejection of it, as offending the national dignity of Portugal, was greeted as a major national triumph by orchestrated crowds, cheering in the streets of Lisbon. But how were the bills going to be paid?

Carmona turned for help to the only source he and his colleagues could think of, the economics guru of Coimbra University, Oliveira Salazar.

Salazar was then thirty-seven years old. He led a bachelor life in austere lodgings near the university, which he shared with a priest, Manuel Gonçalves Cerejeira, who was to become Cardinal Patriarch of Lisbon at around the same time that Salazar became Prime Minister. The Cardinal's life-long loyalty to Salazar was to bring the Church hierarchy into disrepute through association. For instance he consented to the denial of re-entry to Portugal, of the Bishop of Porto, after an official visit to Rome because he had publicly advocated the cause of the urban poor, against the regime.

Salazar himself had spent eight years studying for the priesthood, and was commonly addressed as "Father" on his visits to his native village in the Dão valley. After taking his minor vows, instead of continuing towards ordination he had switched to studying law, qualifying a year ahead of schedule.

The rector of Coimbra decided it was time for the university to begin offering courses in the new and fashionable quasi-science of economics. As there was nobody in Portugal then obviously qualified to teach it, the university staged a competition for the best essay on the subject. Salazar entered and won, and was appointed the country's first lecturer in economics.

His career had had a touch of the maverick. He had been dismissed from the university for engaging in subversive, pro-monarchist policies, but reinstated a year later. He had then stood for and been elected to parliament, for the Catholic Centre party. He took the train to Lisbon, and attended parliament for a day. Then he returned to Coimbra, and declined to take any further role in democratic politics.

Salazar wrote a series of articles on public finance. In them, he called for balanced budgets and a return to the gold standard. He pointed to the huge quantities of wheat being imported as a major cause of the country's economic woes.

Carmona's offer to him of the post of Minister of Finance was the second he had received. The previous negotiations had broken down two years before, because the military junta refused to grant his basic demand, that the spending of all ministries be brought under his control. The government's finances had continued to worsen, along with the national economy. This time, the generals conceded to Salazar, and at last he moved to the capital.

Salazar raised taxes, and slashed government spending so savagely, that he produced a balanced budget in his first year. Soon, his budgets were producing surpluses, which he used to redeem Portuguese debts abroad. This enhanced the country's credit rating, and so reduced the interest Portugal had to pay on its outstanding debt by almost half. Salazar turned his attention to the massive sums deposited by pensions funds, individual savers and others which were lying virtually idle in the state-owned bank, the Caixa Geral de Depósitos. He borrowed the money, and invested it in massive irrigation projects and the modernisation of transport. He greatly increased the production of rice, in which Portugal became the only European nation to achieve self-sufficiency, as a substitute for imported wheat. He modernised the packaging of dried fruit and the canning of sardines, which he began to trade abroad for flour.

Under his management, unemployment was reduced dramatically, and tax revenues correspondingly increased. Though Portugal did not survive the great depression of the late twenties and early thirties unscathed, it was less adversely affected than most western nations. The country gained a new reputation for financial and social stability. This attracted large amounts of foreign money, along with prosperous foreigners, seeking a secure and tranquil refuge from the troubles of the outside world. Estoril, the then recently built luxurious resort to the west of Lisbon, became home to many British tax exiles, and even more wealthy Spanish families, fleeing republican threats. They were followed by a stream of exiled royalty – Prince Juan, pretender to the throne of Spain, King Carol of Romania, King Umberto of Italy, Regent Horthy of Hungary, and Count Henri, pretender to the throne of France.

Within the government, ministers resigned one after another, in frustration at having no real power. As they left, Salazar often took over their portfolios himself. As well as remaining Minister of Finance, he also served, at varying times, as Minister for Foreign Affairs, for War, for the Colonies and for the Interior. Most of those he replaced were army officers, and it was thus, through Salazar, that the government largely returned to civilian hands.

Eventually, General Carmona, the President, took the logical step, of appointing Salazar Prime Minister, and also commissioned him to oversee the drafting of a new civilian constitution. Salazar himself later described the "New State" he created as "anti-communist, anti-democratic, anti-liberal and authoritarian... a dictatorship of reason and intelligence".

The programme he produced with a team of academics from Coimbra University, from 1930 to 1933, was purportedly based, like the fascist constitutions of Italy, and the future Francoist constitution of Spain, on the "anti-modernist" social teachings of Popes Leo XIII (*Rerum Novarum*) and Pius XI. Political rivalry between parties was "inherently evil". The forward path of virtue was to consist of a homogenised blend of patriotism, Catholicism and financial prudence. In a pseudo-platonic perception, human society was distinct from, and more important than the individuals who belonged to it. Its basic unit was the family. Each family had a head: the husband and father. It was the heads of families who would vote in national elections, to elect the head of the Portuguese national family. The lower house of parliament was to become a kind of family conference centre, where members could make suggestions and pleas and comments, but not have a say in how the national family's head allocated its money. This mirrored the legal principles of household finance: a woman or minor might own property, but it was the prerogative of the male head of the household to manage it.

As a family, the Portuguese nation had no tolerance of class warfare or any other form of internal strife. So trade unions, as well as political parties, were to be disbanded, and strikes outlawed. Industrialists were to be organised into guilds, on a quasi-medieval model, as were members of the professions. Manual workers were to be corralled into syndicates. Representatives from each of these three were to compose the upper chamber of parliament. As such they were to resolve all matters between them peacefully and in the common interest. The Church was to be restored to its traditional role as the nation's mother — and so subject, as all other mothers in Portugal, to the head of the family. As the latter, Salazar declared: "There is no authority to be imposed by one upon another that does not come from God. God has instituted human authority and conferred it on those in charge."

To replace political parties, he created the National Union, "to support the dictatorship, its goals and its actions". All state employees were obliged to sign, every year, an oath to oppose communism, and to swear that they were not Freemasons, whom Salazar had outlawed. Their duties as citizens of the New State were to show "respect for the family, as the ideal social unit, the authority and the dictatorship of the new order, and for the Church's spiritual values and hierarchy." They undertook to work hard and recognise the need for virtue and piety.

It was for women to mind the home, visit the shops and frequent the church, and for men to go out to work. Salazar explained: "In countries where women share with men the work in factories, offices and the professions, the family deteriorates. We defend the family as the foundation stone of a well organised society."

A widowed mother went to court, to claim the right to vote as the head of her family. The judge found in her favour. Salazar rewrote the electoral law, so as to deny her voting rights.

The widow's defeat and Salazar's victory were but symbolic. Those who went to the polls, whether to re-elect the President or a member of the lower chamber, found no choice of candidates. Those who therefore did not bother to vote, found their abstentions counted as votes in favour of the *status quo*.

Demonstrations against dictatorship had begun in Lisbon and Porto, in 1927. A succession of smaller protests, led, in 1929, to a police round-up of the organisers, and their exile to a remote island in the Azores. The first large demonstration against Salazar himself, in the town of Marinha Grande, the centre of the glass-making industry, was in 1934. There were over a thousand arrests, and 150 of his leading opponents were deported, also to the Azores.

Salazar created a new force, the International Police for the State Defense. He introduced state censorship, not just over news, but every form of publication, from books to invitations to children's birthday parties. Newspaper and magazine editors found that the power of the censors was not limited to removing reports and commentaries. The spaces thus freed were filled by them, with articles written by Salazar's team of propagandists. A civilian court of no appeal was established, to try lesser political crimes. A new military court heard the more serious ones, of those – including civilians — accused of "crimes against the security of the state".

The waves of protest continued into the following year, 1935, mainly in the form of strikes against Salazar's creation of fascist-style, state-controlled workers' syndicates, in place of the outlawed trade unions. Salazar responded by ordering the building of a concentration camp at Tarrafal in the Cabo Verde Islands, off the west coast of Africa.

The first deportees were transported there in October, 1936. They were between 20 and 30 years old. Portugal had been one of the first western nations to abolish the death penalty, in the middle of the previous century. Salazar had not reintroduced it, formally. Tarrafal was not a concentration camp in the Nazi meaning of the term. There was no gas chamber, nor other systematic programme of mass-executions. The death penalty remained illegal in Portuguese colonies, as it was in Portugal itself. But the conditions were so harsh, that the governor told his first inmates: "Those who come to Tarrafal, come to die."

Several of these young men did so within the year.

Meanwhile, in Portugal, anti-Salazarist army officers twice attempted to overthrow him. The dictator unveiled a huge statue of his eighteenth-century predecessor, Pombal, and reformed the new secret police force. At his request, Mussolini sent from Italy tutors in new techniques of torture, which would leave no visible physical scars. A huge round followed of arrests, imprisonments, interrogations, and incarcerations in concentration camps.

Mussolini also sent, on a visit to Lisbon, a delegation of young black-shirts, led by his own children. Salazar created the Portuguese Youth Movement. Membership was effectively compulsory, even for

234

the children of the rich and powerful. The uniforms featured belt buckles in the shape of the initial "S". The National Union staged a demonstration in Lisbon to congratulate Salazar on his 52 birthday. His friend, Cardinal Cerejeira, held a clerical conference at Coimbra entitled "The Christian Basis of the New State".

Yet, as World War II loomed over the rest of Europe, Salazar, despite the disgrace to come, had built a strikingly broad popular support within Portugal. He had gone to some pains to distance — in internal propaganda — the New State, not only from Nazism, from which it was indeed distinct, but from the fascism of the rest of southern Europe. If, to outside observers then as now, the differences were largely those of detail, he fairly successfully presented Salazarism as a return to traditional Portuguese values.

The main force of the opposition was in the industrial trade unions, which were relatively small. In other quarters, even his creation of a secret police force was looked on with gratitude, as a sign of his commitment to "law and order". Memories were still vivid, of the anarchy of the first republic, and the military dictatorship that had succeeded it. Discipline had been re-imposed on the armed forces, to make another military coup d'état seem implausible.

Economic chaos, in which many had lost both their jobs and their bank-deposits, had been replaced by, for the middle class, at least, a new prosperity. Civil servants and other state employees were receiving their salaries regularly and in full. Farmers again had a viable market for their produce. Public building projects — new roads, hospitals, prisons, schools, sports stadiums — created new employment, and an increase in national pride.

The greatest of these projects were the hydro-electric schemes, to produce the power to exploit the country's large mineral reserves, of copper, gold, tin and, as was to prove most profitable of all, tungsten.

CHAPTER XIX

WORLD WAR II, BETRAYAL
AND THE FIGHT FOR FREEDOM

At an emergency meeting of the war cabinet in London, in February 1943, Winston Churchill showed his ministers aerial photographs taken the day before, by RAF reconnaissance planes. They were of strange cement structures being built around Calais. They resembled inverted ski jumps, and they were all pointed towards London. It was the dramatic confirmation of the intelligence rumour, begun by a Polish anti-Nazi spy group a few months earlier, that they most dreaded.

The Germans had developed a rocket-propelled bomb; and Hitler planned to use it to devastate the capital of Britain and her empire until its civilians surrendered. The rockets were being mass-produced in factories set up in caves, deep in the Drakenburg mountains and impregnable to attack. Analysts at the Ministry of Economic Warfare advised that the project depended on the ability of the Germans to obtain hugely increased supplies of tungsten. If the rockets' jets' nozzles were made of any metal with a lower melting-point, hardness or elasticity, they would disintegrate before leaving the ground.

The Germans had been buying up this rare metal from occupied Czechoslovakia and neutral Spain, to use in the manufacture of bullets, guns, armour-plating and tanks. As a result, its price had increased by forty times, in the month following the outbreak of World War II. Now, the only plentiful sources of this rare commodity, available to the Germans, were mines in the central mountain range of Portugal, much of whose geological terrain is still permeated with tungsten. The biggest of these, Panasqueira, was English-owned, and soon nationalised by the British government, which also had access to ample supplies of tungsten, from the USA.

It was to secure more tungsten — enough to devastate London — that Albert Speer, Hitler's Minister of War Production, drove from Berlin across Nazi-occupied France and fascist Spain to Lisbon, and paid court to Salazar. Portugal was supposedly neutral in World War II. Since the early 1940s, the British ambassador had asked the dictator to cut off supplies of tungsten to the Germans. The requests were based on the claim that the two countries were "oldest allies", and so Portugal was bound, by treaty, to comply.

Salazar refused. He had previously declined Churchill's demands that he bring Portugal into the war, or at least allow British troops to cross Portuguese territory in Africa, or to ban German citizens from entering Portugal, or to stop broadcasting uncoded weather forecasts for the central Atlantic, from the Azores, which the crews of German ships and submarines could hear. These were calculatedly populist moves: resentment towards the British, for their historical penchant for seeking to profit from their "oldest allies" woes.

To add to Churchill's frustrations, British intelligence was investigating allegations that one of the suppliers to the Germans in Portugal, was a British businessman.

The British government tried outbidding the Germans for the supplies, of which they themselves had no need. The price of tungsten soared again, but the shipments to Germany continued to increase. The Nazis had ample supplies of gold, with which to pay for it, from the reserves they had confiscated from the central banks of the Netherlands, Norway, Belgium, France and Italy.

Churchill and his cabinet ordered MI6 to have its Portuguese section use less orthodox means to cut off the supply. The Secret Intelligence Service's Iberian department, headed by Kim Philby, had no Portuguese section. Its sister organisation, the Special Operations Executive, had been operating in Portugal under the cover of the Shell Oil Company. Its agents had been uncovered by Salazar's secret police, and expelled. Kim Philby turned for help to his friend Graham Greene, who had just been brought back to London from West Africa in disgrace. He had been teasing the head of British Intelligence in Lagos, to the degree that London had feared he would give his boss a heart attack. His last proposal had been for the establishment of a Portuguese touring brothel, to move up and down the west coast of

Africa to seduce and debrief the crews of U-boats on shore leave. Greene was appointed head of all Britain's secret activities in Portugal. He recruited a team of officers, male and female, who entered the country under various guises.

Álvaro Cunhal and the other leaders of the outlawed, underground Communist party, were provided with a "safe house". From there the communists issued a manifesto, printed on one of several presses smuggled from England, declaring themselves ready to participate in a united anti-Salazar front. Before long, they were joined by socialists, liberal Catholics and other democrats. They elected as their chairman, General Norton de Matos. He had resigned in the early years of Salazar's rule from the governorship of Angola, in protest against the dictator's abolition of laws protecting the rights of African workers, and cancellation of Norton de Matos's economic development plan. Salazar had replaced this with an order that Angolan peasants grew cotton for export to Portugal, instead of food for local consumption. After Matos's departure this had led to hunger demonstrations, which had been brutally repressed. Salazar had wanted the cotton so as not to have to spend foreign currency buying it from the southern USA. The owners of the textile mills in northern Portugal protested that the cotton from Angola was too short-fibred, but to no avail. The result had been starvation in central Africa, and the ruination of the Portuguese textile industry's reputation for quality.

Matos was the leader of the Portuguese Freemasons, a group whom Salazar had also outlawed. But neither they nor any of the other clandestine groups rivalled the communists in underground organisation. Arno Barradas, in an essay published in 1996, described both the rigours and the courage of the women who ran the clandestine communist centres, printing copies of underground newspapers, giving refuge to comrades on the run, or those who had escaped from prisons or concentration camps, under the constant eye of the secret police. Out of love for the cause, they were expected to deny themselves marriage or motherhood. Several, at least, succumbed to motherhood, only to be arrested and taken off to the secret police cells, with their infants.

It was the impression common to all the anti-fascists, reported by Dr Barradas, as well as by Professor D.L. Raby in his book *Fascism and Resistance in Portugal*, that employees of the British Secret Service, in addition to giving them financial and other practical support, had conveyed a clear promise. In return for helping the allies to victory, the British would guarantee free and democratic elections in Portugal after the war.

A German ship in Lisbon harbour was loaded with boxes of sand instead of tungsten. Soon after it set sail, and before the ruse was discovered, the ship was blown up. Sardine tins, also filled with sand, were loaded on to a ship in Setúbal. Demonstrations and riots broke out in the shipyards. Railway wagons, loaded with tungsten and bound for Germany, were surreptitiously stencilled with notices claiming that they contained "surplus food" as a gift from the Portuguese to the Germans. Housewives, already angered by food rationing, stood on the tracks, preventing the goods from moving. National guardsmen were ordered in, to disperse them. The women stood their ground. The national guardsmen disobeyed orders to move them forcibly. They were young men; the women could have been — in some case actually were — their mothers.

As well as refusing to stop the tungsten shipments to Germany, Salazar had stalled over the allies' request to set up military bases in the Azores. These Portuguese islands were being used by German U-boats as a safe haven from which to attack convoys bringing food and other vital supplies to Britain. With the help of the U-boats, Hitler had come close to realising his dream of starving the British into defeat. Still Salazar did not budge. The Azorian people themselves have long had closer personal links with the USA than with mainland Portugal itself. Indeed more Azorians live there, than in the Azores themselves. There was no question as to where their sympathies lay. A wave of demonstrations on the island demanded independence from Portugal. In the summer of 1943, seemingly abruptly, Salazar conceded to both the allies' demands. He banned all exports of tungsten. A team of military engineers was allowed to come from Britain to Lisbon, to negotiate the technical details of setting up bases in the Azores. At the same time, Salazar's secret police made a series of arrests of leaders of the anti-Salazar underground. They were obviously working from accurate and up-to-date tip-offs as to identities and whereabouts.

British agents in Portugal then, have denied since any deal or trade-off. It is the case, however, that Graham Greene resigned as head of MI6 Portugal soon afterwards. The first thing he wrote after doing so was an ironic story of Secret Service incompetence and betrayal. In it, he portrayed himself as The Chief, living in the relative safety and comfort of London, in the Albany, down the corridor from his mistress and her husband, dining lavishly and next morning dyspeptically manipulating agents in the field as though they were the creations of his hung-over imagination. It was only when they met violent deaths carrying out his orders, that he realised for the first time that they had been real people. He first wrote the story as a film treatment. It was banned immediately by the British government's film censors, and eventually appeared, rewritten years later and in book form, as *Our Man in Havana*.

For most of World War II, neutral Portugal was the only Atlantic nation in continental Europe not to have been occupied by the Nazis. Lisbon remained open to the British and their allies. It was through here that the International Red Cross transferred mail from detainees on each side to their families on the other. The mail to and from England was carried by KLM flying boats. They were also the main means by which travellers arrived in the Portuguese capital, from Britain. The Lisbon that greeted someone newly arriving from a blacked-out, bomb-ravaged London of food and petrol rationing, and barely heated homes and work places, was a city of tranquillity and light. Malcolm Muggeridge, one of Graham Greene's secret service officers, recalled how, after several years of deprivation, the mere sight of the menus displayed outside Lisbon's restaurants was so bewildering that he ended up ordering a cheese sandwich in a café. *Lisbon* became the title of a musical, now remembered only for its theme song, "Pedro the Fisherman", which ran in the West End of London for years. Ian Fleming was another British secret service man who visited Portugal; and his first James Bond novel, *Casino Royale*, was set in Estoril.

It was said later that Fleming's model for James Bond was Dusco Popov, a Yugoslav who lived in Estoril. The real Popov, cool, aristocratic, and a player for high stakes in the Casino and outside it, was one of Britain's most important double agents. Pretending to the Germans that he was their spy, he fed them false information compiled by disinformation experts. The purpose was to delude the Germans into believing that the allies were to invade occupied Europe at the coast around Calais. This deception was highly successful, enabling the allies to land further south in Normandy, with much-reduced resistance from the Germans and the sparing of many lives. Popov was secretly flown to London and awarded a high honour at a secret ceremony in the palace.

It was also in Lisbon that anti-Hitler Germans, notably the lawyer Otto John and several senior members of the Abwehr, sought help to overthrow the Führer and negotiate a peace through a non-Nazi German government. Kim Philby, as head of the Iberian section of the British Secret Service but, as it was to turn out, a Soviet sympathiser, naturally feared that such a scheme could intensify the German assault on Russia. His brisk reply was that Britain would accept nothing other than total and unconditional surrender. A group of high-ranking Germans in Lisbon however supplied British agents with extremely valuable information, at least one of them paying for this service with his life.

Portugal's great hero of the war years was Aristides de Sousa Mendes. At the time France fell to the Nazis in 1940, Mendes was the Portuguese consul in Bordeaux. He was approached by large numbers of Jews fleeing from certain persecution and probable death; and he readily issued them with Portuguese visas, without charge. When his superiors in Lisbon discovered what he was doing, they ordered him to stop. Mendes called a council of his family, who were with him in Bordeaux. They included his recently married son-in-law. He put to them his predicament. His conscience told him, as a Catholic gentleman, that he had to go on handing out the visas. But this would probably mean eventual disgrace at the hands of the Salazar regime and financial ruin for his family as well as for himself. His wife, daughters and son-in-law not only urged him to go on issuing the visas; they all set to work as his clerks, to process them in greater numbers. As word spread, crowds of Jews gathered each day outside the consulate. The Mendes family took to working through the nights. The Portuguese consul in Bayonne telephoned to say that the street outside his office was jammed with Jewish refugees. What should he do? "Issue them with visas, of course," Mendes told him.

As many as 30,000 Jews were rescued from the Nazis. A few can still be found living quietly in the spa town of Caldas da Rainha. Many more went on to North and South America. Mendes himself was suspended and recalled to Lisbon. He was tried in secret by a disciplinary tribunal on a specimen charge of issuing a visa against orders, to a fugitive who turned out to be, to the embarrassment of Mendes's accusers, an eminent professor of international law. Mendes was forbidden from working, and was granted a minimum pension. He spent the rest of his life in rural anonymity. In 1967, the Israeli government declared him to be a Hero of Conscience and a Righteous Gentile. The Portuguese government itself began to honour him posthumously in 1980, and has been doing so since.

If there had been any doubt before, the ending of the war showed where Portuguese sympathies lay. The streets of Lisbon and other cities filled with people waving Union Jacks and Stars and Stripes, acclaiming the allied victory and shouting anti-Salazar slogans. A few days later, Salazar, in something of a funk, staged a demonstration of his own, having himself implausibly applauded for his "contributions towards the allied victory". He also acknowledged the strength of the feeling against dictatorship, by promising "free elections, as free as in free England".

Soon, however, he was to remark: "I admire the English, their way of life, their respect for their national institutions, their love of freedom. Unfortunately, I know the Portuguese too well, to see that these principles could not be applied here."

While the anti-fascist coalition was forming its United Movement for Democracy, Salazar was supervising the modernisation and enlargement of his secret police, presiding over their weekly policy meetings. A cornerstone of this policy was to round up not merely those who were known to be working for the overthrow of his regime, but those who, it was thought, might begin to do so in the future. The opposition found their campaign countered by obstruction, censorship, harassment and more and more arrests. A large demonstration in Lisbon called on the dictator to make good his promise of a free election. A petition for democracy received 300,000 signatures. In Porto, the organisers kept the identitites of the signatories – apparently over 100,000 — secret. When those collected in Lisbon were handed in, they were immediately turned over to the secret police, who ordered the dismissal of all those who had signed, who were employed by the state. Some of Portugal's most respected professors were, similarly, dismissed from their university posts. Employers in the private sector were also pressured to dismiss workers who had signed it. The elections took place without a single opposition candidate standing.

Some members of the democracy movement recalled what they had believed to be the promise of the allies, to guarantee that free elections in Portugal would be held after the war as a reward for their help to the allied cause. The Germans and others, in defeat, were having democracy thrust upon them. The consensus was that Salazar had persuaded the governments of Britain and the USA that the outcome of any political freedom would be Portugal's takeover by the communists. In reality, the Portuguese Communist party probably contained no more than 7,000 activists. They had long had by far the best organisation of any of the opposition groups, and had shown considerable efficacy in organising anti-Salazar strikes. But the evidence was against any notion that a nation as Catholic as Portugal would bring them to power.

However, the cold war was then getting under way, and "the communist threat" as the only alternative to fascism in Portugal, was to remain an article of faith in Washington, uniting politicians there of such disparate views as Henry Kissinger and Robert Kennedy. Even a seven-year ban on *Time* magazine in Portugal for publishing an article critical of Salazar's excesses, was tolerated by the US authorities.

Salazar called another general election in 1952. There were of course no opposition candidates. One of the dictator's protégés who was elected, Henrique Galvão, noted that in his constituency at least, the electoral officers did not even bother to count the votes before declaring him a winner. Galvão, as a young army officer, had reached the rank of captain, and then been transferred to the Colonial Service. He had organised a highly successful exhibition in Lisbon celebrating the alleged achievements of the Portuguese empire. Now, Salazar appointed him Chief Inspector of Portuguese Colonies in Africa.

Visiting Angola and Mozambique, Galvão was appalled to find how the realities there contradicted the official propaganda which he himself had masterminded. He wrote a report describing the human degradation and the official cynicism he had found, to present to his fellow members of the National Assembly. The secret police confiscated all the copies of it that they could find.

Galvão wrote in his report that almost all the able-bodied men who could do so, had deserted Angola and Mozambique for South Africa. There, not only did they enjoy better wages and living conditions, but, despite the oppression of apartheid, better civil rights. Second, of those men aged between fourteen and seventy who had remained, most judged to be fit to work were rounded up by Portuguese government agents, and put into corrals. From there they were rented out to the owners of mines and plantations, and other private employers. He argued that this system of forced labour was worse than slavery itself. The owner of a slave had capital invested in him, and therefore a self-interest in keeping him alive and fit. An Angolan or Mozambican, rented out by the government, who fell ill or who died, was simply sent back by the employer to be replaced free of extra charge.

Third, those men in Angola and Mozambique who remained in apparent freedom in their villages, cultivating their family lands, were scarcely better off. The claim at the exhibition in Lisbon had been that these peasants were given help by Portuguese technical experts to produce profitable cash crops: coffee, cotton, rice, tea. In fact they had been deprived of any such expertise. Those colonial officials and company agents who visited them were compulsorily purchasing what little there was produced, for derisory prices, and reselling it for huge profits. The peasants were thus unable to support their families financially. Medical services were virtually non-existent. Galvão estimated the rate of infantile mortality to be sixty per cent and, in some areas found that forty per cent of mothers in childbirth, died. Many of those who survived, mothers and children, suffered from bilharzia, which was endemic. Sick mothers and orphaned children were to be found everywhere.

Historians of Portuguese colonialism in Africa, under Salazar, have since suggested that his statistics on health were probably exaggerated, but that the rest of his report was a model of moderation. Salazar, had, in all but name, reintroduced the slavery his liberal predecessors had outlawed about a century before. The dictator's philosophy was expressed thus: "The negro does not work, unless compulsorily obliged to do so."

The report was suppressed before it could even be rejected, let alone rebutted. Galvão resigned. He declared that the situation in Portuguese Africa represented a total betrayal of traditional Portuguese values of humanism and justice. The fault was not with the Portuguese people, but with "an illegitimate government that the nation continues to endure only because it is forced to do so by the outrages of the police".

Some of the fault also lay with Britain and the United States, which were providing Salazar with financial aid at home, and diplomatic support abroad. "By their support of the dictatorship, they have not merely betrayed their own ideal of democracy. They have placed obstacles in the way of Portuguese democrats, trying to achieve liberation."

Galvão was arrested, as he later remarked, "by some men from the secret police, behaving like gangsters holding up a bank". They held him in solitary confinement, tortured him, had him found guilty of treason, and sent him to a concentration camp. After seven years of incarceration there, Galvão became seriously ill. He believed it to be as a result of an attempt by the secret police to poison him with arsenic.

He was transferred to the Santa Maria Hospital in Lisbon. Guards worked two at a time in shifts, keeping him under constant watch. The window of his room was barred. Galvão escaped through a small bathroom window on the seventh floor. He edged himself from ledge to ledge, until he reached an open window letting on to a corridor. He found a staff changing room, in which he was able to disguise himself as a doctor. He walked out of the main lobby into the street, and then to the Argentinian embassy, where he asked for political asylum. The ambassador negotiated his safe conduct to the airport, and he was flown to Buenos Aires.

Less than two years later, in January 1961, the world awakened to hear with astonishment the news that the *Santa Maria*, the luxury cruise liner and the pride of the Portuguese merchant fleet, had been captured. Most of the passengers were Americans, on a Caribbean cruise. Some of these reported, via ship to shore radio, that the pirates had moved the third-class passengers into vacant first-class suites. They were organising champagne and dancing parties.

Galvão and twenty-three other exiled Portuguese democrats had boarded the *Santa Maria* the evening before, disguised as passengers and technicians. They were too short of money to buy enough tickets, so others had come on board as visitors and hidden. They had with them a small assortment of weapons they had bought on the Venezuelan black market. In the middle of the night, they stormed the ship's bridge. The duty officer refused to surrender. He was shot and later died. He was the only officer or crew member to resist. The captain himself, awakened in his cabin, surrendered immediately. Galvão remarked later that this man, one moment authoritarian, the next snivelling and cringing, personified the cowardice and moral turpitude to which Salazar had tried to reduce the whole nation. Several of his officers quickly changed sides, and joined the pirates.

Salazar, invoking the Nato alliance, asked all fellow members to help the Portuguese navy hunt and re-capture the *Santa Maria*. He declared that Galvão was known to be a communist, and that the internationally accepted punishment for piracy was to be hanged to death from the ship's tallest mast.

Most Nato nations ignored his appeal. France publicly rejected it. Britain sent two Royal Navy frigates, and the United States a warship and reconnaissance planes. Galvão was no ideologue, but an idealist and a devout Catholic. He renamed the ship *Our Lady of Liberty* and issued a statement by radio, saying that his was no act of piracy. He cited Hayward and Hapworth, the acknowledged authorities on international maritime law, a copy of whose textbook he had brought with him on board. A ship was the sovereign territory of the country whose flag it flies. *Our Lady of Liberty* was a part of Portugal, which he and his colleagues had liberated from an illegal dictatorship, so as to restore it to constitutional rule.

John Kennedy, the new President of the USA, himself took legal advice and concluded that Galvão's case was a sound one. Britain soon joined with the USA in withdrawing its ships from the chase.

Galvão's original intention had been to sail *Our Lady of Liberty* to Angola, as the signal for an anti-fascist uprising there. Shortage of fuel and pressure from the US government persuaded him instead to sail to Brazil. The American passengers disembarked at Recife, virtually all of them — according to the remarks they made to the waiting press — now propagandists for a free Portugal. Galvão himself was escorted with honours to the Brazilian national assembly, where he received a standing ovation.

Salazar remained dictator, but his domestic support had waned. The rising living standards of much of the rest of Europe, the return there to democracy, the free discussion of ideas, values and aspirations, had ever greater appeal to a nation that was growing out of its own ultra-nationalism, and seeing itself as narrowly provincial. Salazar responded to the unease and impatience, by increasing the powers of, and recruitment to, the secret police, imposing still more rigorous censorship, and cutting back on the hidden enemy, education — particularly at university level. Thousands of students were dismissed from their degree courses, and sent to Africa as conscripts, to quell the colonial rebellions.

Abroad, the perception of Salazar changed radically. The stalwart of civilisation, standing alone against the Soviet takeover of Portugal, was now seen as no more than an isolated and humiliated tyrant. That same year, the Indian army invaded and conquered Goa and Portugal's other colonial enclaves in India. Both Britain and the USA refused to intervene with so much as a token diplomatic protest. Amnesty International was founded in London, with its first objective to secure the release of pro-democracy university students being held in secret police cells in Lisbon. Álvaro Cunhal, the legendary leader of the Portuguese communists, was sprung from his heavily guarded prison cell, and reappeared triumphantly in Moscow. General Humberto Delgado, who had stood as an anti-fascist candidate for the presidency in 1958, and had, many believed, received a majority of votes, had immediately afterwards had to flee from the secret police and leave the country. Now, in Brazil, he became the focus of an ever growing opposition to Salazar overseas. Salazar's response to the inevitable surrender of Goa, was to have the commander and his senior officers, who had acted so effectively to avoid what could have easily been a huge civilian carnage, arrested, humiliated by court martial, and harshly punished. His secret police were to murder Delgado in Spain; you can see the names of his murderers today, in the Museum of the Resistance and the Republic in Benfica. In Angola, there was a major uprising against the cruelties imposed by the state. It was ruthlessly suppressed, with the loss of many lives. But a new generation of young conscript officers, while taking part in the suppression, had begun to discuss among themselves how much longer such oppression could or should be allowed to survive in Portugal or in her overseas territories.

CHAPTER XX

FREEDOM AT DAWN

At 24 minutes past midnight, on the morning of Wednesday, 24th April 1974, José Vasconcelos, chat-show host and disc-jockey, was in his studio in Radio Club Portugues. He lowered the needle of his record player on to a single he had never played before, "Land of Brotherhood". The lyric had been banned by the Salazarist censors. Several of the people who heard it were first-time listeners to Vasconcelos's show. They had switched on and tuned in, in response to a review of the show published in the newspaper the previous afternoon saying it had improved so much, it had become "obligatory listening".

These new listeners were young army officers. Both the newspaper review and the playing of the banned record were their coded signal that the moment had come to put into action the plan they had spent the previous few months devising at secret meetings, several of them held at weekends in the Alentejo countryside. At dawn, early-rising Lisboans found tanks and armoured cars positioned so that their guns faced the frontages of key government and military buildings, major police stations, the airport, state broadcasting studios and other key installations.

Salazar had died in 1970. The deck-chair in which he was reclining, while having a pedicure, on the terrace of his holiday home in Estoril, had collapsed. His head had hit the floor, but he had appeared to suffer nothing worse than a superficial bruise. Two weeks later, he began to complain of "feeling very old". He was taken to hospital, where a blood clot was found on his brain. He underwent surgery, but died.

When l visited his birth-place, in the Dão valley, 35 years later, the small town's memorial to him — a mural of painted tiles depicting his life — had neither been removed, nor maintained. It reflected a lingering ambivalence towards Salazar, found in many other parts of the country. The dictator's policies had rescued Portugal from the plight it was in, when he took over, but at the same time, they had branded Portugal, internationally, as fascist, because he had been so influenced by Mussolini and Franco. Yet in imposing his will, he had not resorted to brutality on anything approaching their scale. Possibly less than a dozen of his political opponents died as a result of torture at the hands of his secret police. However, Catholic teaching, which he professed, is clear that how many people you torture to death is not the issue. It is whether you do so at all. The thriving survivor to foreign revulsion of the treatment of political prisoners in Portugal, in the latter days of Salazar, is Amnesty International, which was founded in direct response.

Were he to be alive today, would he have been charged with crimes against humanity? Professor Fernando d'Orey, a strong exponent of Salazar's economic reforms, suggested in conversation, after the arrest of Pinochet in London, that the Portuguese dictator would have also faced a demand for extradition from Spain, for a crime nearer home than those in Chile: his forcible return of Spanish republican refugees, who had sought asylum in Portugal, to Franco's forces, who shot them in the bull ring in Badajoz. His denial of human rights in Africa remains as a terrible stain on the country's good name.

Was he a fascist or an autocratic patriot, in the foosteps of Pombal? *The Columbia Encyclopedia* defines fascism as a "totalitarian philosophy of government that glorifies state and nation and assigns to the state control over every aspect of national life... Its essentially vague and emotional nature facilitated the development of unique national varieties, whose leaders often deny indignantly that they are fascists at all".

Salazar was succeeded as Prime Minister by Marcelo Caetano. Caetano, who had been Salazar's favourite protégé, was a lawyer who had developed an affection for Italian-style fascism as a student, and who had helped Salazar to draft his "New State" constitution. After serving in various ministries, and orchestrating repressions in the colonies in Africa, he had been appointed rector of Lisbon University. He had resigned in protest after uniformed police stormed the campus to disperse a student demonstration. His protest had not been however against the police savagery, but their effrontery for having set foot on university territory without first seeking and receiving his permission. Now, he was awakened at his home at 2.00 am, by his minister of defence, who alerted him of unauthorised troop movements in the capital. Caetano took refuge in the National Republicain Guard's headquarters, in the Carmo barracks.

By late morning, the barracks was surrounded by the cavalry. National guardsmen opened fire, briefly, but Caetano agreed to receive a delegation of young army officers. They told him that during the night Portugal had been freed from fascism, and that he was under arrest. They demanded that he resign immediately.

Caetano said that he would resign, only to General Spínola, whom he telephoned. Spínola said he had nothing to do with the coup, but came to the barracks to confer with the rebel officers. Then, Spinola went in, to talk with Caetano, and accept his resignation, on their behalf.

That evening, the officers named Spinola as head of an eight-man Council for National Recovery. Spinola, until recently a pro-fascist — during World War II, openly pro-Nazi — and a late convert to democracy, was among the many who could not at first believe that a coup could have succeeded so easily. But within two days, Caetano, three of his most senior ministers, and the President of the Republic Admiral Américo Tomás, were flown, under arrest, to exile in Brazil. Almost half a century of fascism in Portugal was now indeed over.

The only resistance to the military coup came from a group of secret policemen ensconced in their headquarters. As soldiers approached the building, the secret police now opened fire on them. The two deaths and thirteen people injured were the only casualties of what quickly became known as "the revolution of flowers", after the carnations which the soldiers put into the muzzles of their guns. Twenty years later, there is hardly a person in Portugal who cannot instantly and vividly recall where they were and what they were doing, at the moment they realised that fascism had collapsed. Journalists who were on the roof of the Avenida Palace Hotel, recall seeing the streets filled with crowds of people cheering and embracing the soldiers. Young conscripts, awaiting with dread being sent to Africa to fight in the terrible colonial wars, remember the gates of their barracks being thrown open, and being told they were free to leave, but must take off their uniforms and put on their civilian clothes.

The daughter of a wealthy family recalls their uniformed maids going out into the front garden, to watch the soldiers' jubilant parade, but being called back inside by her mother, fearful that the sight of so many domestic servants would indicate that they were no friend of the popular masses. Several of the richest families, who had been prominent supporters of Salazar, fled abroad, taking what cash and valuables they could with them, and installed themselves in suites in the Ritz hotels in Paris and London, and similarly de luxe establishments in Rio de Janeiro. But aside from them and from the majority of the secret policemen, who were allowed to flee unmolested and grateful to be left alive, how had the support for Salazar's dark experiment in re-moulding society, the "new state", evaporated?

Although not even Salazar himself, from the evidence of his own conduct, seems to have believed that he had long had the support of the majority of Portuguese, his regime had clearly had its sympathisers. Support for him had been more broadly based than on a handful of families whose business interests had prospered so enormously, during the years of state-directed economy. Very few people had been attracted by his quasi-fascist ideology. There had been middle-class people, appreciative of the peace and apparent stability that they saw as characterising the Salazar years. There had been an aura of order, far removed from the activities of the secret police — one of efficient postal services, of cleanly swept streets, of an extraordinarily low crime rate, of railway stations freshly painted and with neatly tended flower beds, from which, à la Mussolini, the trains left on time. The dictator had also won respect for his lack of show, for a frugality in his personal life, for his genuine financial incorruptibility, for his pose of loving the Portuguese as his family.

The source of the fatal collapse in support for the regime was not within Portugal itself, but its colonies in Africa. As the wars of independence in Angola and Mozambique spread like summer fires, the regime abandoned the benign and cosy family image Salazar had striven for so long to propagate. The telegrams began to arrive at the homes of conscripts serving there, bringing news of their deaths. Photographs of the young men who had been killed, in a cause in which they had no interest let alone belief, were put on the walls of village churches, by grief-stricken parents. In chapels, sanctuaries and shrines throughout the country, there were flowers and candles representing prayers for those who had been killed, and that their comrades might be spared. With the help and encouragement of their families, young men approaching conscriptable age escaped from Portugal, despite strict border, dock and airport checks to prevent them doing so. Professional men who had been pillars of the Salazarist establishment suddenly saw the regime in a new light, as they realised that their sons were seen as so much fodder for the wars in Africa. Substantial communities of young Portuguese draft-dodgers developed in Amsterdam, Geneva, Paris and South America.

To the Portuguese in Africa, Lisbon's policy of armed resistance to the inevitable appeared still more insane. A large number of civilians moved down to South Africa. Today in Johannesburg alone, there is still a Portuguese population of 400,000. Senior officials risked their careers by campaigning openly for the anti-fascist, anti-war movement. To this, by now, the vast majority of officers in the armed forces also belonged.

General António de Spínola was the commander of Portuguese troops fighting against the liberation army in Guinea, in West Africa. His local authority had been enhanced by Lisbon, by his being named also the country's civil governor. In 1973 Spínola told the government in Lisbon that the Portuguese had no prospect whatsoever of victory. The only realistic option was to try to negotiate with the liberation movement a ceasefire during which the Portuguese soldiers could be evacuated. Otherwise many, perhaps most, of these would be killed, to no purpose. Caetano rebuked him. Spínola returned to Lisbon and, after a fierce dispute with the Prime Minister, resigned.

His status as the hero and leader of the anti-fascist military officers was consolidated still further by the book he then wrote. Banned in Portuguese Africa, Spínola nonetheless managed to have it printed and distributed, in Portugal, in February, 1974. It is still the best-selling contemporary Portuguese book. Titled *Portugal and the Future*, its thesis was that the country's system of state control of the economy and society was unworkable. In Africa, Portugal should hold referendums. The peoples of Angola and Mozambique would be offered two choices: to become independent and sever their links with Portugal, or to become independent and join in an association of Portuguese-speaking nations, roughly based on the British Commonwealth. In Portugal itself, there were not only to be elections, but a lot of basic freedoms, as enjoyed in the rest of western Europe. The ex-Prime Minister, Caetano, said later: "The moment I read it, I realised the regime was finished."

And so it was, less than two months later. But this did not mean an immediate transition to democracy, to the disillusion of many. Spínola formed a government in which he included the returned exiles Mário Soares, the socialist leader, and Alvaro Cunhal, the communist. The real power in the streets however seemed to be in the hands of a group of extreme leftist military officers, led by Otelo Saraiva de Carvalho. They set up road blocks, harassing people they suspected of being "class enemies". They stole money, watches, cars; they sequestered houses. They illegally arrested the Duke of Palmela and other members of the nobility. They seized some members of the Espirito Santo banking family. Others escaped abroad.

The revolutionaries nationalised all the banks and many of the major industries, without compensation. Likewise, they seized large areas of farmland and cork-tree estates, claiming to be doing so in the name of the peasants and workers.

Spínola had resigned, and tried to rally right-wing officers to overthrow their communist colleagues, now in effective control of government. This was a fiasco. Spínola narrowly avoided capture by the Marxist-Leninist commissars, by commandeering an army helicopter and escaping to refuge in Spain. The promises of free elections began to seem as illusory as they had been under Salazar. In Washington, Dr Henry Kissinger, the Secretary of State, said that Portugal was a hopeless cause. The country's unavoidable future was to become western Europe's Cuba. The US embassy in Lisbon had taken on the appearance, which it still by and large maintains, of being more a fortified enclave than a diplomatic mission.

Censorship of the press had been abolished, along with fascism. Otelo, as Major Carvalho was by now universally known, sent into the editorial department of newspapers "guiders", who in effect replaced the copy takers, sitting at the right hand of the editors, selecting items for them for publication and rejecting others. As almost all the press had by now been nationalised, there was only one remaining editor, Raul Rego of *Republica*, who held out. He had spent long periods in the Salazar regime's torture cells and concentration camps in the cause of editorial freedom, and was not now going to concede it to a left-wing dictatorship. Journalists and other supporters of the free press organised a demonstration in his defence, outside the presidential palace. Otelo ordered in armoured cars and troops to disperse it.

Television was already owned by the state at the time of the April revolution, when it had been occupied by the military. Marxist-Leninists had accused the military of denying the far-left sufficient air time to present their case fully and in their own words. Liberal programme-managers and journalists were sacked. Their leftist successors arranged for a four-hour live political show, for Álvaro Cunhal to enlarge on his Communist party's plans for Portugal's future. But they also invited to the programme, Mário Soares, the socialist leader, confidant that Cunhal would wipe the studio floor with him. It was, for them, a disastrous miscalculation.

There was hardly a Portuguese who did not watch the television that evening. Though most did not yet own sets of their own, they gathered in front of those in the cafés, bars and corner shops. The two politicians had known each other for a long time. Soares was the son of a headmaster, and, as a pupil in his father's school, he had studied under Cunhal, who was employed there as the head of geography.

Both men were graduates of the secret police cells, of solitary confinement, the concentration camp and exile. Cunhal had spent a large part of his adult life underground, organising the party's secretive network. Soares had opposed fascism in the open: after qualifying in law, he became a full-time civil rights worker, specialising in the defence before the courts of those charged with crimes against the state. He was such an irritant to the authorities, that after he had been arrested and tortured several times, Salazar had had him banished to the tropical island of São Tomé, off the coast of West Africa. There, instead of becoming inactive as had been expected, he resumed his law practice, defending minor officials prosecuted on false charges for trying to organise themselves into a trade union. The response of the colonial judges before whom Soares appeared, was to mete out to his clients much harsher sentences than would have been the case had they been represented by any other lawyer or by none at all. After a customs officer, who should have been, at worst, fined half a week's wages, was sentenced to prison for ten years, Soares was allowed to return to Portugal. There he had been constantly harassed by the secret police. After a few months, he had escaped to Paris where he had founded the Portuguese Socialist party.

After the revolution, Spínola had appointed him Foreign Minister. Soares had travelled around Europe, drumming up support for a free

Portugal. The Foreign Ministry had no funds to pay for this, but socialist parties in other countries, co-ordinated by Britain's Labour party, rallied round. He had quickly established himself as a new and impressive figure on the European political scene. Dr Kissinger had dismissed him, deriding him as "a Portuguese Kerensky", alluding to the liberal Russian politician who had presided over the downfall over the Czars in Russia to pave the way for democracy, only to be toppled by the Bolsheviks. The communists in Portugal were already presenting Soares as Public Enemy Number One, and a traitor to the anti-fascist cause.

The television programme that featured Cunhal and Soares, in November 1975, could not be described as a confrontation, or even a debate, between the two leaders and their ideologies. Soares was alert, warm in his manner, lively in his speech. He addressed the viewers as equals. He seemed thoroughly at ease with the situation, confident but in no way arrogant, friendly and open. Cunhal had been raised in the authoritarian mould. He sat stiffly, upright, unsmiling and seemingly unmoving. He read out the manifesto the Portuguese Communist party had prepared. It was a very long document, written in the frigid, bureaucratic vocabulary used by nobody else but Stalinist ideologists. If Soares asked a question or raised a point, Cunhal would pause to let him do so, but then made no response. Without even an acknowledgement, he would continue reading his tract, droning on and on.

Well before the end of the four hours, most Portuguese had come to the consensus that Cunhal was little else but Salazar in a new guise. That the communist side had been decisively defeated in the public debate, was not lost on Otelo and his fellow extremist left-wing army officers. They ordered in platoons of paratroopers to seize military installations in and around Lisbon which had been in the hands of liberal members of the armed forces. By the fourth week of November, to many more people than Kissinger, the cause of a free Portugal seemed to be as good as extinct.

Then came one of the most remarkable reversals in Portuguese history. General Ramalho Eanes, a liberal veteran of the African wars, and a group of his fellow officers, had kept their beliefs to themselves, for fear of being arrested or even executed. Soares had made such an impression on them, as well as on most civilians, that they found their courage, and resolved to risk all to restore Portugal to democracy. On the evening of 24th November, under Eanes's command, they staged a series of lightning raids on communist military positions, and took them over. Cunhal, to his credit, issued a statement calling on communists in the military to back down, for fear of causing terrible bloodshed. Otelo and his group were arrested, and later tried for crimes against humanity.

The following April, 1976, exactly two years after the revolution, Mário Soares was elected Prime Minister. A grateful civilian electorate voted Ramalho Eanes to the Presidency, with 61 per cent of the vote.

The situation of the Portuguese in many ways remained bleak. Not only was there all the wreckage of the past year, but the deterioration caused by almost half a century of Salazarism. Under him, the country had become the most backward in western Europe. It had the highest rate of illiteracy, and of tuberculosis. Salazar had thought that peasants were happier, the less they knew. His famous, and perhaps most cynical, dictum had been to feed them and the rest of the workers on "Fado, Fátima and Football". He had held that to issue drugs with which to fight TB without charging the patients and their families for them, would weaken the moral backbone of the Portuguese. And Portugal was again facing a national debt to foreign lenders of such immensity, economists in Lisbon said it would take two generations of national sacrifice to bring it down to an acceptable level. Then, with the withdrawal of even token Portuguese rule from the colonies in Africa, Portugal received a tidal wave of 400,000 refugees. Most were the descendants of lower-middle-class and working-class Portuguese, who had gone there to find an environment in which progress in their careers would not be blocked by their low caste. Now, most were penniless, living a family to a room in hotels abandoned by foreign tourists and businessmen, with barely a change of clothes.

There were shortages of petrol, and even of cash in the banks. Francisco Sá Carneiro, the founder of the Social Democrat party, and the highly respected centrist voice of politics, was killed when the small plane in which he was flying, crashed. Many saw behind this tragedy the hand of anti-democrats, whether of the right or of the left. Soares spoke out against a sentiment felt by some Portuguese that they were inherently incapable as a nation, of conducting themselves as a modern democracy and economy.

Under his massaging of the national psyche, signs of recovery became apparent. Part of the post-revolutionary crisis had been caused by the flight abroad of more than 10,000 trained managers, engineers and others, on whom the functioning of Portuguese industry and commerce depended. Now they were returning, and getting the factories and the construction projects going again. While in exile abroad, many of the young draft dodgers had not been idling. They too began to return home, bringing with them qualifications in medicine, technology, architecture, and as university teachers. Among the superficially pitiful refugees, there were found to be not only more doctors, architects, engineers and academics, but energetic entrepreneurs, applying their business expertise to the creation of new industries and other companies. Portugal's rate of economic growth accelerated and then overtook that of the rest of Europe. The country became known, in the financial press abroad, as Europe's "tiger economy". Prudent and highly sophisticated management of the national debt reduced it within fifteen years to one of the lowest in the western world.

New parliamentary legislation made Portugal, in its goals at least, one of the most socially enlightened. Its laws protected the rights of women and children more than those in the United Kingdom. There were huge improvements in the state health service, in hygiene, and in schooling. Government has changed hands peaceably several times. There is no longer a fascist party — the furthest to the right is the Partido Popular, whose ideology is no more extreme than that of other "popular" parties elsewhere in Europe. It seems unable to attract as much as ten per cent of the vote. The communists have hard-earned respect for efficiency, integrity and enlightenment in local government. Their administration of the city of Évora is widely upheld as a model of excellence. But they have never gained a foothold in national politics any larger than that of the right.

For all their continuing problems and challenges, the achievement of the Portuguese during their first fifteen years of freedom became a beacon of hope, when the nations of eastern Europe suddenly found that they could free themselves from two generations of despotism. They saw that Portugal, too, had during this century experienced in succession military dictatorship, fascism and communism. They had been through the sense of blight that followed such a liberation. They too had been told that their case was a hopeless one, and that they could not expect to recover economically, for two generations at least. They too had been told that their only hope was to continue a life of deprivation and self-denial.

From Prague, Havel came to Lisbon on one of his first trips, to confer with Mário Soares, by now Portugal's President. Czech judges were among groups of professionals sent here, to learn how to function under a democratic constitution. Portuguese production engineers went to Hungary, to advise on the modernisation of factories; Lech Walensa came from Poland, and gave thanks at Fátima for his nation's liberation.

Portugal's importance today to the outside world is proof that other countries, traumatised in the twentieth century, have cause to live in hope.

A NOTE ON SOURCES

I am a reporter, not an academic, and *The First Global Village* is neither a text-book nor a dissertation, but a personal narrative, about how the Portugal of today came into being,

It is the result, above all, of eight years spent living, working and travelling among the Portuguese; and of further journeys in search of their history, in North Africa, Andalucia and Burgundy.

I am grateful to our many Portuguese friends, who have contributed their own experiences of the events leading up to the return of democracy, towards the end of the twentieth century, and of the country's remarkable recovery, enabling its entry into the European Union, and participation in the euro.

In addition, I have consulted several hundred written sources, in Portuguese, English and French, in the original languages, and in Arabic, German and Latin in translation. Many are mentioned in the text, others in the list of "Further Rading" below. These sources include not only books, but publications, mostly Portuguese, ranging from daily newspapers to learned journals. Since the ending of censorship in the late 1970s, thousands of previously secret documents have been released, for public inspection. A new generation of archaeologists and historians, freed from the ideological constraints of either the extreme right or left, are re-examining the past, in a new light.

These developments are closely followed by such daily newspapers as *O Público* and *Diario de Notícias,* the weekly *Expresso,* popular magazines, such as *História,* pamphlets published by the British Historical Association of Lisbon, monographs which have appeared in *Brotéria,* the scholarly journal of the Portuguese province of the

Jesuits, and the bulletins of the Camoens Institute, at Columbia University, New York.

The works of Livy, Pliny the Elder and Plutarch provide fascinating information about the immediately pre-Roman and Roman era. This has been greatly expanded by archaeological research, in areas ranging from the Romans' extraordinary feats of engineering — such as in deep-shaft mining and dam construction — to the introduction of Christianity to western Europe, in which recently uncovered evidence contradicts folklore.

The pioneer of research into the Islamic period was Reinhart Dozy of the University of Leyden, in the 1850s. His *L'Histoire des Mussulmans d'Espagne et de Portugal* was the result of his years of studying records of the period, which the Moors had taken with them, in their flight to Morocco. More recently, a symposium at New York University in 1975, chaired by Professor Bayley Winder, brought together eminent western and Arab scholars of the Islamic contribution to the development of European civilisation, starting in Iberia. Their papers were subsequently published by Massachusetts Institute of Technology, under the title *The Genius of Arab Civilisation.*

Perhaps the most contested era of Portuguese history is, as I have mentioned in the introduction, the "reconquest" — the forcible expulsion of the Moslems, and the country's incorporation into Christendom. The conventional Portuguese account is challenged severely from non-Portuguese sources, in particular the records of the Council of Troyes and of the founding of the Knights Templar, and the letters of St Bernard of Clairvaux in Burgundy. I am particularly indebted to Brother Irénée Vallery-Radot, the Cistercian biographer of St Bernard.

My account of the Jews in Portugal, the Inquisition, and their expulsion, is based on Sephardic Jewish sources, and on modern studies of the meticulous records kept by the Inquisition itself. The era of Pombal remains an historical minefield, contested not least by the Jesuits, and those who see them as the opponents of modernisation then. I have depended on both sides for my version of events, so it will probably satisfy neither. My intention has been to be just to both.

By consensus, *The History of Portugal,* written by Alexandre Herculano, during a period of enlightened government, without censorship, in the mid-nineteenth century, is the first major work in the field. Subsequent major and authoritative histories include those of Oliveira Martins, available at the time of writing, only in Portuguese and French. In modern times, the two-volume history compiled by Oliveira Marques — and now translated into and published in English — is an outstanding scholarly work. By far the most popular of Portugal's modern historians is José Hermano Saraiva, who delights in both demolishing ultra-nationalist legends, particularly of the Salazar dictatorship, and replacing them with more convincing causes for his fellow Portuguese to have pride in their past.

In drawing upon foreign — and particularly English — accounts of Portugal's history, I found, repeatedly, that caution is needed. Britain has claimed a vested interest in Portugal, almost since its foundation in the middle ages which has sometimes been in conflict with the well-being of the Portuguese themselves. This bias recurs in ways which are relatively obvious, from grossly exaggerating the role of Henrique the Navigator in the Portuguese discovery of a world beyond Europe, because he was half English, to suggesting that Britain claimed southern Africa from the Portuguese, for the benefit of its inhabitants, rather than for Cecil Rhodes to acquire immense wealth. Other assertions, such as Livermore's, that Portugal has no natural frontiers with Spain — an obvious absurdity to anyone who has travelled along them — represent a view that implicitly challenges Portugal's right to independence.

The noble exception, among English historians of the Portuguese, is Charles Boxer. Ironically he was banned from entering Portugal for many years, during Salazar's dictatorship, though afterwards he became greatly honoured here. His accounts of Portugal's "seaborne empire", some of which appear in the reading list below, are masterly.

SUGGESTIONS FOR FURTHER READING

This list of books, in English, includes publications up to the year 2000. Some are original, others translations or adaptations of manuscripts, going back about a thousand years; or reprints of eighteenth and nineteenth century works. The list is far from comprehensive: the catalogue of the British Library lists over 50,000 items, under the category of "Portuguese history" alone. In my selection, I have excluded college text-books, though I have not sought to avoid academic works, where appropriate. It is intended to guide the reader, who wishes to begin to look more closely into one or more of the topics I have covered. It is eclectic, both in its range of specialist areas, and in the varying points of view they represent, many of which are not my own. The dates of publication (in brackets), given when available, are, where possible, of the latest and so most easily available edition. Spellings of Portuguese names have followed the English form, for readers' ease of reference in library and booksellers' catalogues.

Alden, Dauril
Royal Government in Colonial Brazil (1968)

Andersen, Hans Christian
A Visit to Portugal, 1866 (1972)

Anderson, James M.
Portugal, 1001 Sights, an archeological and historical guide by the University of Exeter (1994)

Baretti, Giuseppe
A Journey from London to Genoa through England, Portugal and Spain (1970)

Beamish, Huldine
Cavaliers of Portugal (1968)

Bernard of Clairvaux, Saint
Letters (1953)

Berneo, Nancy
The Revolution within the Revolution: Workers' Control in Rural Portugal
(1986

Bloom, Murray Teigh
The Man Who Stole Portugal (1966)

Bodian, Mirian
Hebrews of the Portuguese Nation (1997)

Boxer, Charles R.
From Lisbon to Goa, 1500-1750 (1991)

Boxer, Charles R.
Salvador de Sá and the Struggle from Brazil and Angola, 1602-1686 (1952)

Boxer, Charles R.
South China in the 16th Century: Being the Narratives of Galeote Pereira, Father Gaspar da Cruz O.P., etc. (1953)

Boxer, Charles R.
Portuguese Society in the Tropics (1965)

Boxer, Charles R.
The Tragic History of the Sea 1589-1622, 2 vols.
(1959, 1968)

Boxer, Charles R.
The Portuguese Seaborne Empire 1415-1825

Bradford, Sarah
The Englishman's Wine: The Story of Port

Bragança Cunha, Vicente de
Eight centuries of Portuguese Monarchy (1911)

Brearley, Mary
Hugo Gurgeny: Prisoner of the Lisbon Inquisition (1948)

Brett, Michael
The Moors: Islam in the West

Brettell, Caroline B.
Men Who Migrate, Women Who Wait (1986)

Bruce, Neil
Portugal, The Last Empire (1975)

Camões, Luís de
The Lusiads (translated by William Atkinson) (1952)

Charles, Sir Oman
A History of the Peninsular War (1999)

Cheke, Marcus
Dictator of Portugal: A Life of the Marques of Pombal (1938)

Coates, Austin
City of Broken Promises: A Story of Macau

Collins, Roger
The Arab Conquest of Spain (1995)

Corkill, David
The Portuguese Since 1974

Custódio, José
National Palace, Sintra

Duffy, James
Portuguese Africa (1968)

Evans, Gillian R.
Bernard of Clairvaux (2000)

Featherstone, Donald
Campaigning with the Duke of Wellington: Guide to the Battles of Spain and Portugal (1993)

Ferreira, Hugo Gile
Portugal's Revolution: Ten Years On (1986)

Fielding, Henry
Journal of a Voyage to Lisbon (1855)

Gallagher, Tom
Portugal: A 20th Century Interpretation (1983)

Gervers, Michael
The Second Crusade and the Cistercians (1992)

Góis, Damião de
Lisbon on the Renaissance (1999)

Graham, Lawrence S.
In Search of Modern Portugal: The Revolution and Its Consequences

Gunn, Geoffrey C.
Encountering Macao, A Portuguese City State (1996)

Hamilton, Russell G.
Voices from Empire: A History of Afro-Portuguese Literature

Hufgard, M. Kilian
St Bernard of Clairvaux: A Theory of Art (2000)

Isherwood, Christopher
Christopher and His Kind (1988)

Janitschek, Hans
Mario Soares: Portrait of a Hero (1979)

Levenson, Jay A. (editor)
The Age of the Baroque in Portugal (1993)

Lowe, K. J. P.
Cultural Links between Portugal and Italy in the Renaissance (2000)

Marques, A. H. de Oliveira
History of Portugal; Vol. 1: *From Lusitania to Empire*; Vol. II: *From Empire to Corporate State* (1971, 1972)

Marques, Susan Lowndes
A Traveller's Guide to Portugal (1954)

Maxwell, Kenneth
The Making of Portuguese Democracy

Maxwell, Kenneth
Pombal: Paradox of the Enlightenment (1995)

McGuire, Brian P.
The Difficult Saint: Bernard of Clairvaux (1991)

Melville, C. P. (Editor)
Christians and Moors in Spain: Arabic Sources 711-1501 (1992); *Texts of the Reconquest* (1990)

Mendes Pinto, Fernão
The Travels of Mendes Pinto (edited by Rebecca D. Catz) (1990).

Mira, Manuel S.
Forgotten Portuguese: The Melungeons and the Portuguese Making of America (1998)

Molinos, Arturo
The Archeology of the Iberians (1999)

Myatt, Frederick
British Sieges of the Peninsular War (1996)

Nowell, Charles E.
A History of Portugal (1952)

Opello, W.
Portugal from Monarchy to Pluralist Democracy

Paris, Erna
The End of Days: A Story of Tolerance, Tyranny, and the Expulsion of the Jews (1995)

Passos, John dos
The Portugal Story (1969).

Pearson, M. N.
The Portuguese in India (New Cambridge History of India, Vol. 1) (1994)

Pessoa, Fernando
The Book of Disquietude (translated by Richard Zenith) (1997).

Phillipps, Jonathan
The Conquest of Lisbon (2000)

Pierson, Peter
Commander of the Armada (1989)

Pinto, António Costa
Salazar's Dictatorship and European Fascism: Problems of Interpretation (1996)

Read, Jan
The Moors in Spain and Portugal

Queirós, Eça de
The Illustrious House of Ramirez (1994)

Robinson, R.
Contemporary Portugal (1979)

Saramago, José
The History of the Siege of Lisbon (1997)

Shirodkar, P. P.
Researches in Indo-Portuguese History (2 vols.) (1998)

Singerman, Robert
Spanish and Portuguese Jewry (1993)

Sitwell, Sir Sacheverell
Portugal and Madeira (1954)

Smith, Colin (Editor)
Christians and Moors (1990)

Soares, Mário
Portugal's Struggle for Liberty (1975)

Stanislawski, Dan
The Individuality of Portugal (1959)

Strandes, Justus
The Portuguese Period in East Africa (1961)

Strangford, Lord
Poems From the Portuguese of Luis de Camões (1824)

Subrahmanyam, Sanjay
The Career and Legend of Vasco da Gama (1997)

Tamen, Miguel
A Revisionary History of Portuguese Literature (1999)

Vernon, Paul
A History of the Portuguese Fado (1999)

Wheeler, Douglas L.
Republican Portugal: A Political History, 1910-1936

Wills, John E.
*Embassies and Illusions: Dutch and Portuguese Envoys to K'Ang-His, 1666-
-1687* (1984)

Winius, George
The Fatal History of Portuguese Ceylon (1971)

Wise, Audrey
Eyewitness in Revolutionary Portugal (1975)

Wordsworth, William
The Convention of Sintra (1983)

Zilmer, Richard
The Last Kabbalist of Sintra (1997)

WEB SITES

www.portugal.com
A specialist search-engine, providing links to general, business, travel, media and other information about Portugal.

www.well.com/user/ideamen'portugal.html
A wide-ranging list of, and links to home pages of information-providers about Portugal, from the CIA to the University of Minho.

www.the-news.net
News about Portugal in English, up-dated weekly.

www.algarveresident.com
New of the Algarve, up-dated weekly.

www.alemnet.org/aol/elo
On-line news and information about the Alentejo region.

INDEX

A

Abd-al-Rahman dinasty, 56, 62-64
Abis, 34
Abraham, Rabbi, 121, 122
Abu-Thabet-Mohamet, 118
Adahu, 101
Afonso IV, King of Portugal, 86
Afonso V, King of Portugal, 108
Afonso VI, King of Portugal, 181, 182, 186
Afonso Henriques, first King of Portugal, 71-75, 78, 80, 81
Agida, Visigoth Prince, 53, 54
Alarcão, Jorge, 48
Albert, Prince, 215
Albuquerque, Afonso de, 136-142
Alenquer, Captain Pêro de, 125
Alexander VI, Pope, 112
Alexander the Great, 36
Alfonso, Kuke of Medina Sidonia, 117
Alfonso, King of Leon e Castile, 71
Al-Idrisi, Arab geographer, 63
Almeida, António, republicain leader, 222
Almeida, Francisco de, 136, 139, 140
Al-Mu'tamid, Prince of Seville, 66, 67

B

Altabé, David, Rabbi, 162, 164
Altenburg, 197
Amadeus, Count of Savoy, 71
Amélia, Queen of Portugal, 222
Andeiro, João Fernandes, Count, 86, 87
Andersen, Hans Christian, 24, 215, 216
Aquinas, Thomas, 202
Arib bin Said, 64
Aristotle, 65, 202
Arroio, João, 216
Arruda, Diogo, 151
Arruda, Francisco, 151
Auden, W. H., 22
Augustus, Emperor, 40
Azambuja, Diogo de, 113
Azurara, Gomes Eanes de, 95, 102, 104

B

Badomel, King of Senegal, 104
Baldaia, Captain Afonso Gonçalves, 100, 102-104
Barlow, Father, 183
Barradas, Arno, 238
Beresford, Lord (William Carr), 209--211

Bodley, Sir Thomas, 180
Boitac, Diogo de, 151, 152
Boxer, Charles, 125, 261
Braga, Teófilo, first republican President of Portugal, 221
Bragança, Duke of, 108
Bragança, Duke of, see King João IV
Bragança, Princess Catarina of, 25, 183-185
Braganças, 187-191, 205, 206, 215, 219, 222
Brito, Brother Bernardo de, 181
Brito, Gabriel Mesquita de, 9
Brito, João de, 187
Byron, Lord, 21

C

Cabral, Pedro Álvares, 112, 135
Cadaval, Marquesa de, 21
Caetano, Marcelo, becomes Prime Minister, 249, 250, 252, 253
Caracala, Emperor, 45
Carlos I, King, 219, 221, 222
Carlota Joaquina, Queen of Portugal, 212
Carmona, General António Óscar, 229, 230-232
Carneiro, Francisco Sá, 256
Carneiro, Roberto, 27
Carol, King of Romania, 232
Caron, Isabel de, 145
Carvalho, Major (now Lieutenant-
-Colonel) Otelo Saraiva de, later known as Otelo, 253-256
Castlemayne, Lady, 184, 185
Castro, Américo, 56
Castro, João de, 153
Catarina, Princess, daughter of Fernando and Isabel of Spain, 163
Catz, Rebecca, 144
Cerejeira, Manuel G., Cardinal Patriarch of Lisbon, 230, 235

Chagas, João, republicain leader, 222
Chagyat, Juddah, Rabbi, 162
Charles II, King of England, 126, 148, 183-186
Churchill, Winston, 229, 236, 237
Clement V, Pope, 84
Clement XIII, Pope, 201
Clement XIV, Pope, 201
Coates, Austin, 9
Coleridge, 21
Colombo, Bartolomeu, 110
Colombo, Cristóvão, 94, 108-112, 115, 118, 119, 161
Constantino, 46
Correia, Gaspar, 131
Cortesão, Armando, 127
Costa, Afonso, republicain leader, 226
Covilhã, Pêro da, 111, 116-125
Cunha, Pedro da, 9, 25-30, 218
Cunha, Susan, 26
Cunha, Tristão da, 140, 150, 152
Cunhal, Álvaro, communist leader, 238, 247, 254-256

D

Dalrympe, Major, 82
Daniel, Thomas, 88
D. António, Prior do Crato, 176-178
Delgado, General Humberto, 247
Descartes, 201
Deus, João de, 216
Dias, Bartolomeu, 102, 108, 111, 121-123, 125, 127, 135
Dickens, Charles, 215
Dinis, King of Portugal, 83-85, 160
Domitiano, Emperor, 45, 49
Dourado, Fernão Faz, government cartographer, 172
Dozy, Reinhart, 260
Drake, Sir Francis, 93, 173, 176-179

Duarte, King of Portugal, 91, 93, 95, 98, 160
Duke of Alba, 158, 171
Duke of Aveiro, 196
Duke of Beja, 118
Duke of Olivares, 186
Duke of Palmela, 253
Duke of Portland, 208
Duke of Terceira, 213
Duke of Viseu, 108
Dürer, Albrecht, 153
Duzy, Reinhardt, 56

E

Eanes, Gil, 100
Eanes, Major (now General), Ramalho, 255, 256
Earl of Arundel, 95
Earl of Essex, 179, 180
Earl of Sandwich, 183, 184
Eberhardt, 103
Edward II, King of England, 84
Eiffel, engineer, 217
Eliezer, Rabbi, 160
Eramus, 172
Escoffier, 208
Eugene IV, Pope, 122
Eulogius, 58, 59

F

Father Forez, 173
Father Francisco, royal chaplain, 117, 118, 123, 124
Fearless Geraldo, legendary Knight, 72, 73
Fernando I, King of Portugal, 86, 87
Fernando II, King of Portugal (Duke of Saxe-Coburg and Gotha), 215, 217
Fernando, Prince, son of the King João I of Portugal, 93, 97, 98, 118

Fernando, King of Castille, 112, 161--163
Fernandes, Carlos, 9
Fernandes, Mateus, 151
Ficalho, Count of, 107
Fielding, Henry, 21
Figueira, Captain Francisco, 222
Filipe I, King of Portugal (II of Spain), 158, 165, 175, 180
Filipe II, King of Portugal (IV of Spain), 180
Filipe III, King of Portugal (IV of Spain), 180
Fleming, Ian, 21, 240
Fonseca, José Maria da, 45
Franco, Francisco, Spain's dictator, 249
Franco, João, president of Movement of Renewal and Liberty, 222
Frey de Fonseca, Archbishop, 172
Friar António of Lisbon, 122

G

Galvão, Henrique, 243-246
Gama, Estêvão da, 127, 128, 134
Gama, Paulo da, 127
Gama, Vasco da, Count of Vidigueira, 108, 112, 125-135, 138, 152
Gargaris, god-king, inventor of cultivation, 33
Garrett, Almeida, 214, 216
Gascon, Samuel, 160
Geddes, Michael, 168
George III, King of England, 205
Gilbert of Hastings, 80
Glanvill, Herbay, 76
Glória, Maria da, Queen of Portugal, 212, 213, 215
Godofrede of St. Aumer, 69
Goethe, 192
Góis, Damião de, 150, 151

Gomes da Costa, General Manuel, 229

Gomes, Fernão, 106

Gomes, Henrique Barros, Minister of the Colonies, 220

Gonçalves, Antão, 101

Graham, Billy, 26

Greene, Graham, 21, 237-239

Guterres, António, 109

H

Hadrian, Governor of England, 38, 42

Hamilcar, military Commander in Chief of Carthage, 32, 34

Hannibal, son of Hamilcar, 33-35, 44

Hasdrubal, 34

Havel, Vaclav, 258

Henrique, Cardinal Archbishop of Lisbon, 156
becomes King, 158

Henrique, the Navigator, Prince, 91--98, 101-108, 118, 261

Henri, Count, pretender to the throne of France, 232

Henry, Count of Burgundy, 71

Henry IV, King of England, 94

Herculano, Alexandre, historical writer, 216, 260

Hercules, 31, 35
pillars of, 31, 32

Herode Agripp II, 51

Hitler, Adolf, 236, 241

Hoofmann, Cornelius, 173

Horthy, Regent of Hungary, 232

Hypocrate, 154

I

Ibn al-Labban, poet, 68

Ibn A'mmar, poet, 66, 67

Imulce, daugther of the lord of the Silver Mountains, 34

Isaac, Brother, 57

Isabel, daugther of Fernand and Isabel, 162

Isabel, Queen of Portugal, 83, 85, 86

Isabel, Queen of Castille, 112, 161--163

Iserwood, Christopher, 22

J

Jaffrey, Medhur, 148

João II, King of Portugal, 107-115, 117, 118, 121, 123, 126-128, 162, 226

João III, King of Portugal, 155, 156, 176

João IV, King of Portugal, 180, 181

João V, King of Portugal, 189, 190

João of Avis (King João I of Portugal), 87-89, 90, 93, 95

João, Prince Regent of Portugal, 205, 206
King, 209, 212

John of Gaunt, Duke of Lancaster, 86, 89, 90

Jonah, 31

José I, King of Portugal, 113-200, 203

Juan I, King of Castille, 87-89

Juan, Prince, pretender to the throne of Spain, 232

Julian, Pope, 119

Julius Caesar, wins governorship of Hispania Ulterior, 31, 36

Junot, General, Duke of Abrantes, 206-208

K

Kennedy, John, 246

Kennedy, Robert, 243

Keroualle, Louise de, Duchess of Portsmouth, 185

Kissinger, Henry, 243, 253, 255

Konetske, Richard, 56

L

Lancaster, Terence, 18
Lane, Salles, 23
Leão XIII, Pope, 232
Leonor, Princess, 155
Linshotten, 172
Livingstone, David, 221
Livy, 260
Lopes, Fernão, chronicler, 87
Louis XI, King of France, 108
Louis XIV, King of France, 183
Luís, King of Portugal, 215
Luís Filipe, Crown Prince, 222
Luísa, Queen of Portugal, 181, 182, 186

M

Madjid, ibn Ahmed, 127
Mafalda, Queen of Portugal, 71
Maia, Manuel da, 197
Major, Richard, 92-94
Mântua, Duchess of, 181
Manuel I, King of Portugal, 123, 126, 127, 134, 142, 150-152, 154, 156, 162-165
Manuel II, last King of Portugal, 222, 223
Maria Anna, Princess of Austria, 189
Maria de Bragança, Queen of Portugal, 205
Maria Francisca, Princess, 203 Queen, 203-205
Mariana Ana von Hapsburg, Queen Mother of Portugal, 195
Martins, Lourenço, 88
Martins, Oliveira, 261
Maschioni, Bartolomeus, 118
Massena, General, 207, 211
Master Rodrigo, 115
Matos, General Norton de, 238
Maximus, Emperor, 50
Medicis, the, 107, 112, 119

Giovanni, 152
Lourenço, 152
Melo, Paulo de Carvalho e, brother of the Marquês de Pombal, 201
Mendes, Aristides de Sousa, 241
Mendes, Álvaro, 170
Mendes, Diogo, 171
Mendes, Graça, 170
Mendonça, Colonel Salvador de, 188
Miguel, Prince Regent, 212, 213
Miller, John, 186
Molay, Jacques de, 84
Moore, Susan, 9
Mohammed, profet, 57, 59, 76, 134
Muggeridge, Malcolm, 240
Mulachik, King of Fez, 118
Musã ibn Nasser, Khalif, 55
Mussolini, Benito, 229, 234, 249, 251

N

Nacalao, Father, 68
Napiez, Captain Charles, 213
Napoleon Bonaparte, 205-208, 211
Nasi, Josef, 170
Noah, 31
Norris, Sir John "Blackjack", 176-179
Nun'Álvares, Portuguese Commander in Chief, 89
Nunes, Pedro, 153

O

O'Connor, John, 9
O'Daly, Father Daniel, 182, 183, 186
Oliveira, Father Fernando, 105
Oliveira Marques, historical writer, 107, 261
Orey, Fernando d', 9, 29, 249
Orta, Garcia de, 154
Osório, Jerónimo, Bishop of Algarve, 188
Otto, John, 241

P

Pannick, K. M., 126
Pascal, 201
Paynes, Hugues, 69, 73
Pedro Hispano, Portugal only Pope (João XXI), 65
Pedro I (IV of Portugal), Emperor of Brasil, 212, 213
Pedro I, King of Portugal, 83
Pedro II, King of Portugal, 182, 186
Pedro, Prince Regent, 91, 93, 96
Pessanha, Admiral, 83
Pessoa, Fernando, 152
Peys, Samuel, 184, 186
Philby, Kim, 237, 240
Philip IV, King of France, 84
Philippa, daughter of John of Gaunt (Queen Filipa of Portugal), 89-91, 93, 96
Pinto, Fernão Mendes, 143-146
Pius XI, Pope, 232
Pliny, the Elder, 43, 44, 260
Plutarch, roman biographer, 36, 260
Pombal, Sebastião José de Carvalho e Melo, Marquês de, 193-205, 234, 249, 260
Popov, Dusco, 240
Prester John, 122, 123
Priscilian, Bishop of Ávila, 52

Q

Queirós, Eça de, novelist, 217
Quintilian, Iberian historian, 49

R

Raby, D. L., 238
Raggesvinth, Visigoth King, 53
Raleigh, Sir Walter, 179
Rego, Raul, newspaper editor, 254
Reis, Alves dos, 227, 228
Reis, Jaime, 9
Rex Argentonius, the Silver King, 31

Rhodes, Cecil, 220, 221, 261
Richard II, King of England, 88-90
Richard Lionhearted, 68
Richelieu, Cardinal of France, 180
Roderico, Visigoth King, 53, 54
Roth, Conrad, German banker, 157
Romanov dinasty, 223

S

Saher, Lord of Archelle, 9, 30, 72
Salazar, António de Oliveira, 9, 30, 72, 230-234, 237, 238, 240-249, 251, 253, 256, 261
Saldano, António, 9
Samorim, the Lord of Oceans, 125, 131, 132, 134, 135, 140
Santos, Eugénio dos, architect, 197
Saraiva, António José, 165
Saraiva, José Hermano, 72, 128, 261
Sarfati, Isaac, Rabbi, 170
Searlatti, Domenico, 190, 193
Schomberg, General, 180
Scipio, Gaius Cornelius, Roman General, 35
Sebastião, King of Portugal, 156, 157, 158
Seneca, 42
Shakespeare, William, 151
Silva, Aníbal Cavaco, 27
Silva, Paulo da, 190
Siqueira, Bartolomeu, 188
Sisenand, 57
Soares, Mário, socialist leader, 20, 253-258
Soult, General, 207, 210
Southey, Robert, 21
Speer, Albert, 237
Spender, Stephen, 22
Spínola, General António de, 250, 252-254
St Bernard, Abbot of Clairvaux, 69--74, 80, 81, 83, 87, 260

Stephens, William, 82
St James, 49-52, 70
St John the Baptist, 72
St Martinho, Bishop of Braga, 53
St Paulo, Deacon, 58, 61
St Peter, 72, 201
Stukeley, Sir Thomas, 157

T
Talleyrand, 206
Tarik, Arab General, 54, 55
Távora, Marquesa de, 195, 196
Teles, Leonor, Queen of Portugal,
    86, 87
Tennyson, Alfred, 21
Teresa, Princess, Alfonso's second
    daughter, 71
Tiberius, Emperor, 39
Timoja, Hindu emissary from Goa,
    136
Tirdo, Josef, Rabbi, 171
Tomás, Admiral Américo, 256
Tomlin, Geraldino, 9
Torralva, Diogo de, 152
Toscanelli, Paolo, 111, 112
Tristão, Nuno, 100-103

U
Urban VII, Pope, 182
Umberto, King of Italy, 232

V
Vallery-Radot, Brother Irineé, 70,
    260
Vasconcelos, José, 248
Vasconcelos, Miguel, 181
Vasques, Fernão, 86
Velho, Álvaro, 128-130, 132
Velho, Captain Manuel Garcia,
    188
Vicente, Gil, 216
Victoria, Queen of England, 215
Vieira, Father António, 169
Viriato, Lusitanian leader, 36
Visinio, José, 115
Voltaire, 201, 202

W
Walesa, Lech, 258
Wellesley, Sir Arthur, Duke of
    Wellington, 209-211
William IV, King of England, 171
Willis, Doctor, 205
Winder, Bayley, 260
Witiza, Visigoth King, 53, 56
Woodsworth, Dorothy, 21
Woodsworth, William, 21

X
Xavier, São Francisco, 19, 137, 138,
    144-146, 200

277